BUILDING INTEGRITY

—— *IT'S YOUR CHOICE* ——

A STORY OF BUSINESS, LIFE, AND THE JOURNEY

✝

Mark A. Bartkoski

Copyright © 2016 by Mark A. Bartkoski

Second Edition.

All rights reserved.

No part of this publication may be reproduced, distributed, or transmitted in any form or by any means, including photocopying, recording, or other electronic or mechanical methods, without the prior written permission of the copyright holder, except as provided by USA copyright law.

To obtain more copies of this book and other resources, visit our website below.

www.IntegrityDevelopment.us

Printed in the United States of America

ISBN-13:

978-0-9914226-1-6

CONTENTS

Dedication — vii
Introduction — ix
Objectives — xi

I. CORPORATE HISTORY
1 The Business Condition — 1

II. OPERATIONS OVERVIEW
2 Straight Ridge Mine — 11
3 Broad Run Mine — 23
4 Deep Hollow Mine — 33
5 Lucky Star Mine — 43
6 Lucky Road Mine — 57
7 Taurus #1 Mine — 69

III. RESTRUCTURING THE ASSETS
8 Reallocating Facilities and Equipment — 79
9 Developing the Team — 89
10 Operating Style Shift — 97

IV. PROCESS DEVELOPMENT AND PRESENTATION
11 Building the Foundation — 105
12 Selling the Change — 113
13 Integrity Process — 119
14 Building the Process Pillars — 127

V. MONITORING AND MATURATION
15 Progress Reports and Creep — 135
16 The True Winner: Earning Balanced Security (Corporately & Personally) — 141

TABLE OF APPENDICES

APPENDIX A Notable Quotes   149

APPENDIX B Support Resources
    B.01 Suggested Reading List and Bibliography 175
    B.02 Property Evaluation Categories 176
    B.03 Process Study Obstacles 178
    B.04 Mine Economics 101 179
    B.05 Super Unit Comparisons 180
    B.06 Critical Performance Efficiency Ratios 181
    B.07 Mine Planning 201 182
    B.08 Typical Time Distribution 183
    B.09 Cost of Loss: Safety 184
    B.10 Cost of Loss: Production 185
    B.11 Heinrich Triangle 186
    B.12 Reasons for Loss 187
    B.13 Parallel Processes 188
    B.14 Maximized Scheduling 189
    B.15 Mine Support 301 194
    B.16 Proactive Employee Relations Programs 195
    B.17 Deep Mine Performance Indicators 196
    B.18 Key Performance Indicators 197
    B.19 Trending Categories 198
    B.20 Restructuring Forecast 199
    B.21 Process Coordinator Responsibilities 200
    B.22 Corporate Transformation Downfalls 201
    B.23 Prevention Tenets 202
    B.24 Corporate Communication Plan 203
    B.25 Bulletin Board Components 204

B.26	Weekly Crew Communication Meeting	205
B.27	Training Lay-out	206
B.28	Definitions of Complacent	207
B.29	Reasons for Not Breaking a Habit	208
B.30	Integrity Process Basics	209
B.31	Work Request Flow Chart	210
B.32	Prevention Projects Form	211
B.33	Action Plan Form	212
B.34	Loss Symptoms vs. Root Causes	213
B.35	Preventative Maintenance System	214
B.36	Integrity Growth Assessment	215
B.37	Personal Efficiency Challenge	216
B.38	Examples of Creep	217
B.39	Integrity Process Flow Chart	218
B.40	The SHARE Plan	219
B.41	Digging Deeper...Into The Source	220
B.42	*Refining Integrity*	224

DEDICATION

To my father, who is a relentless example of a true servant and a living testament of commitment beyond emotion. He taught us that service to one another is a decision worthy of our focus. Whether it is in the workplace, marriage, parenting roles, and/or church ministry, elevating others is a calling we all should aspire to perfect.

My father provided a secure, stable home, and mentored a firm set of values. For those foundation blocks, I am eternally grateful and I am pledged to continue *paying them forward*. His determination and sacrifice defined for me what the truths of love and integrity meant. As I have tested those definitions throughout my life in my home and at work, I have begun to realize that my father had not been just good, he had been right. By the way he lived he had revealed truth, a truth that never diminishes in its affect but actually grows stronger with each test it endures. And it's that maturation of principles which defines us. We realize integrity is not only what we have done but who we are. That statement of value is one of the greatest gifts we can share. I can honor my father in no greater way than to strive to pour into others what he poured into me. May his legacy of INTEGRITY live on.

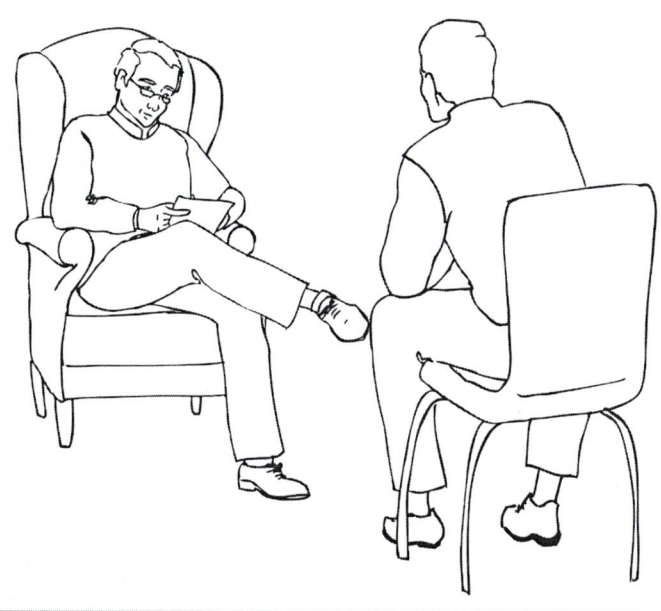

WISDOM

INTRODUCTION

Today's companies are being pushed to a heightened level of excellence due to market challenges, therefore new business strategies must be explored. This book offers a sequenced plan to retool, empower, and energize the entire team for a common goal. Integrity Process is a comprehensive operating system that is integrated in every aspect of the business. Integrity Process sows a detailed loss prevention concept intertwined with accountability that produces individual efficiencies and system effectiveness. The results are balanced in priority and will yield a win-win for the owners, management, workforce, and the community.

Integrity Process has five distinct areas of refinement. The operating plan module is built on a procedural structure called MVP Plan. The unifying **M**ission Statement is developed and introduced first. Upon that, a list of foundational **V**alues is sewn into the operation's cultural fabric. Completing the plan, focus is then turned to the **P**rocess. The process is a grouping of management techniques used to charge continuous improvement. Specifically, it is based around three Process Pillars. Each pillar Gathers information, Refines process, and Monitors results. When correctly customized, appropriately introduced, and completely supported, the results of this process with respect to safety and productivity have been extremely strong.

THE AUTHORS VIEW

Understanding the perspective of a book's author is critically important. Even in the discussion of facts and experiences, interpretations are going to vary. As you read through the text, my intent is to offer insight, suggestions, and stories that will hopefully help you in the continued refinement of your character, operating style, and calling. I believe we are all endowed with a basket of strengths that are unique, and when matured, each one of us can be a positive influence to the world around us. Accepting that challenge to perfect *our own basket* is the initial step. While the experiences shared are framed within the context of the underground coal mining industry, the personal lessons, process sharpening, and management techniques can be used across many fields.

My career has been extremely expansive. With over 33 years in the mining industry, I have been exposed to many facets. After earning a couple of engineering degrees from Virginia Tech, I spent the next eight years underground learning the hands-on side. Assignments varied from beltline work, ventilation support, and maintenance, to equipment operator positions. I would not claim to be the strongest operator, but the familiarity with each type of equipment and their process challenges has helped me immensely in my ensuing management duties.

Being able to relate to the struggles of the industrial process should be a required prerequisite for every budding manager. The next 25 years of my career have been in senior management. I have come to realize that whether the operation has accompanying surface mines, preparation plants, a rail load-out, and/or barging facilities, the technical challenges may have varied, but the basic leadership and management issues are similar. The locality differences are real, but sound operating techniques are always applicable. I have been responsible for operations in nine different states and over three different coal regions, and the basics remain the same. Consulting work internationally and in differing industries has also added its salt, in that cultural and past practices do affect the plan development and presentation even if the basics stay consistent. With respect to workforces, 70% of my assignments have been union-free and 30% union-represented. In my opinion, people are people, and they respond the way they are treated. Due to differences in operational history and past personnel relations, each operation requires customized planning but I believe common ground can be found in every case. Diversity is also found in the business' season. I have had start-ups (greenfields), expansions (brownfields), and rebuilds, and each has a unique personality of its own. I have found that before the management and a growth plan can be developed, a complete understanding of the past technical challenges, agency perceptions, management/workforce personalities, and business constraints must be fully vetted. By way of the fictional story that follows, I have addressed many of the obstacles and issues that I have lived and learned through.

During my career I have been cast into numerous extremely difficult management roles, but have always viewed them as an opportunity to build. Most of my early superintendent assignments followed a serious accident or collapsing economics, so the initial focus was naturally on that specific area. After reading the industrial masterpiece, *In Search of Excellence*, by Tom Peters and Robert Waterman, Jr., and a number of the W. Edwards Deming Books, I was challenged to develop a detailed, step-by-step, operations template. Then, I was given the opportunity to work with Dr. James Bennett. He is an international expert with respect to employee behavior effects on business results. After being exposed to his loss prevention concept, I discovered his explanation of loss was the key I was looking for. Coupling Bennett's view of loss with Deming's push for quality work, I was determined to model a win-win management technique. Surviving some tough early lessons kept me striving to learn. I have had the opportunity to work for some industry icons, have been responsible for more than a dozen companies, conducted over 40 operation evaluations, and visited over 150 operations—and I am still learning. I believe there is a lesson to learn from every assignment. Battle worn I am, but I still consider myself a student of the field.

The vision—an integrated, transformation system that could marry corporate goals with employee needs and community requirements, seems like an onerous task. But this vision of complete transformation has to be possible. I have seen solid safety programs, but not an inclusive, business balanced, bought into, plan for security—so that became the dream.

The definition of security is very personalized to each of us, but there are some basics we can agree on. Let's build an operation where we proactively earn a safe, stable future from which we can provide for our families—A tomorrow that is available, because of the teamwork successes of today. Viewing security through these glasses, ties us together in unity and casts a mutual accountability for the outcome.

Over the last four years of domestic and international consulting experience, I have refined Integrity Process. *Building Integrity* introduces a management model that offers short and medium-term goals and strategies, which earn the long-term goal of security that we all seek. Side paths will take you into exploring the challenges of our personal calling and creating balance within the numerous facets of our lives. Integrity Process is a high value, win-win approach to business that centers around the belief *integrity of character will yield integrity in process*. It is an employee empowered process that provides return to the investor, offers security for the employees and their families, and illuminates a positive influence toward the community. The result is a true win-win-win outcome.

OBJECTIVES

The goals of this work are to offer you an alternative management perspective and operating style. It is one of focused vision, foundational values, and balanced processes. It is centered around building a *character of integrity* personally as individuals and as an organization. It is a philosophy of team empowerment that undergirds the common goal of earning security—a win-win from the boardroom to the employees' homes. The case will be presented that the most supportive management style for this type of build will be one of *servant leadership*. Uniting these techniques can catapult success to a level that only true teams may go. As you invest your time in the reading of these thoughts and stories, I would like to challenge you to consider the adoption of the optimizing procedures that are shared. The choice is yours as to the level you wish to engage. But as is often the case, the amount of effort you exert and follow-up you apply, will determine the reward received.

HOW TO USE THIS BOOK

This book is organized to facilitate its study at three different depths:

Level I

Read it as an entertaining, motivational, and informational collection that is set in the industrial process world of underground mining. The management stories and information are equally applicable in any people-oriented business where process abounds.

Study Suggestion: Read the book, highlight pertinent notes or ideas, and briefly glean the appendices. A month after reading the book, review your highlights and the Notable Quotes in Appendix A.

Level II

Consider the book as a direct challenge to find your own professional calling and pursue it, utilizing some of the offered techniques. Recognize the multi-roles of your journey—spiritual, family, career, and health/hobbies, and how you can optimize your influence and giftings.

Study Suggestion: Reread the text and relevant appendices, regularly review* Notable Quotes and cumulative highlights from both readings, and adopt a couple techniques or ideas to add to your arsenal.

Level III

Utilize Integrity Process as the building blocks for a customized transformation plan within your circle of influence. Develop the pillars presented and be sensitive to the precise timing required to usher-in change. Be affirmed and challenged to prove integrity of character yields integrity in process.

Study Suggestion: After completing Level I and II study suggestions, complete the formulation and implementation of a customized Integrity Progress Plan. Simultaneously develop and commit yourself to an individual effectiveness improvement journey. This personal improvement plan could be supplemented by the reading of the Appendix B.01 book list and a monthly self-audit of Appendix B.36.

*To assist in your review of the Notable Quotes, a recorded MP3 or audio CD can be obtained from **www.IntegrityDevelopment.us/purchase**

WHAT OBJECTIVES DO YOU INTEND TO GAIN FROM THIS STUDY?

- OBTAIN A HIGH LEVEL OF UPPER MANAGEMENT LEADERSHIP SKILLS & TECHNIQUES
- BUILDING CO. SECURITY / INTEGRITY
- DEFINE LEADERSHIP VIA LEADING, GUIDING MENTORING & SUPPORTING YOUR TEAM.

We only improve, when we maintain an open mind and a desire to excel.

I. CORPORATE HISTORY

Chapter 1
The Business Condition

The day started like many others, with the alarm clock shattering the darkness—but I caught it on the second burst. As I navigated to the sink in blindness, the minefield of toys left by the twins became adversarial. How could such sweet little three-year-old girls be so diabolical? But I survived, with only four hops and a bruised instep. It could have been worse. As I showered and prepped for another day, my cell phone went off. Glancing down, I could see it was the corporate secretary. I cleared my throat and answered, "Hello Ms. Margie, what can I do for you?"

"Mr. Brothers, we need you to come by the main office at 9 a.m. The board is meeting formally and they have requested your presence."

"Am I in trouble?" I sheepishly inquired. "Is it another round of cost-cutting?"

"I don't know, but something different is going on. I am just praying there is good news for once."

I pocketed the phone and started the trek to the big office. I played a lot of scenarios over in my mind and finally landed on—*fate will decide*. As I pulled into the parking lot, the normal cast of cars was there, plus a big black Lincoln bearing New York plates. Not exactly the common ride for a small Appalachian coal town. Walking past the car I could not help but notice in the back seat two file boxes labeled with our company's name, Profit Coal. On the rearview mirror hung a medallion that said, HE HAS CHARTED YOUR DESTINY, BUT THE CHOICE IS YOURS. I found that phrase puzzling, but quickly dropped the thought. I had too many other things to worry about.

Margie met me at the door saying they were ready for me. Inquisitively, I opened the door to find the usual three board members and a visitor. *Who could that be?*

Chairwoman Amy Daubert stood up, greeted me, and invited me to be seated. After glancing around the room, she proceeded. "Dirk Brothers, we asked you to come in today so we could announce a shift in corporate ownership. Effective immediately the major shareholder will be a capital venture group represented by Jeff Page."

Mr. Page quickly came over to me and firmly shook my hand. "I am really looking forward to our new relationship and journey, Mr. Brothers."

I was taken back by his confidence. His demeanor seemed warm and sincere, but I was still cautious. *What was all this about?*

Mrs. Daubert took charge and clearly delineated the ownership percentages. She explained that the fund investors she represented had sold their 60% controlling interest in Profit Coal to Jeff Page's syndicated group. She then gave the floor to the other two board members. Marci Franco led next stating that her investor group would retain their minority interest of 20% and was prepared to weather the recent market downturn. As I had heard her say in the past, their group believed the long-term coal markets would come back and that they were satisfied to be a passive owner. She went on to explain that she believed most other coal companies were losing the financial and mental drive to embrace the battles and pro-actively plan ahead. She assured us that her group was in it for the long haul.

The third board member, Fred Miller, bellowed out, "I am going to try to be passive but—we'll see." He continued, "After my third heart attack and second wife's urge to travel, my orders have been to slow down and disengage."

Fred's reputation cast him as an intense, driving mine operator. He had been a career father to me, but the tough love scars were deep. He was old school, and proud of it. I was raised up through the safety department, so he hardly noticed me until I started face bossing. My style did not fit his mold, but even still, he commonly commented on my solid results. Over an eight-year period, he shuffled me around to various problem areas and the results always seemed to meet his approval. I was never considered one of his boys though, since I lacked the cussing, hard-nosed reputation his team was known for, but he seemed to respect me, none-the-less.

Fred continued to explain that he would be more removed, and thus would be relinquishing the operation manager title. His next comment was a bombshell launched without warning, "Dirk, we would like you to temporarily fill my spot."

With surprise still registering on my face, I immediately refuted his logic and assured the whole group that I was not ready.

Fred interrupted, "I don't think you are ready either, but I think you will be the best fit for the new majority owner."

I was dumbfounded and pretty sure that was just Fred's way of complimenting me, but I still felt inadequate and very weak at the knees. The entire board just stared at me waiting for my next response. I was trying to say "no thanks" but nothing was coming out.

Finally, Jeff Page came over to me. "We have a strong developmental plan for the future and we need your help, Dirk. Will you please help us refocus, restructure, and build a stronger future?"

I could see Jeff had an uncanny way of being positive and encouraging, yet he seemed to be enticing me toward a forward moving, bigger picture. Normally I liked this approach, but this time I was solo in his sites. He scared me and challenged me in the same breath. He detected I was still petrified, so he eased off and asked, "would you consider it overnight?" I stuttered, but then agreed I would think about it.

Marci took the remainder of the meeting to review last quarter's flat financials and dismal market trends. At one point she looked at me and said, "Dirk, this is where you need to make sure rumors of bankruptcy do not start."

Fred interrupted, "Just tell them they will lose their jobs unless they cut costs. They need to get on board or get off the bus."

"No!" Jeff erupted. "Building our security will not be started this way! We will analytically evaluate and gather input from the team *AND THEN* redesign a business plan. In a down market there are a lot of opportunities, and we are blessed to have one. If we do not react decisively to the industry change besieging us, we will be left behind. The faster and more efficiently we retool, the further ahead in the pack we will start. We are here to affect positive change and we need the entire team. Threatening our partners is not an effective way of engaging and empowering them." Jeff then turned to Fred, "Over ten years ago you masterfully built and synergistically merged together six underground mines into one company. This company has survived in a multi-year rolling market, but continuing to progress forward will stretch us even further. May I suggest to everyone—go home tonight, think about our challenges and goals, and come back tomorrow to continue to work on forging our plan."

Fred glared at me and murmured, "Boy, you got your hands full." I felt like a man without a country.

As we started dispersing, Jeff came over to me with some words of encouragement. "Leadership has varied moments, some are meant to build your character, while others lead to victory, but both make it all worthwhile. You are part of a plan, Dirk—you just have to figure out where you are supposed to fit."

I was feeling conflicted—energized but scared, motivated but threatened, alone but needed. All the way home I rehearsed how I would handle myself in tomorrow's meeting. My mind said bail, but my heart had a check. Usually I was all about logic, but this time something was unsettling, it was like an internal war. Part of me felt I was supposed to say yes, due to blind company loyalty, and the other part was hesitant and fearful of the unknown. I had always been taught never to turn down an opportunity, even if you are not excited about it. My dad had always lectured, "Take care of the team first, as there will be times they will carry you." My heart was hinting that this was going to be one of those times where my prints were not the ones found in the sand.

> "TAKE CARE OF THE TEAM FIRST, AS THERE WILL BE TIMES THEY CARRY YOU.

†

When I arrived home I was still preoccupied. After dinner, Nikki got the kids ready for bed and I came in for the nightly bedtime story. Normally we put the twins down first and then Colt, our six-year-old, but tonight seemed to call for something different. As Nikki finished a short prayer, I said I wanted to share about something that had happened at work. I explained unenthusiastically about the temporary appointment the board had asked me to consider. I said it would require more time away from home, a lot of stress, and long, long hours—I emphasized that they would be giving up their daddy for a while. I glanced around for their responses. In my heart, I knew I had tainted the story enough to get my preferred answer.

To my surprise, my little boy crawled over into my lap and with big, loving eyes said, "Daddy, we will share you. If you can help save those other families' jobs, how can we say no?"

Unprompted, the twins came over and one whispered, "We will be here waiting for you every night, Daddy."

With a solo tear trailing down my face, I looked helplessly at Nikki. With a little tilt of her head she quoted, "Out of the mouths of babes…"

I cut her off, "Sure, I get the message," and I reflected on the kids' unselfish answers. That was a long night. I wrestled with Mr. Page's provocative question—"where was I supposed to fit?"

†

Jeff Page opened the board meeting the next day and set the agenda. He proceeded to lay out initial goals, which were to evaluate the needs of each operation and look for any potential area to recapitalize monies from current assets.

"We have to improve our balance sheet," Jeff lectured.

Fred piped up, "That sounds good but we have been draining our assets and starving our rebuild programs for the last two years already. Federal and State operating policy changes have also levied crippling constraints, even above the normal capital expenditure requirements. It's like a perfect storm and we are in the eye of the hurricane."

"When it was bad in the past," Jeff challenged, "you got creative. If you hadn't, we would have joined that other 30% of the industry that did not make it."

In her usual quiet but profound way, Marci spoke up, "We have waged war on the cyclical coal industry before and won, but this time the clouds look thicker. It seems that not only is pricing down, but global climate pressures are climbing and agency attacks keep escalating. Reserve qualities are eroding, costs are growing, and the coal supply competition is more aggressive than ever."

Jeff stood up, "I agree with all the realities presented, but I also see our families partnering with us, and I believe if we come together, we can out-perform the field."

Fred chimed in, "These people are fighters and will rise to the occasion. They just need a plan, but I am afraid we are out of magic rabbits."

"You know," Jeff continued, "the challenges or giants in our land are real obstacles, but it is our choice as leaders to decide what we will focus upon. Some consider obstacles to be these frightful things that you see when you take your eyes off the goal. I will assure you our camp will focus on pursuing the prize. They had to be good to survive this far, but we must agree to aspire and achieve greatness together. All this sounds like an advertisement for the Jim Collins' book *Good to Great* but I am convinced we can be one of the GREAT companies if we decide to be. I would like to make a proposal. Let's have an independent operational review completed on our company. I have worked with an individual who has a couple of engineering degrees and over 30 years of experience in the mining industry. He has over 20 years in senior operations management. Although he has recently retired, he would be available for a couple months study."

"Well, my first reaction is normally to be defensive and reject an outsider," Fred interjected, "but we are desperate. Any help would be appreciated. I have even asked my wife to remember us in her church's prayer meetings, and that's not normally my source for solutions. If we used this guy, what would his study scope be?"

"He could visit each operation for a week, and just be a quiet observer." Jeff took a sip of his water and continued. "At the end of the week he would provide a review and suggestions, and at the conclusion of all the visits he would compile a comprehensive Operational Development Plan."

"That would give us an excellent third party evaluation," Marci commented. "Is he detailed and could he also do a management review?"

Jeff quickly answered, "May I suggest we bring him in and let him provide those answers himself? When I called him last night on his potential availability, he said he was coming through our area and could come by this afternoon."

Nods and gestures of approval swept over the board members. All agreed, saying it sounded like a really good plan.

†

After lunch, the board meeting reconvened with Jeff introducing the consultant, Al Hunt. An hour was spent rehashing the study parameters and obvious challenges. Al seemed technically sound and well versed. When Marci inquired about the operational detail to be provided, Al explained that he had conducted numerous reviews in the past and would be happy to send in a copy of his standard Property Evaluation Categories check sheet (Appendix B.02).

Seemingly satisfied, Marci continued, "Our company's safety performance is considerably better than the national average, so I am assuming we are okay there. Could you also incorporate in your study a full management review and formulate an overall corporate business plan recommendation?"

Al hesitantly looked at Jeff for a release.

Jeff nodded, smiled, and turned back to the group, "Al would love to take it there, but I must warn you, that is his calling. If you study his résumé, the resurrection of struggling operations has been his career focus. He has even gone so far as to develop an operation transformation model."

Al stepped in, "It is a raw template, not a model plan. Every operation is different in history, conditions, management personality, timing, equipment constraints, skill and talent levels, scheduling, and workforce make-up. An outsider can mess up an operating plan if the plan is not completely customized and everyone is not on board. Even if the technical facets are perfect, the plan presentation and acceptance is critically important. Developing a complete business model is the ultimate goal, but I warn you there are many potential pitfalls and it takes a couple years to weave it into the cultural fabric. I have seen many companies push for the flash in the pan results. In the long run, it splinters the company, misses the creative input of the employee base, loses buy-in, and the GREAT status is never achieved. I would caution this group, don't embark down this road unless you are completely sold-out to a higher standard and willing to lay the complete foundation. Another additive issue is the differing goals of the ownership between the board of directors and the employees. The corporate agenda of profit does not completely translate to the employees' need for a secure job. The disconnect is real. Motive diversity across all the layers of the organization is usually the turbulence—but bridge that, and there is a win-win for those willing to change. A divided house will not stand. The common goal of operational security is where the owner/employee covenant must unite. That commitment must start and radiate from this room. An operating plan can be built and a process designed, but I will reiterate, the foundation has to be laid first. Those building blocks come from your values—the values you support are those you live and promote. We honor what defines us. The type of company I am describing is spun from the heart and what is truly important to us must permeate every level and process we sanction."

> **THE VALUES WE SUPPORT ARE THOSE WE LIVE AND PROMOTE. WE HONOR WHAT DEFINES US.**

"Now you know why Al has been nicknamed The Strategist," Jeff said, enthusiastically. "He is passionate about the building process!"

Little by little it seemed like the atmosphere of the meeting was beginning to ignite...

"You mentioned good and GREAT earlier," Marci continued, "How do you define them?"

Al elaborated further, "Good is achieved by a solid plan and aspiration, GREAT is achieved by the refining of the plan and perspiration, but we have to earn that level to start refinement. That's the second book of the journey. Initially our focus must be on the business plan and foundational values. But it is not about my beliefs, it is about yours." Al looked at each board member, as if sizing them up.

> **GOOD IS ACHIEVED BY A SOLID PLAN & ASPIRATION; GREAT IS ACHIEVED BY THE REFINING OF THE PLAN & PERSPIRATION, BUT WE HAVE TO EARN THAT LEVEL TO START REFINEMENT. THAT'S THE SECOND BOOK OF THE JOURNEY.**

"My vote is yes on this type of attack," Marci voiced with a bit of excitement. "With margins tighter and costs higher, we have to raise the performance bar to survive. I can see what Al is saying on creating a sustaining plan. We must view and treat our employees as equal business partners and work toward a larger common goal. Communicating the driving economics sensitizes them to the challenges ahead. If they understand the *WHY* and *HOW*, we engage, empower, and energize the team in one direction. When we improve the safety and productivity, and therefore economic performance, investors see profit and employees see safe job conditions and employment opportunities. The result—security is earned. I can sign on to this. Even my conservative investor group will back this approach."

To that, Fred spoke up with increased hope, "I will be the first to admit this warm and fuzzy approach is not my style, but that is probably the ticket for today and especially for this newer generation. I was raised in the era where you hired the best superintendent you could find, crowned him king, and he told everyone else what to do. That style sometimes got us to good, but never to GREAT. We now live in a society of low values, tolerance for everything, and rampant dishonor. Maybe this higher standard approach is what we need."

Jeff stood up to emphasize his point to the board, "When business deals a crisis, successful companies use it as fuel, a catalyst for change, and view it as an opportunity. Let's be a GREAT company, first class, a united contributor, with high integrity."

Al was right in there with a warning, "Integrity is a strong word with a lot of responsibility; don't go there unless you are sold out 100% to its mission. It is a position and a lifestyle, which once announced, will invite close judgment. If you make a mistake of the heart, the sale is over. If you hold to your values, the team can be impenetrable. May I suggest that we reconvene in a couple months, and I will submit a technical operations review with operation planning suggestions. If you want to continue a discussion on the corporate business/management plan, we can do that then."

"We can do better than that," Jeff excitedly affirmed, "In two months, we the board, will submit a mission statement and foundational value list for a group discussion."

Everyone energetically and unanimously agreed.

†

As I was walking out of the board room, I was overwhelmed. My competitive and leadership side was fired up by the challenge, but my managerial side felt the enormous load. I had never been in an executive meeting where that magnitude of change was the topic of discussion. I was reminiscing about how nice it was to just follow orders, when suddenly there was a firm hand on my shoulder, stopping me.

Jeff spun me around and looked deep into my eyes, "Can the people count on you to help?"

I responded protectively, "Sure—but I know I am inadequate to build the boat you all have described."

Jeff encouraged supportively, "We will all design and build the boat together, but we need someone like you to keep a hand on the rudder."

"For now, temporarily—I will try," I answered.

As I drove home, I was in a stupor-state, feeling overwhelmed. *What had I signed up for?*

II. OPERATIONS OVERVIEW

Chapter 2
Straight Ridge Mine

As previously arranged, I met Al Hunt the next morning at the main office to start the operations download. We spent a couple hours reviewing records and transferring files on all the mines. He was extremely thorough on the detail and insisted on prying into past technical layouts, run schedules, and personnel policies. Al also asked me about each of the mine superintendents we were going to meet. He probed me for information about their personalities, family, and hobbies. My expression must have given away my confusion as to why this information was pertinent.

Al coached, "People understand best when you speak in their native language and through their interests. This is where most presenters are left behind. Most cannot get out of their world long enough to think of another's perspective. If you do not really know your audience, how can you write your speech? The presentation must be about them, not you. Remember Dirk, you must first decide what type of communication best serves the situation. *Basic communication* is for them to understand and relate. *Advanced communication* is achieved when you get them to buy-in to the solution. *Progressive communication* is a style in which involves your audience by having them inject input into a collaborated solution. *Influencing communication* is when you are able to earn their technical and/or moral respect, which will be vital later in the building of relationships. This is important when you are introducing and selling change. As a leader, you have to see yourself as a facilitator, salesman, designer, and builder. Your communication style should promote gathering the input, designing a plan, refining the solution, and aid in the selling of the change. Since each phase of the project has a different goal, time frame, and possibly participants, the communication type may also vary. A communication plan must be thought-out in advance. Again, most people communicate subconsciously

> **MOST PEOPLE CANNOT GET OUT OF THEIR OWN WORLD LONG ENOUGH TO THINK OF ANOTHER'S PERSPECTIVE.**

through their own perspective, thus not earning the buy-in of others. Optimum performance is achieved when every detail is delineated and executed, and that occurs when communication successfully threads all parts together. The other aspect of communication is mastering the art of *WHEN TO*. You can be the greatest orator around, but if the timing is off, your message will not be well received and good seed will be wasted. Look for times when the ground is fertile."

I didn't follow Al completely, but I was getting the feeling the accelerated course was just beginning. By lunch we were heading to the mine to meet and start our shadowing time with the mine superintendent.

Al wanted to swing by the local burger joint to get a bag of food for the mine.

"Getting them to share their hearts, sometimes requires that you feed them first," Al explained. He smiled, inhaled a test burger, and said, "Food works great as an opener, and that is legal if it is for a sincere cause—gathering information to help them refine their process is a sincere cause. And don't ever discount the belief that employees are constantly checking your sincerity. They are gifted with the ability to dissect your true motive. If it supports their gain, they will continue listening. If you are really good, they may even participate."

On the drive to the mine, I briefed Al on the operation. The Straight Ridge Mine is a solid performer, with decent conditions, and has an excellent management group. Their superintendent is a devout family man, avid hunter, and strong in people skills and communication.

"Thus I bet he is well respected?" Al questioned.

"You bet, he is our best," I boasted. "He defines the plans clearly, people receive him well, and they accept responsibility."

Entering the mine office building, we made a quick tour before finding our superintendent, Cody Meyers, who was back in the maintenance room talking to some mechanics. Cody introduced us to the hourly guys and then bragged on their recent accomplishments. We then joined Cody in his office to lay out the visit plans. At 2 p.m., Cody's watch alarm went off. He apologized for the interruption but said that was his reminder to visit the afternoon crew before they went underground. We lost him for about 10 minutes. While waiting for his return, we heard an eruption of laughter. We tracked the noise to the elevator where there was a young man bound-up in electrical tape and whimpering for release. We rolled him out of the elevator and cut him loose, to the disappointment of all the on-lookers. In collecting the story, we found out he was a new employee that "green-horned his car cable," which is when you pull your trailing cable apart—a rookie mistake that happens when you don't check the cable length. As we cut the poor guy loose, he grumbled, "I will never do that again."

Cody rejoined us in the crowd, leaned over and quietly whispered, "That is peer pressure at its finest." He turned to the jeering crew, "Don't you guys think you may have been a little hard on him?"

A tall lanky man in the back yelled out, "No, it cost us 30 minutes downtime. If you figure the cost of downtime at $100/minute, like they showed us in the last business workshop, that mistake cost us $3,000. We figured the $10 of tape was a good investment to stop it from happening again, since he was the root of the problem."

Cody, winked, smiled, and crowed, "As you can see, the crew is self- policing. We communicate the business cost so they understand it and challenge them to do better. We actually involve them in developing our *Best Practice* standards which improves buy-in; they are the experts."

Al questioned, "How do you then use and follow-up on those standards?"

"That's where we are weak," admitted Cody, "Do you have any ideas for ways to reinforce awareness?"

Al offered, "I was a part of an operation where we reviewed one specific operator's list of Best Practices (BP's) in each weekly communication meeting. Over the course of two months, we covered every position. We also required every operator to keep a laminated copy of their specific BP's with them. In the mine office we posted pictures and played a video that showed good and bad operating procedures. Repetition is an important key in making a new procedure a habit. Repetition via visual signage is free, and it subconsciously keeps the advertising constant and the desired behavior in-focus. With respect to BP follow-up, operation audits are the most effective, but let me defer until later, about explaining audits. Whether it is introducing BP's or any other process enhancement tool, each needs to be fully vetted for every operation, and the timing of their introduction is critical."

I chimed in, "Change must be orchestrated and supported. It's like preparing the ground, there is a time to plow and then a time to sow. Get that right, and there is a harvest."

Al returned, "Excellent analogy, it's also critical that the ground is not rocky or overcome by weeds, management must be wise as to where to plant the seed and when. Said another way, if the foundation is not laid correctly and timely, we labor in vain— we will discuss the foundation later."

> **IF THE FOUNDATION IS NOT LAID CORRECTLY AND TIMELY, WE LABOR IN VAIN.**

We followed Cody around, meeting more miners and then he again excused himself. After a few minutes he came back saying he privately needed to address a negative performance issue. We spent the next hour circulating as the crews came out. I gathered up a box of shift reports for Al to study overnight. As Al was leaving, I mentioned, "You probably noticed I have been taking a lot of notes throughout the day. I hope that's okay."

Al smirked. "If you hadn't have been, I would have figured you thought you knew everything and were above learning from my mistakes. If a lesson is important enough to share, the intelligent ones will write it down and reuse it," he affirmed. "That holds true for every site visit you make. Each should be an open challenge for you to find that group's creative pet peeves and learn from them. Your personal growth is a choice."

†

The next morning we were heading underground with Cody. As was a ritual for him, this involved a lot of greeting and visiting with the workforce. Attitudes seemed extremely positive, and someone even asked if I had a good rumor from the corporate office. Al nosed in and volunteered to trade one for one. The guy complained, "That's the problem, I don't have one to trade, Cody tells us everything."

Al looked at me and said, "That's the way it should be."

We spent the entire shift at the production face area with Al discreetly taking notes and jotting down cycle times. I was so impressed with how detailed he was, and yet he never put people on the defensive. He asked numerous questions and prompted a lot of discussion on their input. He also challenged them to search for process improvements. I probed Al, "What is the key to getting employees' input?"

Al responded, "Convince them your focus is on the process, not people and names. Show them you are willing to get in and understand their world, and give them the assurance their input will be considered—then they will join in the solution. As an industry, we lost a tremendous tool for studying efficiency when we abolished the comprehensive time study programs. In the name of cost reduction, most companies eliminated these study personnel in the 1980's and 1990's. From a total cost effect, that was a mistake. Studying cycle and individual process times are vital in bottleneck reduction, but they have to be done in a way that does not demoralize the workforce. I like to see this information gathering done under two programs. The first is called a *Process Study*, where we observe, time, and analyze all affecting conditions, downtimes, and processes. It is a numbers study to define the flow restrictors—be it situational, equipment oriented, section layout, or behavioral based. The second slice of information critical to the equation is operator input. We truly miss the whole picture, if we do not drill down on their observations and ideas. They live the daily frustrations, thus why do we not take time to weigh their suggestions? I term this collecting vehicle, *Efficiency Surveys*. As we incorporate both these information gathering techniques, a realistic Best Practice can be developed and then continually refined. Utilizing these tools correctly will achieve major efficiency gains and operator buy-in. Cody, I will send you a cheat sheet on do's and don'ts for Process Studies that may help (Appendix B.03)."

Cody shook his head, "I would appreciate those notes. My people's attitude toward time studies in the past has been bad because the results were not handled professionally nor were the findings acted on."

Al offered, "Here's a story along that same line. One time when I was doing some consulting work for a friend of mine, he asked me to help him with a Process Study at one of his mines. He had warned me there had been numerous management consultants in before and the results were poor. He feared mine management and the workforce probably would not be very open to my presence. I decided to start my study with one production crew who was on their week of second shift rotation. I went in with them every evening shift for the week. While I worked with them, I got the chance to study each operator's habits, observe the cycle flow, and yes, gather time study data. Over the week, I spent at least an hour individually with each employee in not only observation but interacting with them personally, asking for their input, and discussing process improvement ideas. The crew and their face boss accepted me very well and had hopes their comments would help. Once I promised no names would be used in my report regarding negative information, they were open to share. The crew nicknamed me Timex. After the first week we rotated to the day shift. As we were getting ready to go underground the first morning, I overheard an equipment salesman, who was visiting the mine, talking to one of the guys on the crew. Referring to me, the vendor said, 'What is that guy doing here?' The crew member replied that he was just a time-study guy, here to help us. He is a good belt shoveler too. He falls in and helps wherever needed. The salesman replied, 'Do you not know who he is?' The operator replied, 'Sure, his name is Al, we call him Timex.' The vendor said, 'I don't know why or how that guy is here, but he is not just a time-study guy. He is one of the better mine operators in the industry and has been the president of a number of coal companies.' As I came around the corner, their conversation stopped and I realized my cover had been blown. The enlightened crewman spouted, 'All right, we just got the whole story, and your name has just been changed to Rolex.' Moral of the story—*once you have lived their world, shown humility, and earned their trust, they will share information because they believe it will add value.* Remember, if you sincerely convince them you need and value their input, and that names will be protected, they will open up."

Cody interjected, "Let's head back outside now as I start my monthly superintendent meetings with crews. I would appreciate it if you both would watch a few of my presentations and critique me. I am struggling a little with meeting control, particularly when a heckler fires-out a negative question with a nasty spin. Any suggestions?"

Al paused for a moment and then said, "Dirk tells me you are a hunter, we've got that in common. I am also very passionate about hunting. I was on a grizzly hunt in Alaska a few years back, and when you hunt dangerous game, you have to take it very seriously. You have to learn your adversary's strengths and plan to keep the upper-hand. Research their habits so you can predict their response. I remember a story that an experienced guide shared with me about a Kodiak bear hunt that almost went bad. After his client shot the bear, it headed deep into the alders and with three feet of snow, mobility was limited. As the guide proceeded into the brush following the wounded bear, he proceeded very carefully. Since Kodiaks are known for charging back on their pursuers, the first tracking rule is to watch the tracks 30 feet in advance of your position. As the guide and the hunter came around a big downed tree, the guide halted. Something didn't look right. He backed up and climbed a large rock to his left, and glassed the tracks ahead. Sure enough, the tracks were double toed, which meant the bear had back-tracked in his own footsteps to bushwhack his pursuers. As the guide looked around, he found a pile of disturbed snow only 15 feet from their original position. Careful examination revealed steam coming from under the snow where the ambusher awaited. Four shots later not only assured the story would have a positive ending for the hunters, it reaffirmed the importance of knowing your aggressor and their habits."

Giving the hunting story a minute to sink in, Al then continued, "Before every meeting, I rehearse the top five negative questions with which I think I could be assaulted. It's like the hunt, I keep my safety on but I have the gun loaded. If I think there is a good chance of a sniper set-up, I will be proactive and I will bring up a loaded question myself. You might say, 'Some of you might be wondering...' that way you can phrase the question in a more neutral way and get credit for being honest and open. By bringing it up yourself, you can figure out where in the meeting to fit it in and still maintain a positive atmosphere, and also protect your closing remarks. It also defangs the heckler, since you can be assured there will always be one around. I want people to feel free to ask questions, but you have to protect against negative motives." Al went on to exhort Cody, "Remain focused on teaching and encouraging the neutral and positive employees. We all have a habit of spending too much time with the negative people. The 80/20 rule applies. We spend 80% of our time with 20% of the people, and commonly a disproportionate number of them are the disgruntled ones. People-investment is always good, but with limited time you are charged to get the most out of every minute you have." Al pulled out a little note pad and drew the following chart:

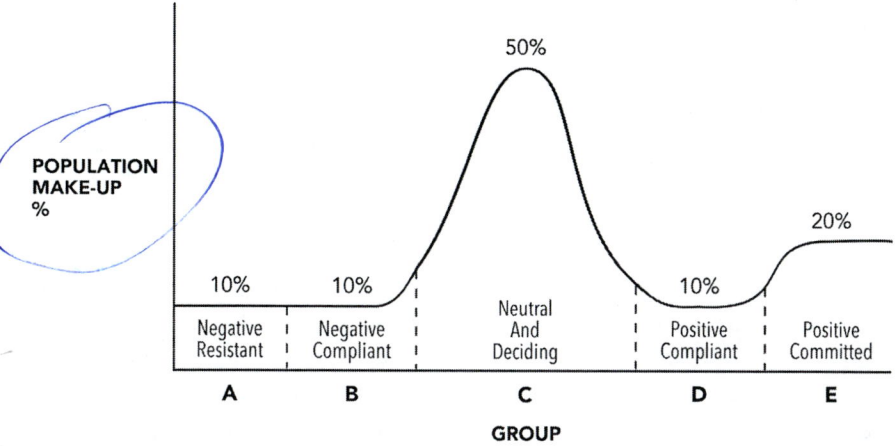

Al continued, "Let's talk a little about what the goal is when we're developing our team. We want people to be committed and genuinely onboard with us. There is a big difference between being committed and being compliant. Compliant is doing something because we are told to do it. There's no mental or buy-in investment. Committed is doing something because we believe and want to do it. A conscience decision has been made to join the program. Leadership must foster the correct motives. When a manager addresses their work group by saying, *they told me to tell you,* they are spreading compliant values and you need to remove them from leadership. It may not mean he or she is a bad person, but just unwilling to carry the flag high. We must build a committed base if we aspire to get to GREAT. Our managers must be focused on growing *positive committed* Group E employees in numbers."

As he further explained the chart, Al emphasized, "I believe in time everyone can be matured to the *positive committed*. But there are time constraints involved. We must prioritize the majority of our time investment to the *neutral and deciding* employee Group C. Groups D and E deserve some of our time to show appreciation and encouragement for the positive support and growing commitment. Another small portion of time should be invested in Groups A and B to give them a chance to change their position. Unfortunately, most of Group A usually stays *negative resistant* and thus an elimination plan should be enacted swiftly. As an industry, we are way too passive in letting these attitudes infect our companies. This is the tough part of management, but we have to remember, we are charged to *protect the house*. Studies have shown weeding out the negative not only protects the positive, it promotes creativity, and encourages growth and retention of the strongest. The *negative resistant* are those that should be hurled off the bus. Sounds cold, but we have to learn to expediently remove the detractors who won't join the team."

Cody admitted, "That's where I have a hard time since those people have families too. But I must admit, I get too distracted with all the second chances and I let the negative people deflate our progress."

Supportively, Al replied, "We all can migrate there, but we must remember we have a responsibility to the entire group. Early in my career I made the same mistakes; I always thought I could help everyone come around. Some never did, and some took so much of my time the whole team suffered. I've learned that dropping our expectations temporarily for a few, shows inconsistency. It's a delicate, fine line. If we continue accepting lower standards and attitudes, we won't achieve GREAT. In my career I have had to discharge about 80 people, but operations growth has allowed me to hire over 1,600 and tear up 2,000 WARN shut-down notices, thus my record is a net positive 3,520. You have to defensively protect progress. If you go back to the chart and look closely at the A Group, you'll usually find that these people are the same ones who have other authority issues. Their negative attributes show up a great deal in their lives. And yes, they have families, but so does someone else who is looking to be a positive part of a new company. The majority of our managerial time needs to be spent on Group C, to help move them to the E position. Their loyalty must be earned, as they first will need to believe in the cause, then the leader, and finally the program."

†

The next three days was more of the same—meetings, tours, and observations. Cody continued to pick at Al for communication pointers. Al was trying to be a quiet observer, but since communications was a pet area of his, and Cody was an eager learner, Al let loose a full critique, "Okay. Here's my critiques:

> **EFFICIENCY IS DEFINED AS MAXIMIZED SAFETY BALANCED WITH OPTIMUM PRODUCTIVITY.**

1) I recommend that you always comment on the safety results, injuries, and violations first. By keeping safety your lead-off issue, you are re-enforcing to your team that it is an uncompromisable core value. I prefer to view efficiency as a complimentary term and as our focus goal, whereas I define efficiency as maximized safety with optimized productivity. If you sell safety as the single goal, then the most successful operations are those that are shut down, since potential safety issues have been eliminated. We have to get in the habit of teaching efficiency: *The*

balanced attack to the earning of security. In fact, that would sell well on a sign. Hint-hint.

2) You do a good job of touching base with many employees, but sometimes you get into a prolonged visit with one employee that robs time with others. Try to be sensitive to the whole group, not just a few. Another time-utilizing technique you can use is to join an employee in their work as you talk and listen. Since over 50% of our communication is through non-verbal means and the first impression carries heavy weight, falling in to help someone as you communicate is extremely effective. The obvious main goals are to gain input and express your personal interest in them, but at the same time, if you can help them on their job, they don't have the frustration of getting behind while you are visiting them. People don't remember how long you worked with them, but they do remember you were humble enough to help. Don't forget, they are constantly reading your heart.

3) Your pre-shift meeting with the foreman is an excellent idea, but it sometimes drags on too long. Use a Stephen Covey principle, 'Begin every meeting with the end-in-mind.' Use the meeting to emphasize key focus points and stay on track.

4) In your cost cutting communication, make sure you are balanced and the focus areas are based on the correct unit measurement. For example, if you only post the parts and supply cost per item, and not the frequency of use, you are only giving your people part of the prioritizing equation. In the case of mining, the item should be viewed from a cost per the final product (i.e. cost/clean ton). General cost reduction programs are okay, but specific prioritized attacks will yield more immediate results. Highlighting the low hanging fruit is the manager's job. I have seen so many people emphasize the wrong things in cost control. I once saw an operation put in a washing machine and dryer to recycle cloth gloves. It was a fetish of the superintendent to stop buying replacement gloves. Yes, it saved money, but the intangible negatives far outweighed the possible positives: The employees' distaste in reusing old gloves, and the management follow-up needed to keep the program running, just wasn't worth the effort to wash and process the reused cloth gloves. There were other *low hanging* projects that benefitted far more from equal focus. Many old-style managers address cost as though they can save their way to a profit. Most progressive leaders realize improving efficiencies pays better dividends. Helping educate people in mine economics is a good investment of your time. I will send you some workshop notes of Mine Economics 101, from a past project (Appendix B.04), that I believe you'll find helpful.

5) In your superintendent meeting presentations, you do a good job of staying on your Power Point items, but you need to be a little more flexible in running applicable rabbits. An effective leader reads his audience, uses stories and events

from their shifts, matches their terminology, explains things in the way that they think, and motivates in a style to which they can relate. In short—speak their language through their eyes. Our people are listening to their filtered channel, WIIFM —What's In It For Me? Once you show them *the pot of gold*, they will be more open to the plan to follow the rainbow.

6) You are a strong presenter and do well in one-on-ones. But here's a tip to help enhance your influence. Getting people off their own agenda to listen to what you have to say is always a challenge. Dale Carnegie wrote, 'Most people don't listen to understand, they listen to reply.' So be patient; sometimes it's a good idea to restate your points multiple ways and times.

> **DO AN EXCELLENT JOB OF PRAISING YOUR PEOPLE IN PUBLIC AND DISCIPLINING IN PRIVATE.**

7) You do an excellent job of praising your people in public and disciplining in private, I saw that on several occasions. When maximizing the effect of your positive motivation, you might consider using a compliment for a dual purpose.

Offer the sincere specific praise for one situation and then cordially encourage them on another project. This technique utilizes momentum to help propagate continued progress. When you achieve a smile, people are a lot more amenable to follow the direction. That is true not only in a speech but also in postings. When you post a success note, you can also emphasize the trend direction and/or project progress, and then offer a specific challenge. Keep in mind, once you earn their respect and trust, and they are listening to WIIFM, you will have an opportunity to lead them across the rainbow. Communication, in all of its forms, is a vital tool in that leading.

8) It is critical to sincerely show your team that everyone is needed and equally valued. The ownership buy-in felt among your people is testament that they are sharing in the business accountability. Most companies never get there.

9) Posting publicly is a wonderful opportunity to praise positive efforts. I used to require three positive notes on the wall or bulletin board for every negative one. Here's a tip for balancing criticism with praise: If you have a criticism to share, lead with an honest compliment, then deliver the negative, and end with a positive. Creating the right environment increases the acceptance of all the communication.

10) You and your team should be very proud of the positive morale and buy-in, but I feel you could help them achieve even more of their potential. If you truly believe you are helping them earn security, you should expect a faster response in the raising of standards. If you run 5 miles/hr, your team may keep up at 3, but

on a whole, they won't pass you. You are the pace-setter. Your team knows they are performing substantially below their potential. Our job is to tool them, lay-out the plan, and help them maximize their potential. I once read, 'Morale is a barometer of engagement,' By that definition you guys are on course."

As I looked over at Cody, he was scribbling away. Holding up his notes, he said, "Al, these are insightful, invaluable, and challenging. They will help us."

Al pointed to the sign on the bathhouse wall which read, ATTITUDE IS A DAILY CHOICE, LET'S ENJOY TODAY. Then he told Cody, "Keep building it, they will follow."

On our walk to the car, I looked at Al and said, "I am in awe of your experience and knowledge."

Al humbly replied, "Dirk, I have been given a lot of opportunities to learn and mentor under many strong individuals. I have always pushed myself hard to learn something from each. I have never gone to an operation where I did not take away notes. That's how I got labeled a strategist. I was always scheming to customize the best plan. I don't consider myself to be that smart, just a well-seasoned student. My views and quotes in many cases, trace back to those I worked for, pastors I have sat under, and authors I have read. I am inbred with a little Carnegie, Covey, Maxwell, Warren, Collins, Blackaby, Robbins,… and His Word. Reading outside your normal environment continues to sharpen your sword, as scripture shares, 'iron sharpens iron.' In a comparative way, we should all be wearing a multi-colored coat, with threads woven from all the opportunities, individuals, and teachings in our lives. That coat is a protection from the weathering trials and darts to which we leaders are subjected."

"Al, that's inspiring. Could you send me a copy of your top ranked reading list?" (Appendix B.01).

"Sure, Dirk, but keep in mind that my studying favorites are a reflection of my heart and my values. You have to choose for yourself, 'whom and what you will serve.'"

II. OPERATIONS OVERVIEW

Chapter 3
Broad Run Mine

The sign on the haul road coming in gave us a prelude of the mine's personality: NO PAIN, NO GAIN. In my operations summary I introduced Broad Run as our flagship mine and explained that it was being run by a very strong-handed superintendent.

Luke Couch is a repressive dictator, and he is proud of it. His sergeants are clones, who very forcefully carry out his style through every facet of the operation. As we entered the office, Luke was conducting a meeting with a couple vendors on a new productivity tracking system. He called a break and formally welcomed us. After the usual pleasantries, he invited us to catch the remainder of the meeting. Watching Luke rant about the mission of the project and people's resistance to accept accountability made even me feel uncomfortable. I knew Al would not take it well either. Luke was disrespectful in the way he challenged the potential monitoring system providers, and his comments about our own employees were degrading. His final statement summed it all up—"I want a real-time report showing when every car is loaded and dumped, and how long it takes to do every facet of the cutting cycle. I want this automatically analyzed, and a productivity score assigned and displayed on a ticker screen as the crew comes out of the mine. If a minimum score is not realized, I want the people responsible in my office."

When the meeting dispersed, I looked at Al and said, "I wish I could lie to you and say that Luke was just showboating but I can't. That is vintage Luke."

Al held back as Luke charged up to us.

Luke blared, "What did you think?"

Al said, "Your idea is tremendous and will be huge in helping to follow up on accountability. The immediate feedback of the crew's results will be very valuable as well. But I can't agree with your motivation technique. We should use productivity tracking as a positive accountability tool and as a method to teach improvements, not to instill fear."

Luke rifled back, "Fear is a great motivator, and micro-managing allows me to keep a hand on their throats."

Al responded, "I did not come here to argue, I will respect your opinion."

Luke knew he had not won, but he decided to move on, "I have another meeting with my senior staff on a production method change, if you would like to join us."

We nodded in agreement.

Luke started the meeting off by saying that with recent safety law changes and the rumored policy agendas, he believed *split air* super sections would be the most productive continuous miner layout. He then informed the group that all three of their current single miner sections would be expanded to the new layout asap. He then added we would be putting a second boss in each enlarged unit. After a short discussion of the supporting changes needed to make the transition, Luke set a one-month deadline and adjourned the meeting. As we followed him into his office, Luke spun around and asked, "Was I wrong about that too?"

Al took a moment before responding, "I compliment you for being proactive with the recent safety policy pressures, and I do agree that the *dual split* is the most compliant and efficient system in most situations. I have always subscribed to the philosophy that working with the agencies where possible is a better strategy in the end. Especially in this case, where as an industry we have to improve our operating layouts with respect to dust exposure to our people, and yet at the same time, more effectively utilize our equipment and people."

"So you do agree that *split air* ventilation on super units is the best choice?" Luke questioned.

Al answered, "I am always reluctant to recommend an equipment type or unit layout in general, as every case is different. In this particular case with the mining conditions that I understand you have, I think you have chosen wisely. I definitely favor *split air* versus *sweep air supers*. I'll send you a system comparison that I worked up for a former client (Appendix B.05). Because you are so dialed in on efficiency, correctly I might add, I am sure you realize that the exact way a super unit is staffed and run depends on the bottlenecks in the process."

"Oh, yes," Luke added, "I'm all over that. For us it's the roof bolting cycle. We have to manage around our bolters, not the production crews. The production crews pace themselves, conscientiously or subconsciously, behind the bolters. As we have made the bolter up-time availability a higher priority, we have seen strong production gains. This is a diametric change from the past, as we used to only focus on loading crew efficiencies."

Al agreed, "This is a fundamental change throughout the industry. With the easy mining gone and mining conditions eroding, the roof control issues have risen to the lead. If and when a bottleneck is mitigated, it pushes the problem somewhere else, but to a lower degree. The surviving companies must learn to evolve their operating techniques. If you want to lead the field, you have to be willing to break from the old paradigms. Being a student of the environment and adaptable to change, keeps you from being one of the extinct dinosaurs. Some companies are so resistant to change they die without accepting the new book."

Luke pressed, "I am curious what measurements you use to track the bolting bottleneck. How about elaborating?"

Al answered, "I like building through positive accountability, but with a laser focus on the critical path or bottleneck process. In your case, one of the *Key Performance Indicators* (KPI's) would probably be *Bolting Efficiency*, defined as the bolts installed per up-time minute. The bolting rate will directly influence the cut cycle sequence and unit management. As bolting rates improve from everyone's focus, this will then turn the bottleneck back to the production crew where it should be. At that time, the focus KPI is the *Production Efficiency*: tons mined per up-time minute. This KPI follow-up technique closely parallels a version of the old Management By Objectives (MBO) style. It keeps us in line and maintains a correct emphasis and monitoring on the driving factors. Another way to phrase it is: an interactive industrial process is more like a game of chess rather than checkers. Every process change cascades a new line of limiting factors and opportunities. The faster those challenges are dealt with, the greater the chance of survival. To combat all the dynamics, I like to use KPI's as a total process check and balance. This keeps efficiency evolving. The major KPI's for an underground section are listed on a sheet I will send you (Appendix B.06). Trending these KPI's also moves competition for improvement to the forefront and visual. *As we monitor, they will manage and we all win.*"

"The next point I want to mention," Al added, "is the difference between efficiency and effectiveness. We can be efficient but effectiveness pays the bills. I preach efficiency, maximized safety with optimized productivity, to everyone individually. But management's job is to then take all the best performances and strategically coordinate optimal effective team performance. This again, is where KPI's come into play. The heart of ensuring effective output is to address the correct KPI's, and then to make sure smart, hard work gets rewarded in earned security."

Luke proclaimed, "I like another method: When they screw up or don't react fast enough, I kick them in their rears. Then I fire the weak ones. That's why I fire so many managers. They don't react fast enough."

"You might try the education route first," Al offered. "Teach them the KPI's to manage by and the process clues to look for. I would also encourage you to involve your workforce in the same thought process. The best teams are those that pull together and understand the dynamics of their load. With respect to the earlier question on two face bosses for the dual section, I strongly agree. The face boss position is one of the most difficult positions at the mine, and their follow-up is critical. A dual split would be overwhelming to manage with one person, and certain follow-up details would be lost. Having two also provides a very progressive way to train new foremen under the tutelage of the veterans. I recently did this at another operation and just by adding the second foreman, we picked up productivity rates by 15%."

Luke interjected, "Because there was a second foreman with a whip."

"I would hope the real reason was better coordination, accountability, and positive follow-up," Al refuted.

I stepped in as the peacemaker and said, "You guys just have different outlooks, but at least you are heading in the same direction."

"One more little thing we learned," Al said. "We had each boss fill out a report on the side he managed. We picked up another 10% on our productivity rates, supporting the saying, 'The closer and more often you monitor, the better the results.'"

It was getting late, and we were all done in. We decided to reconvene in the morning.

As we were leaving I turned to Al, "I credit you on this one. Luke listened more to you than I have ever seen him listen to anyone."

Al responded, "That's because I spoke his language on his WIIFM channel."

"Calling him wise and correct, didn't hurt either," I added with a smile.

"Those were sincere words that opened him up to the listening and learning," Al said. "Sometimes by feeding the lion, we can focus and direct its attack."

☨

The next morning we went for a tour of the warehouse. Luke was quick to brag about all the cost saving ideas he had implemented. He was especially boastful about the continuous miner cutting bits. "We had been paying $4.50/bit and now I am getting used bits from a neighboring company's prep plant's magnet for $2.00/bit and they are only 30% used. At our old usage rate of 9,000 bits/month, that's a savings of $15,000/month. This reinforces my favorite cost saving line, 'Do more with less and cheaper, faster.' Those are the kind of reasons why I deserve a raise," Luke spouted.

The remaining part of the tour was more of the same. As we headed back to the office, Luke stopped to talk to a foreman who was on the phone. The foreman prematurely finished the call.

Luke tartly asked, "What are you doing outside? Surely your production crew isn't waiting on you."

The distraught foreman replied, "No, the shift foreman took my crew in. That was my wife and she just called to say we have a major water leak in the basement. She's falling apart."

Luke sternly asked, "And are you a plumber?"

The foreman looked confused and replied, "No, but-"

Luke cut him off and said, "Then tell her to call one and let you try to save the job you have." As we walked away, Luke looked at us and said, "People are just not committed to their jobs."

Luke's secretary, Peggy, motioned at us that Luke had a call from the main office.

I looked at Al expecting a full sermon. All he said was, "The way we treat people and handle trials broadcasts our character and values. Our mouth speaks our heart's response. I am not going to waste my time on Luke's style critique or offer any constructive advice; it's like continuing to throw pearls to the swine. His beliefs are printed all over the building: He personally assigned himself an extra-large parking spot with his name on it; the lights are dim in every office and hall except his; and all his chairs in his office, except his, have had the legs cut down a couple of inches. Do you not see the game?"

"I had not noticed those things, but I figured you would comment on the two signs in the foreman's room that read, THE TOUGHER THE MARKET, THE FEWER THE SURVIVORS and MEASURE WITH A MICROMETER BUT CUT WITH A KNIFE."

Al reeled, "My point exactly, I will give him this, his fear message is consistent. On mining skills, I give him an A, but he fails in presentation and inclusion. A one-man army does not win many wars. It pays to enlist the troops. His cost containment ideas are very old line also. On his bit-saving example, he left out a number of other consequences. The used duller bits have bad effects on dust generation, cutting rates, bit block wear, and motor amps. They also increase bit change downtime. Figuring a normal change time of 30 seconds/bit, and that only half of the bit change time actually translates into *delay to load time*, the downtime cost increase per month for his plan

> " A ONE-MAN ARMY DOES NOT WIN MANY WARS. IT PAYS TO ENLIST THE TROOPS.

was about $67,000. This far overshadows the saved $15,000 in purchase price. In mining, since the downtime cost is so high, most of the time, the default should be on the longer lasting and better performing part. Buying poorer quality supplies can have intangible effects on employee morale and in many cases can be linked to injuries and violations. This reinforces the statement, *'the right and best practices yield top safety and productivity performance together.'*

When Luke returned from the call, Al suggested that he'd like to dive into the equipment maintenance records, since it would take him a couple days to finish a complete review. Al still managed to catch numerous daily meetings and mix in with the people.

Luke found us the next afternoon and asked for some more of Al's time. "I consider myself a master of mine layouts," Luke announced, "But I want to pick your brain. Tell me the top ten operational layout rules."

Al said, "Let me think on that one and I will send you a couple dozen (Appendix B.07). As we discussed before, since each operation, and unit for that matter, varies in conditions, equipment, schedule, workforce and management, the most effective layout must be flexible and adaptable. With respect to the production face, I am a fan of developing a detailed pie chart of delays and then studying that chart for focus areas. There is usually low hanging fruit that gets the progress momentum moving the fastest. Usually the largest category for potential improvement is Operational Delays. Getting everyone in line with these areas of improvement can be huge in terms of the bottom line and security. Our people want to be communicated with and involved. If you want to give me a stack of your shift production/delay reports, any available time study data, and any loss investigations, I will try to build you an example."

"Great," Luke reacted, "I will look forward to picking your pie chart apart."

The next day Al returned with his homework assignment. Handing Luke three pages he said, "This exercise could have been worked up for any industrial process. It should help you prioritize your downtime focus. Assuming your data was correct, here is how I assess your specific issues. The first page (Appendix B.08) is the *Typical Time Distribution* so we can focus on high impact areas. From here I built a *Cost of Loss for Safety* (Appendix B.09) and *Cost of Loss for Production* (Appendix B.10). The Cost of Loss sheets are the teaching backbone for improvement. They are to be custom developed from every work site. Our employees understand dollars, so arming them with the cost of our losses helps them relate to the WHY we need to change and the information to prioritize which areas to change first. It is like raising teenagers—train them right and with the correct values, and they will make the right decision (most of the time) late at night when you are not around. Our employees respond similarly. If you don't take the time to teach WHY and foster solid values, you will have to be there for every decision. And you can't be there for everyone! Nor should you."

As Luke reviewed the sheets, he admitted, "This is really good, but the hourly won't understand it."

Al refuted, "Yes they will, if you explain it correctly. They are smarter than you are crediting them. This information communicates to them: 'I am going to treat you like an equal business partner, because you are,' and then proceed to explain the performance effects to the bottom line." Al explained that it's important to always emphasize that total economics determines our future, BUT safety failures are also factored in because they have huge costs. More importantly, we all have a moral responsibility for being our brothers' keepers. "That's just not lip service," he said "that's an uncompromising value that WE WILL NOT break." Al continued, "After reviewing the Cost of Loss items, individual action plans can be created with everyone's input. When handled correctly, I have seen efficiency gains (safety and productivity) of over 30% in just a couple months."

Luke said, "Okay. I will make the action plans for them."

"You can do that," Al added, "but you will stifle peak performance. If your true motive is the operation security, earning your people's buy-in must be part of the solution. Granted it commonly takes longer to achieve their ownership, but I promise you it will be worth it. People always perform better when they feel they are sincerely valued and their ideas are considered. The second reason to adopt this approach is that multiple inputs are ALWAYS better than one perspective. I love this saying, *'none of us is smarter than all of us.'* The natural deterrent here is time. If better Best Practices come from taking the time to gather input, shouldn't we modify our style to build a better set of job and process guidelines?"

"I am all about the win," Luke resounded, "Look at my numbers."

"Just make sure you are looking at the right numbers, and remember, it's the total performance at the end of the game that counts," Al warned.

Luke wasn't won over. He said, "I hear you, but I am going to hold my course."

†

On the final day of our visit, Luke invited us to join him in a meeting with some of his production foremen. He began the meeting by announcing that their mine had again achieved the best quarterly cost numbers for Profit Coal. To be precise,

Broad Run provided 51% of the profit for the company. They had maintained that title over the past two years. Luke then reviewed a new program that he had started: Every operator had been assigned a primary job function and secondary *prevent project*. Prevent projects were cleaning equipment, housekeeping, safety checks, or productivity enhancers. Luke closed the meeting by emphasizing law compliance, and sent the managers underground to audit adherence to the policy. We joined in the audit. Al and I went together and were very impressed that all four employees we interviewed had done their prevent projects. When we asked why they did it, two answered, "because they will fire us if we don't." Another stated, "they will catch us," and the last was afraid to answer.

Al looked at me and growled, "This lack of respect being shown to the workforce is why unions evolve. Most operations that are unionized violated employee respect somewhere in the past. This is a good example of the difference between being committed (due to belief and praise) and being compliant (due to mandates and punishment). Management builds the atmosphere and employees copy the attitude. Negative atmosphere yields low personal efficiency and thus a failing team effectiveness—the result being: operations economically fold and families go hungry. A lose-lose."

> **MANAGEMENT BUILDS THE ATMOSPHERE AND EMPLOYEES COPY THE ATTITUDE.**

"If that were to happen, it would clearly be our fault," I embarrassingly admitted.

I felt bad that the week had been so confrontational. Although Al seemed fine, I knew he was frustrated for the employees. To decompress, I suggested we grab some Chinese take-out and that he come over to my house for dinner.

Al seemed eager, "I would love that, if your wife is agreeable to a surprise guest."

"As long as we are bringing food, she will be fine," I laughed, "The twins are already in bed this time of night."

☦

Nikki and Colt met us at the front door. Colt exploded, "Daddy, Daddy! Is this him?"

I said, "Yes, this is Mr. Hunt. He has been helping me at work."

"We know all about you," Colt announced, as he dragged Al by the hand through the house. "Daddy says you're a savior."

Broad Run Mine 31

Al humbly said, "No, there is only one of those, and I am learning from Him every day. I am just a guy sharing stories from things I have learned and mistakes I have made in the past. Colt, you need to make sure your Daddy teaches you about all the things he learns. This is one of the greatest gifts a father can give his son. You need to be a good listener. Remember, it is better to lead wisely, than to rule sternly."

"What do you mean?" Colt asked.

Al hit a knee next to Colt, "It is better to gently lead the team or a flock, than to beat them with a stick. If you guide people through respect, you will earn their best."

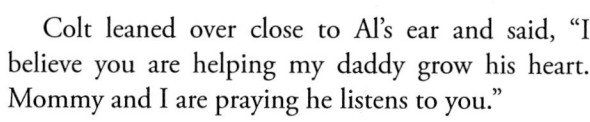

> IT IS BETTER TO LEAD WISELY, THAN TO RULE STERNLY.

Colt continued, "Daddy tells me about a lot of the problems at work and how hard it is to know what to do. He really wants to help the workers and their families. Mr. Hunt, how do you figure out how to help people solve hard problems?"

"I ask them for their ideas and I ask God for His," Al replied.

Colt asked, "How do you know what God says?"

Al whispered, "Sometimes God just gives me a good idea and other times He gives me a warm feeling in my heart that I am doing the right thing. Has He ever talked to you through your heart, Colt?"

Colt nodded and confessed, "If I do wrong, I don't feel good inside, Mommy says that's God."

"That's how God steers us to make the right decisions. If we stay sensitive, God will help lead us through the tough times and be a blessing to others we are around," Al assured.

Colt leaned over close to Al's ear and said, "I believe you are helping my daddy grow his heart. Mommy and I are praying he listens to you."

Al shared back, "You keep the prayers coming, I will work on my end, and I believe He will not let us down."

Colt smiled big, offered a knuckle bump of camaraderie and said, "Teamwork, right?"

Al winked and said, "In Him everything is possible and to the Greater End."

GUIDANCE

II. OPERATIONS OVERVIEW

Chapter 4
Deep Hollow Mine

It didn't take much prodding to get Makirra Cole, superintendent of Deep Hollow, to launch into an enthusiastic discussion about her ideas for improving things at the mine, especially her #1 passion.

"Training is my favorite subject; it holds so many keys to our future." Makirra lit up as she spoke. "It truly empowers every part of the employee, specifically, learning about the concepts of business and operations costs." This knowledge enlightens employees so that they can make better decisions. I firmly believe that with this foundation, employees can use problem solving skills and loss prevention techniques to proactively address actual and potential issues. When you connect all that with skills training, for specific job functions—whether it is managerial, technical, maintenance, or operations—our team becomes energized. A balanced training program invests money in our greatest resource, our people. The pay-off not only shows up in performance numbers, but it is good for morale and reduces turnover."

"I agree, it's a win-win for everyone," Al added.

"Having a strong training program also allows us to hire for character, and then we can train the skills our way. That gives us better employees in the long run. We have found that more experienced employees sometimes carry many bad habits and attitudes from prior, poorly run operations," Makirra expounded.

"I have done it both ways," Al commented, "and I agree. If you can stand the initial inexperience wave, the resulting newer workforce, in the medium and long term, will more closely match your values and expectations. I had a *brownfield* build-up (an operation that is dramatically increased in size and scope) where we hired 200 people in four months to fill operator positions. The majority were inexperienced in underground coal mining, but 70% of them had maintenance backgrounds. We taught the new employees that every operator also had the basic maintenance responsibilities for their equipment, as long as they were certified for the servicing and/or repair. After an initial training period, this employee group became one of the best all-around groups I have ever seen. They took personal pride in taking care of their equipment. It was a classic case of investing in your greatest asset—your people."

Makirra went on to explain her points, "Not only do we have class training and pre-shift workshops, we also have an elaborate on-the-job training rotation, and skills auditing follow-up. Talent-management has traditionally been very poor in the mining industry, but we focus heavily on it—and it pays off. Following-up on the needed skills for our employees' current job and future career growth is a commitment we take very seriously. Improving skill sets are important but it also shows commitment to our employees when we help them advance their career."

Al interjected, "You might like to try using a *Job Book* to compliment your employee development program. I've witnessed how successful it can be. A Job Book is where employees put their name in the book if they would like to be considered for a future open position. If a position comes open, management can move fast to fill the vacancy, while at the same time trying to fairly offer opportunities to those wanting a change. The positions would be filled on interest, seniority, skill set, and employee record. Makirra, earlier you mentioned something about balanced training. What did you mean?"

"Balanced training has two parts," she explained, "I am going to let my partner, Pete, explain the first part."

Pete introduced himself as Prevention Pete. "That's what they call me and I consider it a compliment. We look at everything as a potential loss. A loss is an injury, violation, downtime, rework, or waste. Most companies have different programs for each of these areas and the employees are always trying to figure out which is the *priority of the day*. We believe each of those five losses is the symptom of a failure, and we have one system to find the root problem. It is like finding a log jam in a river; you must first find the problem log. When we first introduced the prevention concept, we focused on investigating losses after they happened, but now our goal is to be studying the near misses, not just the failures. If you refer to the Heinrich Triangle (Appendix B.11), it reminds us the value of learning from multiple events, not single failures. We believe that if our employees don't have losses, they will safely produce, and that efficiency yields operation security. One of my sayings is, 'Prevention accomplished, yields security.' The most enjoyable shifts are when no one gets hurt and we run a large quantity of coal. The full prevention training covers root versus symptom analysis, reasons for losses (Appendix B.12), and parallel processes, if losses occur (Appendix B.13)."

> " PREVENTION ACCOMPLISHED, YIELDS SECURITY.

Al poked at Pete, "You really believe that stuff, don't you."

Pete reacted, "Yes, Sir, and apparently our people do also. We have decreased our injuries and violations to below half of the national average; we won the Sentinel of Safety Award for *no loss time* injuries last year; and our production rates and costs have improved dramatically over the last two years."

"You guys are truly building a powerhouse," Al congratulated, smiling broadly.

I knew Al was enjoying the energy, so I continued to spur it on by asking Makirra, "What was the second part of balanced training you referred to?"

She started, "Thanks for listening to Pete talk about prevention. He is so passionate about prevention, and he is leading us on the journey toward his challenge goal of the flawless shift. We tease him that he is allergic to loss. The second part of balanced training is awakening people to process improvement. As an industry, mining is so far behind in process improvement techniques it's unpardonable. Maximizing process is about protecting flow. Even the best time studies do not show the complete effect of flow disruption or capture the momentum gains seen in a good shift. Studying flow is like looking for the single weak link in a chain. Strengthening all the other links does not make the chain stronger. Strengthening or eliminating the true weak link is the only thing that will release the flow. We are studying process cycles, getting input from our people, and learning things we have never seen before. Some of the ideas are very simple, but they are having profound effects."

I added, "One of our other superintendents is focusing similarly and calling it 'studying the bottleneck.' But your style is more empowering to your people, since you are getting their buy-in."

Makirra continued, "The Dr. Deming purists tell us that 'when you see a result in variance of more than 10%, a process study and improvement must be made.' In mining, we have so many sub-processes that rely on each other, that shift production rates commonly will vary to +30%. Our focus should be to attack the variances in the highest priority categories affecting the sub-processes first. As we reduce the issues in the specific functions, the whole variation comes down also. Step one is to open our people's eyes and plow the ground. Then when the ideas appear, seeds are planted, and finally everyone will work together to reap the harvest. To challenge our people, we chart our results and strive for less than 10% variation. Our goal is a sequenced process with minimized losses and low variation. Even though most of the actual losses result from behavioral mistakes, we focus initially on the process side. This non-blaming positive approach has yielded strong results. As we improve process, and are open to ideas, our people also improve their personal work performance. Along with those facets of improvement, we also look at technology changes. I use the Jim Collins saying, 'technology can accelerate change but it does not cause it.' Continuous improvement benefits from many inputs. Today we are even charting our production variation as a score. For example, last week we had a swing of 36% between our top shift and our worst shift. Even though it's not yet reaching our goal of 10%, its better than the 57% average of last year."

Al was impressed and said, "Your direction is fantastic. Protecting flow is so very important. I would challenge your group with this question, 'What one bad management habit has probably the greatest negative effect on flow? Here is a clue: It's not one of the Deming main points.'"

No one dared to venture a guess.

Al took the lead, "Running manpower short on our production crews is a cardinal sin. We, senior management, typically sanction it on a case by case basis and it destroys flow. This was one of my worst repetitive mistakes, before I realized the damage it causes. The operating process is changed for every crew member when we run shorthanded, because everyone is covering for the missing person. Quality and morale suffer because everyone is stretched thin. We do not perfect our process and maximize flow, because the crewing is inconsistent. If it only happened infrequently, the affect would be minimized. Fill-ins could cover the spots. However, when working shorthanded becomes normal and accepted, at budget crunching time any extra positions are commonly reduced permanently. This manpower shortage issue has been exasperated recently because many operations have reduced their operation-wide vacation shutdown periods in favor of individually scheduled vacation times. When the total mine shutdown period is eliminated, daily absenteeism rates increase, as employees have to work in their vacation time, and the system is taxed even more. Another example of inadequate manpower support occurs when we don't provide the third car driver on a single miner section. Mathematically it can be shown that you need 2.7 cars per section to keep the normal continuous miner maximized, assuming the section is not severely limited by bolting. Since infrequently, two cars would be adequate, too often we only staff two, with the promise we will send another operator later—which almost never happens."

Makirra sheepishly admitted, "Guilty as charged." She added, "As an excuse, I have had mine foreman argue that numerous times during every shift the third car does not gain anything. That is true at certain times, but if a man-shift costs $300 and we use the $100/minute downtime cost, the third car staffing pays for itself when we gain at least 3 minutes of production time/shift. I have never met a production foreman who wouldn't agree that the third car gained at least an extra three minutes."

Al pointed out, "And look at the message we are sending to our people—we, management, have decided that saving a penny in labor by running short is worth losing dollars in safety and productivity, and we ask the workforce to try to cover it up by working harder. That's a true lose-lose. Commonly the answer for ensuring correct staffing is realistic absentee expectations, improved vacancy filling procedures, stricter absentee policies, and a fair system for pre-scheduling and controlling employees' scheduled days-off. Being sensitive to employees' needs, while correctly staffing the operation is a formidable challenge, but it is one we need to take on. Even though it makes it more complicated, offering a number of different schedules at each operation is commonly part of the solution. This allows for personnel preferences and still covers the work needs. Once you get the master schedule figured out, short term flexibility is also needed. I have had mines where we allowed crews to work previously planned idle shifts in return for having time off for some of deer season. Everyone was a winner. There was less absenteeism and efficient production while giving people hobby and family time. This type of consideration should be considered a priority. Dirk, I will send you a good article I saw a few years back on scheduling options that may give you some ideas (Appendix B.14)."

"On to a second subject," Al continued, "If I asked you, Makirra, what was another of the largest self-inflicted process flow inhibitors on the section, what would you say?"

Makirra had no answer, and silence again ruled the room, so Al jumped in, "The answer is—not following an optimal mining cut cycle. Mining out of cycle can have disastrous effects on the process and flow, yet we commonly do not take the managerial follow-up time to enforce it. I had an operation one time that was so bad on their cut cycle, that the mine manager dictated the *accepted sequence* and made a rule that a crew could not deviate from it unless they called him personally. Immediately the mines productivity went up 20%. We revised the policy by teaching that if and when the sequence is altered, which seems to happen every shift due to a localized catastrophe, the crew must start making a provision to get back on cycle. If you couldn't get back in line, the next shift had to keep it a high priority. From the flexibility and accountability, we picked up another 10% efficiency gain. The dictated policy enforcement got us to Good (+20%), and the principle teaching and flexibility allowance took us to GREAT (total +30%). I mention both of these typical mining process-flaws just to make us aware of the immense potential ahead."

Pete interjected, "Our general operating process has been very good and buy-in strong, but we have honestly hit a plateau. Any suggestions Mr. Hunt?"

"Maybe go back and strengthen your information gathering phase," Al suggested. "Develop an Efficiency Survey where you ask for specific details on process losses and improvement ideas, and then you raise expectations. Ramp-

> **THE SEARCH FOR EXCELLENCE IS A JOURNEY NOT A DESTINATION.**

up your questions to get people to dig deeper. Since it sounds like you have already built trust with your people, probing deeper should not be received skeptically. Just keep explaining that the search for excellence is a journey not a destination. Also, remember to celebrate the victories from your monitoring program. Your approach will keep you atop the field."

†

The next day Al, Makirra, Pete and I headed underground to participate in a loss investigation. It was a text book case where asking WHY five times revealed the true root cause. The production conveyor belt had pulled apart causing two hours of downtime. The initial report stated it was a piece of bad belt. Pete and the belt foreman led the investigation, which revealed a very different story: The belt pulled apart because the tail roller locked-up with coal fines. The tail roller locked up with coal fines because the bottom scraper on the belt was knocked off. The bottom scraper on the belt was knocked off because a rock had come off the belt line. Why did a rock come off the belt line? That happened because the belt was out of alignment. The belt was out of alignment because a hanger chain supporting the belt line had broken prematurely. Unless all those symptoms were fixed and a new hanger chain replaced, the system would have kept failing. The initial report recommended replacing $30,000 worth of belt. The more thorough investigation and correct analysis suggested replacing the old hanger chain with a new $4 hanger chain, thus the root problem was solved. As Pete wrote up the findings and recommendations he emphasized the point that the loss could have had any, or a combination of, all the five loss types. The belt failure could have just as easily led to an injury or violation, along with the downtime.

While we were on the working section, we decided to look at the deteriorating roof conditions that had been reported. I took the time to talk to both roof bolting crews for their input. It always amazed me how little we used the on-shift bolters information in everyday decision making. These guys are real-time drilling the roof and can recognize potential issues before they even happen.

"I have seen companies give extra geology training to their bolters to increase their input value," Al volunteered.

"That's a good idea," I replied. "We will incorporate that. As far as I am concerned, every miner cut-depth decision should be made with the input of the resident on-shift geologist, the bolter operators."

The last day of our Deep Hollow Mine visit began with following Makirra as she interacted with the crews in the portal staging area. The atmosphere was upbeat.

Since she had already heard that Al noticed wall signs, she asked, "Mr. Hunt, how do you like my signs?"

The first one read, YOUR ATTITUDE IS THE BANNER OF YOUR VALUES AND CHARACTER.

Al nodded approvingly. He then commented on the second sign, "This one's good, too, but it could be dressed up a little."

> **YOUR ATTITUDE IS THE BANNER OF YOUR VALUES AND CHARACTER.**

Curious, Makirra asked, "What would you add to it?"

Al returned, "Well, currently it says, THE LEVEL OF LOSS YOU ACCEPT IS THE INVERSE OF THE SUCCESS YOU WILL ENJOY. I think I would add a few words so it would then read THE LEVEL OF LOSS YOU ACCEPT IS THE INVERSE OF THE SUCCESS AND SECURITY YOU WILL EARN AND ENJOY. Just a subtle change, but it drives the point closer to home that fate and destiny both are in our hands. I know I am being picky but you asked."

"Give me some other ideas," Makirra encouraged.

"You could put some music in the changing area for atmosphere and try keeping all your bulletin board charts updated. Three are two months behind." He offered.

"I appreciate that. Feedback helps steer my improvement focus," she admitted.

As we headed to her office, Al encouraged Makirra and Pete to continue the 'good fight in faith.' Makirra reminded everyone that we had a 1 p.m. Cost Control Meeting, and we were running a little late. When we arrived at her office, her staff was there so we filtered straight on in. A directive memo had come to each mine to reduce inventories, and the board was asking for an action plan. Makirra led the group discussion and put the suggestions on the white board. The first was to roll some of our owned parts into a consignment program with the vendors, who would then credit the value of our stock back to us. The next idea was to put bar codes and readers at all inventory sites. This would help reduce stock levels since more accurate inventory counts could be maintained and automated reordering could be started. The third idea was to install cameras at the inventory sites to help deter theft. The fourth point is where the war broke out. When the warehouse manager offered to cut stocking levels dramatically, the production coordinator started to go ballistic. His position was that he already had escalating delays from the previous month's cuts. Makirra looked at Al, "Okay maestro, want to take this on?"

Al turned to me, "Let's review the drivers, do we have all of our production sold?"

I said, "Yes, and another 20% if we produce it."

Al continued, "If that's the case, we need to stand on the principle that reducing production volumes drives up the fixed cost ratio, which increases the cost/ton. In most cases, we need to protect our production volumes and resist any detractors to efficiency. I have seen many companies try to save their way to being profitable and/or cut off spending to claim money was saved. In most cases, assuming the parts and supplies were needed, the incurred downtime effect would be dollars lost compared to the purchasing nickels saved. Another way of saying it is—common cost cutting techniques in a tight economic market are counterproductive to progressive *value added* decision making. You must protect your production volumes. I will send you an economic review (Appendix B.04) that I completed for another client that dives into fixed and variable costs relationships. The focus should be on efficiency first, not reduction. Any cost reduction decision must be weighed with the downtime effect considered. Bottom line: never let reactive policies dictate or alter principles. Policies should always support sound principle. Two areas for potential reduction are waste and support functions. Waste reduction is always helpful, but usually to a smaller degree, and it keeps people sensitive to the tight economic pressures. The support functions, on the other hand, are commonly a large dollar item that can be shaved at least temporarily, without direct effects on the production rates. However, I must warn you to be very careful in analyzing all the ramifications of projected changes. I will send you a list (Appendix B.15) of potential support improvement areas that you may want to consider."

"Well that gives us a good framework to build our plan," Makirra concluded. "Let's break for the day and everyone take the evening to review our notes. We will convene tomorrow at 1 p.m. to finalize our plan. As Mr. Hunt emphasized, let's be protective of the efficiency gains. It's consistent with our driving principles."

As everyone filed out of the meeting, Makirra approached Al and said, "You made a profound statement. You said, 'our policies should always support sound principles.' I agree, as long as everyone's motives are the same. In so many cases these days in society, they are not aligned. I believe most people are naive and do not realize the 'head games' that are occurring. There is an open attack on moral values, with the cover-up excuse that we are being flexible to all beliefs.

Our society is an example of this. We keep experimenting and trying to create a valueless world. The result is that the system is birthing poison fruit. Why are we so afraid to admit it's just not working? Let's not repeat the same mistakes and failures that I see happening to many organizations that have focused on being politically correct. In many cases the corporate world runs so hard away from higher values, it indirectly encourages lower standards. Some use the tolerance stance as an excuse to justify the convenient, easy position, or in other cases, it encourages the *no decision*. The cry from a few to neutralize our workplaces and society is proving to be counter-productive and apathy is replacing determination. I am not trying to push a specific religion, but rather I am wanting to help purge the diluted values result from our workplace."

"Makirra, you have a valid point. We have culturally dropped moral values and tried to write enough vague laws to cover the holes. Unfortunately, dumbing-down our conscience is a grave mistake and we are then surprised when principles creep in that are based on evil motives.

> **VALUE-DRIVEN DECISIONS HOLD UP TO THE TEST OF TIME.**

The truth is, value-driven decisions hold up to the test of time. As taught by Stephen Covey, 'staying principle-centered is the right way to operate.' This holds true in business and our personal lives. I believe these are dark times if we do not stay aligned to the truths on which our country was founded and upon which His Word teaches. We must decide upon which rock we are going to stand."

II. OPERATIONS OVERVIEW

Chapter 5
Lucky Star Mine

When Dustin Sturgil, superintendent of Lucky Star Mine, called early in the week to invite us to breakfast, I accepted. "Sounds great. Al will enjoy a hearty meal, especially when it serves the dual purpose of interviewing the chief."

Al wanted to know some of the history of Profit Coal. The drive over to the restaurant to meet up with Dustin gave me time to fill him in.

"The first three mines, Straight Ridge, Broad Run, and Deep Hollow, have been around fifteen plus years. Then ten years ago, Taurus #1 was bought because they had a strong sales contract to the local steel mill. It had good market synergy, but was only a fair producer. Two years later, Lucky Star and Lucky Road were purchased out of bankruptcy. Even though they were union operations, they brought the advantage of having an excellent grade of coal that blended with our base product. In hindsight, it probably was a bad investment. There have been a lot of problems, especially pertaining to Lucky Road. Amidst the challenges, we have traded dollars (one mine temporarily subsidizing another) and kept people working, so that has been a positive. I know that does not sell in the board room, but it is how I feel. Maybe you can come up with a way to save some of their futures. There are many good people in both of those mines, but unfortunately the union has protected some *bad eggs*."

Entering the restaurant, we spotted Dustin seated in a booth with an older lady. As we approached, he shot up and greeted us. "Al, Dirk, I would like to introduce you guys to Mrs. Tara McGinnis. Her husband worked with us at the mine for 20 years, until he retired and later passed. He was a special guy."

Tara smiled and offered a handshake to each of us before she began speaking. "My Barry worked for Dustin the last part of his career as a loader operator. Dustin always made him feel so important; it was like he was a co-owner. I remember one time Barry put an idea in the suggestion box at work. It was for a better brake pedal design to reduce accidents. They tried it and now all the loaders have these non-slip pedals. Barry did not win the monthly Best Idea award, but he did get a letter from Dustin, thanking him for the idea.

We were so proud of that letter that we taped it to the refrigerator door so all the grand kids could see it. Barry would always encourage them by saying, 'When you do the right thing, the right people notice.'"

Al patted Dustin on the back, "Sometimes it only takes a small amount of encouragement and a 'thank you' to bring out the heroes. Once they are out in the open, they are contagious—a working army."

"It was really great to see you again, Mrs. McGinnis," Dustin said as he broke away. "I hope you have a very nice breakfast and rest of the day!"

We all thanked Mrs. McGinnis for her time, excused ourselves, and moved to our own table.

Settled into our booth, Al continued, "But it took you, Dustin, to convince the hero that you needed his help. Barry believed that the effort to think of and submit the idea would be worth it. When he stepped out and trusted, he challenged management to do three things:

1) Respectfully consider his idea—even if they decided not to pursue it, they would let him know why. If they decided to explore it, they would communicate their plans and provide updates.

2) Show some type of appreciation or maybe even a reward—some people like public acknowledgement and some don't.

3) Protect the contributor against personal repercussions.

If we cover all three challenges, the fly wheel momentum starts and our people begin believing in the system. The more they engage, the better we become, and the self-fulfilling prophesy picks up steam. As Dustin demonstrated, it is up to management to convince a couple people to trust that the gain is worth the pain. James Conant is quoted as saying, 'Behold the turtle, he makes progress only when he sticks his neck out.' That's a cute reminder to encourage people to get *out-of-the-box*. Shifting away from old paradigms is against human nature. We all have the habit of *continuing yesterday's course* and at times we'll even follow a dead horse to the ground. I saw a project summary from NASA that said over 10 years and $12 Billion had been spent to try to devise a gravity-free pen that would work in space. Finally, the decision was made to stay with a pencil. Openly re-evaluating our course regularly is critical, not only due to financial implications, but sometimes because the goals change. When the old style typewriters first came out, the proficient typist could type faster than the strike-arms could retract and reset. To slow typing speeds down, a new awkward keypad arrangement was devised. It was very successful then, because it slowed the top speeds down by

20%. Embarrassingly, that is the same keypad we use now with the electronic speedsters. Why have we not upgraded to the fast keypad layouts? Resistance to change! Another example is the 20-year U.S. struggle in switching from standard bolt sizing to metric. No one has been committed enough to make the change. The *pain of change* can be onerous, or at least it is perceived that way. Sometimes our greatest obstacles to solutions are our own paradigms. Another stumbling block is the fear of failure. We need to remind our people we expect some ideas will flop, and that is okay. I love what John Maxwell said, 'People who don't make mistakes end up working for people that do.' Our people should be the experts in process improvement since they are integrally involved and invested. Helping them get creative is very rewarding. Creativity could be defined as *a vision unshrouded by limitations of the past*. Many of the most unique inventions and process changes come from the newer employees who have a fresh look. They do not know all the reasons why a change would not work. My first patented idea came after only two years in the mine. Personally, I am not a gifted operator. It does not come easily and I always seem to be fighting the machine. I am embarrassed at how much damage and downtime I caused in my early operating years. One day after I cut my shuttle car trailing cable, because I was over steering the car into the rib, or side wall, I was determined to design a protective shroud to stop knuckleheads like me from cutting their cable. After six months of design evolutions, I came up with a success. The final design reduced cable damage and subsequent losses significantly. That was over 25 years ago and now a lot of shuttle cars in the U.S. are utilizing my design. I was actually doing some consulting work in some Russian mines last year and saw my shroud there also.

> CREATIVITY COULD BE DEFINED AS A VISION UNSHROUDED BY LIMITATIONS OF THE PAST.

There are many other lessons to be learned from equipment improvements. I birthed another idea from my poor operating skills. I was struggling with a roof bolting machine that required me to control two levers with one hand. Working with a shop machinist, we devised a joystick that inter-connected the two levers. The ergonomic design made operating the machine safer and more efficient while also improving results. Over 80% of the roof bolter machines in the U.S. are now using our joystick design. The need for improvement was definitely the mother of the invention. In many cases, it is management's role to make sure to point out the improvement needs and then step back and let our people invent. There are so many other examples of ergonomic advantages we commonly miss. I would estimate potential productivity gains of 5% to 30% are available if we did better at designing our equipment in line with our operator's preferences. How often do we take an operator to inspect a new piece of equipment when it is still at the manufacturer? We commonly take a mechanic for repair suggestions, but we don't pro-actively address the operator. In one instance, I involved some operators in the designing of shuttle car sideboards. The redesign improved visibility, decreased spillage, and increased payloads by 20%. I came back to the operation a year later and they had stopped using the new, more efficient design. In probing to find out why, I was told a senior manager had reverted back to the old style saying, 'If the old style was okay for 50 years, it will be fine again.' In another example, I worked with an *old school* dictator that once said the seat on a piece of equipment had no effect on the productivity rate of the operator. He couldn't have been farther from the truth. My experience has taught me that there are large gains available for those who care for and support their operators. So many managers have missed this lesson, 'pamper them and they will take care of you.' Plus, it is just the right and respectful way to treat each other."

"I agree that many of the best ideas are so simple and easy to accomplish," I added. "We had a truck dump-area where we were backing into a certain pole about six times per year. At an average damage cost of $4,000 per event, it was a pretty costly problem. Dustin challenged everyone to come up with an idea. The loader man, who had hit it twice last year, said it was in a shadowed spot, but if a normal flood light was installed there, it would be blinding. He suggested a string of Christmas tree lights. So for $5 worth of lights, we saved over $24,000 per year in losses."

Al smiled and said, "That's super. That idea consequently saved equipment damage, downtime, potential injuries and thus, it also built security. Reinforcing these victories is a key to keeping the momentum going and everyone engaged."

"I have to brag again on Dustin," I said, "He has more ideas come from this mine than all the rest put together, and it's a union mine."

> **TO MANAGE IS TO DIRECT AND COORDINATE A PROCESS OR PLAN, TO LEAD IS TO EMPOWER THE HEART.**

"That tells me a couple things," Al said, "they trust you and you openly encourage their input. You also have obviously learned an important truth—that walls will come down as management steps forward first and shows sincere appreciation. That goes along with the sign I saw in the foreman changing area, TO MANAGE IS TO DIRECT AND COORDINATE A PROCESS OR PLAN, TO LEAD IS TO EMPOWER THE HEART. I commend your team on the progress."

I agreed, "However, it was not always like this. Three years ago, the mine was struggling due to poor production and safety results. That is actually when the union came."

Al stopped me, "You mean that is when the employees invited the union to represent them."

"Yes," I replied, "I guess that would be the truer statement. Anyway, things got very bad and the agencies even shut us down over safety problems. Then Dustin joined the group. It has been a difficult couple years, and we are just now barely in the black."

"I interrupted you," Al said, "because I wanted to make the point that in most cases, if a union comes into a mine, it is because relationships have broken down and management has failed in directing the operations. The workforce is smart enough to know that bringing a union in adds cost, but they obviously decided it was worth the gamble in order to solve the poor management and/or mistreatment problems. If you are having financial issues already, that could be the final straw. My experience has been the union cost-baggage is between $1-$4/ton for tangible charges and $3-$15/ton on the intangible. The intangible would be the effect of 'past practice' rules, limits on outsourcing, high absenteeism, scheduling restrictions, etc. Your people's choice indicates the workforce must have felt it was their only option. From what I understand, that was the old management group. Dustin, you obviously chose not to be a part of a solution that meant everyone losing their jobs."

"Exactly right," Dustin replied, "The first order of business was to meet with the agencies and the union officers, and get everyone's perception of what needed to change. I let them know I was willing to get into the transformation trenches with them. We opened a dialog that had been absent. I committed to facilitate the formulation of a plan, and we called it, *Project Almost Perfect*. It was then presented to our management and employees for review. It overhauled our normal operating procedures.

The agencies and union officers were proactive in their suggestions and many of their comments were incorporated. The joint plan was better because it included a diversity of viewpoints that balanced the approach. And it achieved buy-in and acceptance of all the groups. We agreed up front, our enemy was the *at risk behavior* not the individuals. We also decided to abolish the normal reactive safety department, retaught that every employee was part of the 'safety department,' and assert that 'Safety was everyone's core value.' We committed to having prevention coordinators who would help concerning compliance issues and support proactive programs. All of the programs had accountability tied to them. The workforce's progress has been fantastic, but we are not there yet. It's a shame that it took the meltdown to wake us up, because now we have an extra

> **OUR ENEMY WAS THE AT RISK BEHAVIOR NOT THE INDIVIDUALS.**

cost of about $8.00/ton. That's the scar we inflicted from our past. Our operations revival came when everyone saw we were going under and realized a higher standard had to be set. Security had to be earned, not negotiated. I had read *The Toyota Way*, by Jeffery Likerner, and decided that their 3C's theme—consideration, communication, cooperation—would be our foundation. The 3C's would become the avenue that we could travel to transform trust into performance. We gained ground as people were engaged to improve work standards and come up with new ideas. We called those good ideas, Kaizens—which, in Japanese, means 'improvements' or 'changes for the best.' At one time, we were getting over 100 Kaizens per month. People believed in us, but we were failing to act on a lot of the ideas. I heard a fair criticism, 'many good ideas were shouted, some heard, and yet few done.' Our progress was regressing until we started prioritizing. Now we have adopted an evaluation procedure. When an improvement idea is turned in, it is rated with respect to the expected return versus the cost. The cost is viewed as the money needed and the implementation and follow-up effort required to complete the project. The exception is that any safety related idea must be automatically catapulted to high priority. The rankings are:

A-High priority (must)–excellent return for the cost invested

B-Medium priority (should)

C-Low priority (could)

The goal is to complete the A's within 45 days. As we knock out the A's, we re-evaluate the B's and C's, and continue moving them up the priority ladder. It's funny, the better we do at getting projects done, the more ideas we get. We joke that there seems to be a penalty for progress. Seriously, we have received some really good Kaizens that have made this a better place to work. We do a number of Appreciation Programs to encourage people, but the biggest motivation seems to be completing the 'A-Priority' list and publicizing the progress."

Dustin suggested, "Let's move our discussion to the mine. I would like you to meet the union officers and hear their stories."

When we got back to the mine, Dustin checked with his secretary to see if any of the officers were outside and available. She told us they were all off-site in some secret district meeting and would be off work for the rest of the week.

"Some days I love them and other days I could strangle them." Frustration was written all over Dustin's face. "They want us to be transparent with them, but they play their cards close to the vest. Honestly, our officers do a good job for the people here and work well with our united plan, but they are spread out trying to help other failing union operations. Being focused on our survival plans in many cases is diametrically opposed to some of our competition's needs, and they find themselves conflicted. In the current market, there is not room for everyone. At one point, over 75% of the mining industry was unionized and it is now less than 13%. Every time the market gets squeezed and costs start paring out the more inefficient, higher cost operations, the union overhead is commonly the last straw."

"Speaking of costs, Al," Dustin continued, "I would like some advice. We asked the warehouse to give us two lists monthly. The first is the twelve most frequent items purchased and the second is the twelve highest cost items. We post them on the bulletin board and call them the dirty dozen lists. Obviously the plan is to communicate concern and lower cost, but I am not sure it's working."

"Investing effort to communicate and educate is always good for the team," Al offered, "but you have to reduce that information into a conclusion and plan. You have to lead the way. You can't expect them to decipher all that data and prioritize the correct way. My recommendation would be to have your senior staff analyze the two lists and pull out three to five target items. Then develop an improvement plan with an employee *action team*. The group will give you input, buy-in, and will continue to foster cost education. Spreading your base by using certain influential employees on the action team is a smart move. Relying wholly on the union officers to communicate the awareness and the business plan can be a mistake. Another way to educate and steer is through the information and operation results we put on the bulletin boards. We want people to glance at a posting or chart, and see the summary comment or trend interpretation. If they want to validate your conclusion, the information is there, but most people will respect your conclusion, appreciate being included, and follow the plan for improvement."

"I can see this being successful for us, because mutual trust is something on which we have worked hard," Dirk commented.

Al continued, "I have seen operations start with your type of cost containment/reduction approach, resulting in huge savings. That momentum has carried over into safety achievements and productivity gains. As you build success on the easier initial projects, your people gain self-confidence and become ready to handle the tougher loss challenges. Most major victories must first be set up in the hearts and minds of the people, and then they will flow into the field situations. We, the leaders, must choreograph those victories."

T

We spent the next couple days meeting people on the working sections and looking at conditions. Since they were having an unusual amount of maintenance downtime, Al did numerous equipment inspections. He also wanted to spend a night on third shift to see their world. Dustin was busy, and so we went alone.

"Third shift is where the new day starts. How well the day shift is set up has a huge effect on resulting production rates," Al instructed. "You will never have a GREAT shift that does not have a strong start, and you will not have a strong day shift start, if thirds do not have it prepped. That's why I believe in tracking the day shift crew's production amount after the first two hours. It is a critical Performance Indicator of how day shift got started."

I chimed in, "The best Performance Indicators to track are ones in which an employee group can control the outcome. People are more open to accountability, when it is within their circle of influence."

Al smiled, "You are learning quickly, Dirk."

As we were ending our time on thirds, we observed the day shift arriving on the section. They pulled up to the power station. Everyone got off the mantrip, sat down, and took a 10 minute break.

The foreman was fumbling around with his notes and finally said, "I must have lost the pre-shift report, so let's all get to the faces, find your equipment, and get started."

It was another 15 minutes before I heard the first car start up and another 12 minutes before the first car of coal was being dumped. What a comedy of errors—37 minutes lost due to a poor shift start. In this case, thirds had done a decent job and everything was ready. The problem was a failure to communicate and manage the start-up.

I looked at Al, "When they start with a 10 minute *cupcake break*, what would you expect?"

Al calmly turned to me, "That should be an easy habit to track and break. Remember, you will achieve it only if you can monitor it."

"I guess you could purchase, install, and monitor a belt scale to know exactly when they started loading the belt, but at $15,000 that would be a costly solution," I said, shaking my head side to side.

"Actually, even though that would probably be cost effective," Al offered, "I can still think of a cheaper way. Let's monitor the amps on their unit belt drive. It will show relative belt load rates. It will even show the time of the last car dumped. We'll be able to see if some crews decided to stop early."

†

By the time we arrived outside, Dustin had heard about the debacle. He was waiting for us at the elevator. He expressed his frustration and asked for our comments.

I couldn't hold back. It was a classic management failure. No direction, no plan, and low expectation, so—chaos ruled. "You need to have a serious talk with the foreman," I said, "and please also make sure the crew's poor start is not a reflection on the third shift. They had prepped well."

Dustin was already primed, "Dirk, I will have an action plan on your desk Monday. I need the couple extra days to get to every crew for their input. This is a problem mine-wide that needs addressing, and there is no better time than right now."

I nodded in understanding and told Dustin I looked forward to seeing his plan. We followed Dustin back to his office.

Al turned to Dustin, "What was the largest mindset change in safety during the transformation?"

"When our employees started seeing safety as the result of doing their job right, not what inspectors caught us doing or not doing, then the blame-throwing slowed down. If you rely on authorities to motivate your safety and legal compliance, you are not committed to the principle." Dustin pointed to the wall sign, SAFETY COMMITMENT – THE ULTIMATE SHOW OF RESPECT TO EACH OTHER AND OUR FAMILIES. "Safety is for our benefit, not because of the agencies. That pretty well says it all."

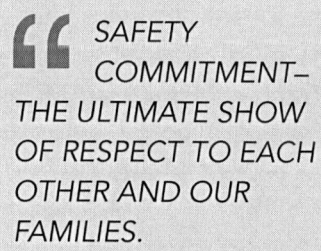

> SAFETY COMMITMENT– THE ULTIMATE SHOW OF RESPECT TO EACH OTHER AND OUR FAMILIES.

About that time we were interrupted by a call from the main office. The Board was meeting and they wanted Al and me to join them. We thanked Dustin for his time and hospitality and headed to the main office.

†

As we walked in the front door, Margie greeted and invited us on in and down toward the conference room. She said she had been hearing very positive things about our travels. "Two or three have told me it is like a breath of fresh air."

When we arrived at the conference room, the door opened and Jeff Page stepped out to welcome us inside. He looked at Al and asked, "How is the review going?"

"Very good and extremely informative," Al said in an up-beat way. "I should be on schedule to present my technical review two weeks after the last mine visit."

"Are the managers opening up? Are you getting a flavor for the operations?" Marci questioned, curiously.

"People are guardedly open," Al responded, "more so at the middle levels. Commonly, the workforce is the most open, as they have nothing to hide and can see the potential for improvement. Senior management is usually either all in or resistant, once they figure out the favored management style and critique the new goals. Middle and first line management is where the walls are. They usually see my type of questions as judgmental and searching for blame. Their reactions are defensively led. If my review yields change, they commonly translate that into a power shift to the workforce and instability issues for them. They see no gain in being transparent. Since this middle and first line management tendency exists, we have to be very careful in how those managers are brought along and involved. They must be kept in the loop for change to succeed going forward. A positive and creative workplace environment can be initiated by senior management, but it has to have the full support of the middle and first line management. Most transformations either die, or are ignited through these managers."

"Am I detecting that you are emotionally connecting?" said Jeff. "You know the saying 'a ship does not sail on yesterday's wind.' We need a new vision and plan, but without the right Senior Team, it is rudderless." Looking right at Al, Jeff asked, "Are you game?"

Unwavering, Al warned, "The change-process leadership cannot be delegated or hired out. If a new operating system is to be brought in, the smoothest transition will be to work through a respected long-term manager. The rallying leader must be able to sell the common goal of security, before the people sign on to the mission, value, and plan. In this case, I think Dirk has the passion and team respect. He is also very teachable. I would be willing to help him on a transformation program. Let's talk about my specific potential long-term involvement later, after the board approves the future direction."

"We have talked internally and believe a radical change in the business philosophy is warranted and we are ready to start," said Jeff. "Surviving companies in this market will not be *luke warm;* they will be proactive, aggressive, and sold-out committed. We must have a new face. Luke warm is a transitional state, it's either moving towards HOT or COLD, but it's not a static state. We can't stay there. Al, you kicked us in the teeth when you said most companies fail because the owners do not relate in motive to the workforce. With a name like Profit Coal, we are engraving that same mistake. Since change must start at the top, we have decided to rename the company Integrity Coal."

Al responded, "That name says a lot; it's a big commitment if it is sincere. You, the board, have to decide what type of motivation will drive this company, then we can design the rebuild plan with that as its foundation and core. The character of Integrity Coal will be birthed in this room, but only after you realistically understand the cost. Most companies are not willing to invest in a foundation of values and the structural framework necessary to build a balanced, unified organization. They want to go straight to progress and payback. I will submit, you can build faster growth and payback using a *compliant approach*, BUT you do not have the potential to attain the eventual altitude toward the GREAT status, as what the *committed path* offers. This is an important difference that must be weighed. If you remember our previous discussion, committed is when people join because they believe. Compliant is when they participate because it is required.

Al walked over to the white board and sketched a graph. At the top, he wrote: "How are our employees to be engaged?"

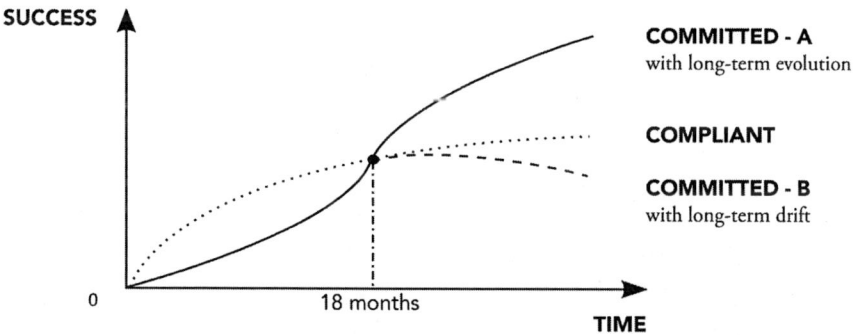

Al explained: "The committed path takes a little longer to get started, since the foundation (trust, communication, education…) must be established first, whereas the compliant approach launches quickly through new rules and mandates. My experience has shown the committed path usually overtakes the compliant approach at around 18 months with respect to success achievements.

Before you decide on the engagement plan, I want to reiterate that you must choose the designed motivation for transformation. If you choose the committed transformation, then you have truly chosen an operation life change. The potential security earned is huge, and it will be a dynamic, breathing, evolving operating process. This path is denoted on the graph as the solid 'A' line. There will be ruts veering left and right, but for your team this is a *best* path. Once momentum gets going, the steering needs to be constant, although probably not dramatic. Holding to your foundational values and just altering your course as new challenges or rocks appear, will be the duties of management. The gamble with the committed path is that if you don't stay involved and sincere, the workforce will feel betrayed, and ground will be lost. As trust erodes, it will be harder to regain previous levels. The graphed 'B' line depicts those results. If you choose the compliant transformation approach, then you have chosen an operation based on requirements and rules. Its longevity relies on enforcement and is usually fear-controlled. Both strategies work. But before you decide, take an honest assessment of your business plan, management beliefs, and expectations, and then chart your course."

Marci piped in, "We are committing to achieve GREAT. The transformation must be a win for the entire team. We do not take this change lightly, Al. In our first meeting you warned us that the word integrity carries huge responsibilities. We are willing to back it up and commit to that level of excellence. Going forward, we want the employees to see themselves as partners and co-owners. We all just bring different resources to the table—some bring financial investments, while others bring managerial skills, and there are others who bring operational abilities. We are all interdependent on each other, but for a body to function at a high level, we need all of its parts moving in sync with one another." Unexpectedly Marci swung around to me and asked, "Can you sail that boat Dirk?"

"Yes Ma'am," I firmly answered. "I strongly believe in our people. If ya'll and Al help me design it, we will get it built."

Jeff spoke up. There was a sparkle in his eyes. "While you've been underground, working the mines, we, the board, have come up with the new mission statement: *'Integrity Coal was founded to be a positive contributor, influence, and supporter to our community. We are committed to earning security for all of our partners. And to unify resources and people in building a first-class organization with a character of true integrity. In using our endowed gifts, we aim to be a blessing.'* Can everyone sign on to that?"

There was a resounding "Yes" all the way around.

Jeff continued, "In business, a successful company strives to synergistically increase value using available resources like investors' money, employees' giftings, community support, and our natural resources. The challenge is to achieve the commitment from everyone, along with all their resources, and get them working together. We can be a Great company if we begin with a foundation of solid values. This company had a good start; let's build on that. Marci, Fred, and I on the board, worked on developing a list of foundational values, but we felt it should represent the hearts and needs of the people."

I stepped forward, "I can do that. I will draft a list of values and present it to the board for approval. We have shortcomings, but we have also done a lot of things well. I will pull out our strong traits, and they will be our cornerstones. Al has been teaching me to recognize and build on operational strengths, and to use them as a platform for development. We have some strong pillars, for which we can thank Fred's tutelage."

Fred grinned, "I appreciate your words, Dirk. Frankly, I'm pretty surprised by what I'm seeing—I've never seen that fire in your belly before. I think you might just pull this off."

Jeff added his encouragement, "Dirk, I believe you have found your calling. Now let's get 'er done!"

Everyone came over excitedly and shook my hand. I was inspired by their energy—but at the same time, I almost feared the extent of the changes we were agreeing to carry through.

When I looked at Al, he was beaming. As we walked out to the car, he said, "I saw passionate leadership birthed today. We will need that energy and persuasion to win our peoples' hearts, but when we do, and we will, a GREAT Company will be born." He continued, "Your comment earlier about expanding our platform was very insightful. I believe God meant for each one of us to build a platform from which we can share our gifts. As we refine our strengths and character, our elevation is raised and the light that is generated illuminates a broader area. On our journey, our gifts determine the road alternatives, but our choices map our potential. You are beginning to wear your mantle well, my friend. I am very proud of you."

ENCOURAGEMENT

II. OPERATIONS OVERVIEW

Chapter 6
Lucky Road Mine

Per our normal Monday ritual, I picked Al up at the hotel and headed to the new mine site. It would be about an hour's drive, so I planned to air out some laundry with Al. "Okay, counselor, I need an ear to bend. The board meeting the other day left me reeling. For starters, I really appreciated your vote of confidence and commitment to help me, but it made me feel a little inadequate admitting I am going to need so much help."

"Don't ever hesitate to ask for help, all that says is you have either tackled a project that is stretching you beyond your experience/skill set—and that's admirable—and/or you are sharing ownership to empower someone else's help. Either way, you are pushing your effectiveness. That's what we are all supposed to do. 'To whom much is given, much is expected' is a biblical quote reminding us that God has gifted us to in turn *pay it forward*. Accepting the calling to be a value-influencer or mentor is a very high honor. Jeff Page and the board's challenge for you to sail Integrity Coal, will be formidable, but I know you have the heart and character for the job."

"I may have the heart and drive, but is that enough?"

"No, it's not, but you also have shown you have the desire to refine your character. Your character is the testament of your values. *Integrity of character will produce integrity in process*, and both are required for a GREAT Company. I can help you on the mechanics of process building, but your character will set the standard. Leading by example with respect to values, will be critical."

> **INTEGRITY OF CHARACTER WILL PRODUCE INTEGRITY IN PROCESS, AND BOTH ARE REQUIRED FOR A GREAT COMPANY.**

"I am excited about building the foundational values list. I plan to derive most of it from what our teams already are doing right. That way they will be familiar with them."

Al agreed, "We are going to call our total transformation plan, Integrity Process. The core components of the operation's plan, which is part of Integrity Process, form the acronym is MVP.

1) **M**ission–know where we are going and why

2) **V**alues–understand and agree to the rules of engagement

3) **P**rocess–develop a tool set that crafts the prize

The Board articulated the mission. It's our job to explain the WHY and HOW-TO. You are going to develop the values from the company's strengths and beliefs. Then you and I can work with each superintendent to teach process and customize a tool set to support the corporate mission. Most companies attack change haphazardly. Our MVP operation module will help us be methodical, thorough, and choreograph every step. We will earn commitment and we will succeed through everyone's contribution. For me, it is truly satisfying to help people maximize their potential and unite with others to weave the common thread of security."

"Once again, I am thoroughly motivated," I said. "I am beginning to slowly see this coming together. I had heard you say the operating plan was a part of the total transformation. What are the other parts?"

Al responded, "The other four focus areas are asset allocation, personnel placement, operating style, and the motivation of transformation, which we have already discussed. The first three will be addressed in due time."

"The other area I am still a little confused about is how everyone's management diversity is going to gel into one plan. In some respects, each operation is going in a different direction and struggling to perfect its approach."

"Good observation, Dirk, but we are a ways from starting to unify the operating plan. What we need to do now is let them continue their focus, with a little guidance, and build our values foundation. As the foundation solidifies, we can then develop the process and eventually start monitoring the progress."

"Let me ask you a personal question, Al. How do you know so much?"

Al smiled solemnly, "As I have told you before, I have learned from numerous mistakes and I have had many smart partners and teachers. I frequently turn to God for wisdom. The older I get and the more sensitive I become, the more I realize He wants to share knowledge and timing into our lives. But we have to choose to enter into that type of relationship with Him. That's the personal decision we each must make. I believe you will choose well, my friend."

†

When we entered the Lucky Road Mine Office, the superintendent, Seth Martin, was meeting with the union officers. He had left a note that he would be with us shortly. I gave Al an operation review while we waited. I explained that at one time, it was a strong mine. But the previous superintendent had gone rogue and was caught embezzling bonus checks from the workforce. He was subsequently criminally indicted. This is when Seth was brought in. Seth has now been at this war site now, for ten years. The seeds of distrust toward management were so well planted that the union representation election was a landslide. Seth's nickname is the *hammerhead* and he is proud of it. Sometimes I think he is more committed to the war than to its resolution.

Al asked, "Why have we not changed the general?"

"Seth is board member Fred Miller's son-in-law," I said in a low voice.

Al's face registered understandingly, "Got it. Let's move to another subject. What are the union officers like?"

"They are pretty much always on the defensive because they are positioned in the corner," I explained. "The newly elected chairman of the safety committee is a big improvement over his predecessor. The union's old game was to call everything into the government safety agency's hotline. We were getting 5 to 10 *code-a-phones* every week, with 90% of them being false accusations. Seth took the call-ins personally and the grudge match started. The inspectors were constantly put in a bad position. To cover their rears, the inspectors started writing safe-guards in order to custom write new laws against the mine."

"So the reactive war rages on." Al shook his head. "When it gets this way everyone loses. An immediate change has to be made. We need people to think like owners, look and listen like inspectors, and be a part of the solution. All our people must realize they are on the same side, not adversaries. But you can't get there without a leadership change and trust being restored."

I continued, "The new safety committee chairman means well, but he can't control all the vigilantes. The chairman of the mine committee is very proud of the thick stack of past practice rulings they have won. He will tell you, 'That is the way they control management. And when management violates *union law*, a grievance is filed.' They average 30 grievances per month. You can't imagine the tension."

"Oh, yes I can," Al sighed, "I was assigned to a large embittered union/management battle similar to this one. They were averaging 45 grievances a month and the mine was quickly going under. The mine had already been put under a WARN shut-down notice of two months. The company fired the superintendent and transferred me from another site to fix the problem. I was at the ripe age of 33.

With the average union member's age being 57, I was not beginning from a position of respect. The tone for our relationship was tested before I even showed up for work. The weekend prior to my start someone bashed in all the windows of my personal vehicle as it sat in my own driveway. With more forgiveness than was natural for me, I decided to stay focused on the victory. When I showed up at the mine on Monday morning, the entire union committee was waiting for me. They asked for an immediate private meeting in the conference room. As we filed in the room, six of them sat on one side of the table. The seventh member had gone to the restroom. With one temporarily open chair on THEIR side, I filled it. They all looked flustered. Finally the union president informed me that I was breaking protocol. He said, 'you need to get six other management representatives and move over to the other side.' I cordially thanked him for the information and told him I would represent management solo, and that I would rather sit amongst the team I was joining. They were caught off guard. Finally, they all got up in unison and moved to the other side. The union president, 30 years my senior, stood up and said, 'Mr. Hunt, we have heard you have come here to save the mine, and we want to know how you plan to do that. We also want to know if you know our by-laws,' and then he waved his little green handbook at me and set it on the table. 'We know you have come from a *scab mine*. I am here to tell you that you need to know the rules on how we run this mine.'"

"I wanted so much to say, 'and how's it working for you?'—but I swallowed the sarcasm. Respectfully, I took the floor. Not knowing how I was going to respond, I quietly murmured, 'All right Lord, this is Your show.' I walked around the table and shook each person's hand, just to give God a little extra time for my prayer to reach His chamber. Then I proceeded. 'To your initial question, our transformation plan will be crafted with input from everyone who is willing to help. I hope I can count on you guys to lead the ranks in participation.' An icy stare was flashed in return. 'As far as the rules of this house are concerned' (I reached in my brief case and pulled out my pocket Bible and held it up), 'these are the foundational principles from which I will work. If I violate one of the rules in your green book, I figure you will know the page and can show me. I do not mean to be rude, but when my beliefs are attacked, I will defend them.' I laid the Bible on the table next to the union handbook and sat down. I can guarantee there was no eye contact. After what seemed like an eternity of seconds, I broke the silence and proceeded to quickly review a safety and production report from the previous month. I encouraged everyone to believe that security was our highest priority and still within our grasps. As I closed the meeting, everyone bolted for the door.

Over the next six months the union president slowly gained respect for my style and our accomplishments. He came up to me one day and said 'Al, we had a rough start. I have never had someone embarrass me like you did when we went book to Book.'

Without hesitation, I told him, 'I am sorry if you took the attack personally, but I will firmly defend the principles I believe.' From that day, he was my best supporter. As middle management softened in their approach, the workforce joined management in one accord. Together, we saved everyone's job, had a super safety record, and made the company a lot of money. After I left, the mine operated for another ten years, until the reserves were exhausted. There were a couple of morals to this story: Meet people where they are, but stand on strong principles. They may not like or agree with you, but a common direction will be respected and supported. A second lesson learned was the obvious need for leadership. I had a first line manager come up to me and say 'it's harder to forgive someone after they've thrown a brick through your window.' My response was that I never said being a leader was easy—I said it was a calling. It's your job to determine the platform from which you are going to operate.

This leads me to share another story that reiterates the leadership calling. A number of years ago I took a management class. The lecturer asked each individual if they considered themselves called to management or leadership. She warned everyone that only a few have the heart and tenacity to actually lead. She challenged the group to list the strongest, most effective leaders in history. Names offered included Abraham Lincoln, Gandhi, Jesus Christ, Adolf Hitler (negative yes, but a strong influencer), Martin Luther King, and JFK. The professor then asked what they all had in common. We listed: passionate, strong speaker, dynamic, and value driven. She stopped us, yes those were important traits, but another was that each of those leaders had been assassinated. The room's disposition changed. She warned us that leaders are sold out to their beliefs, are totally committed, and are loved AND hated. 'If you lead because you think everyone will appreciate it, you picked the wrong profession.' I reflect back on that story, when the detractors show up, and I mentally survive the sniping. Your resolve to leadership must come from your passion to influence positive change, even if some do not appreciate it. A supporting statement is, 'Improving tomorrow requires forgiving and often forgetting the past, and the leadership must help that transition

> **YOUR RESOLVE TO LEADERSHIP MUST COME FROM YOUR PASSION TO INFLUENCE POSITIVE CHANGE, EVEN IF SOME DO NOT APPRECIATE IT.**

> **IMPROVING TOMORROW REQUIRES FORGIVING AND OFTEN FORGETTING THE PAST, AND THE LEADERSHIP MUST HELP THAT TRANSITION BY TAKING THE FIRST STEP.**

by taking the first step.' It may not be your fault that you are in the hole, but it is your fault if you stay and wallow in it."

Seth came out to greet us in the lobby and invited us back. He was visibly shaken, "I just found out the union has filed another stack of grievances. These are side shows to the true economic calamity we are in. Why can't they see that?"

Al asked, "Are you respectfully communicating the economic facts and updates to the operation's challenges developing? Are you including them and asking for their input?"

Seth shot back, "The union is here to do as we tell them."

Al came back, "And how's it working?"

"Terrible," Seth announced, "I told them I would not give in, and planned to keep firing people until the attitude improved."

"Seth, I am trying to help you," Al replied, "I would look at a grievance as a grudge symptom. Usually the complaint is just a vehicle to vent frustration. Leadership must rise above the pettiness, and build a bridge for a greater connection—we need to earn their buy-in by asking for their input."

Seth recanted, "The main office made me put out suggestion boxes a couple years ago, and I never got any input, other than *to fire me*."

"What was your response?" Al asked.

Seth said, "I had a meeting, threatened the group, and said I would be watching for the next hateful note. I secretly installed a camera, but I never got another note. That was fine with me. Enough talk, let's go underground."

As Al and I went to the changing room, he looked at me and said, "Guys like this who have no desire to change are not worth my time or breath. I feel sorry for the management group and workforce who have to live in this atmosphere. Remember, attitude is a reflection of the atmosphere."

I agreed.

Al continued, "I have spent half my career with union and half with union-free workforces, and my conclusion is that people are people and they respond to the way they are treated. I have been through six organizing campaigns and have defeated unionization every time because the majority of the employees respected and trusted me. If the union posed a threat, in my opinion, a door was left open for them. I consider the union-free status of the workforce an honor to work within and I have always been committed to earning and deserving it daily. Dirk, a number of years ago I worked up a list of proactive employee relation programs designed to deter the need for a union campaign. I will send that to you (Appendix B.16).

The underground trip in was very impressive. Al and I were very complimentary on the housekeeping and the orderliness of the supplies in the mine.

Al asked, "Does your support foreman have a military background?"

Seth replied, "Yes, sir—served in the Marine Corps. Does it show? He runs a disciplined outfit. We fired three people last year for littering."

I was dying to ask how they identified the offenders, but Seth beat me to the punch.

"Got them on hidden camera and the union grievances couldn't beat that," Seth boasted.

Al asked to stop at a belt transfer station. It was equal to the same standards as the roadway—well lit, rock dusted, the chute work was enclosed, and it looked structurally solid. Al again complimented, "A classic case of getting the standard that you expect and inspect. I bet there is a checklist for each drive installation?"

Seth was right on it, "Forty-two lines to check off and it is turned in daily. It's a lot more thorough than the law requires."

"The law should always be the minimum standard," Al said. "I bet your belt availability is better than the *1% lost per beltline industry standards*."

Seth was filled with pride. "The #3 unit has 12 belts, industry standard would be about 12% lost or 88% availability. We are running 97% availability—four times better than that same standard. Our goal is 99% and we will get there."

Al encouraged, "And I believe you will. When you do, have you thought about a reward to show appreciation?"

Seth smirked, "Yeah, it is called a paycheck."

Al professionally controlled himself, choosing to change the subject. "Do the underground sections have a good working relationship with the survey crew and engineering department?"

"It's real simple," Seth announced. "We mine it; they map it. They come in off-shift and stay out of the way. Out-of-sight, out-of-mind."

Al suggested, "I think you are missing out on the check and balance that can be offered. Creativity is lost when departments run solo. But I will give you credit, the engineering map-work looks in order and projections are up-to-date."

"They were lucky I guess," Seth replied.

Irritated now, Al added, "That response just means we are not supportive or caring enough to find someone to honor."

We proceeded to the working section. The unit looked fair, it was obviously at a different standard of inspection as was the belt system. Just as we came through the ventilation curtain, we saw a shuttle car run over and damage its trailing cable.

Seth fumed, "I will make sure that cable doesn't get replaced for a while. They will learn best from their own mistakes!"

As Seth marched off looking for the foreman, Al turned to me. "That is not a good method of controlling cost. By delaying the evidential cable replacement, we are going to incur more downtime in the interim. This vengeance actually escalates the total cost effects. It also compromises our standards and conflicts with the loss prevention message we are selling. Remember our actions communicate our true message, and our people are always listening for inconsistencies."

As Seth brought the foreman back to look at the cable damage, he was still ripping him, "I want a letter in the operator's file and I want his name publicized on the bulletin board!"

The foreman reluctantly spoke up, "Normally I might agree, but in this case the car has a steering issue that makes driving it difficult. The operator had been nursing the car along all shift until the new steering link arrives."

Seth stomped off.

I stepped over to the foreman, "Very good explanation and defense of your operator. It does not make damaging the cable okay, but it should influence the penalty. Our autopsies of a loss should be centered around the root cause and preventative counter measures, not the blame. I prefer to teach that I will take responsibility for the first mistake, but we all must pay the tuition. Repeating errors is where it can get ugly. Research shows that over 85% of losses are behavior oriented, but if we lash out after our people up front, the situation usually gets adversarial. If we look for all the contributing factors first, operator admittance usually comes out. The final outcome is always best when the defensive weapons are left holstered. We should be working with our operators to define the Best Practices, and then do standardization training. The final step, that we commonly leave out, is the auditing follow-up. Some need praise for doing it right, some need a reminder, and some are waiting for us to mandate the action. There are those few who only understand compliance enforcement. In any case, management has to follow up. We must communicate and follow up our expectations."

Al migrated to the working face, talked to a number of people, and did a thorough equipment condition inspection. After about two hours, we all met at the mantrip to head outside. Seth said he wanted to visit an isolated area in the mine, so he said he would meet us in the office later.

†

On the way back out, Al asked if we could travel a different route to the outside. "Sure," I said, "but why?"

"I was always taught to try to travel alternative paths to increase exposure for learning and follow-up opportunities. It helps to keep you sharp and deters your mind from mentally drifting."

When we got top-side, we were immediately met by the head security guard who seemed agitated. "We have not been able to reach Seth. He must be in part of the mine without communication, so Dirk you are the reigning official. We have a *Code Green*. Can we launch?" he urgently asked.

"Slow down a little," I responded, "Take your hand away from your pistol, and tell me what a Code Green is."

"It is an Eco-Terrorist Attack. Seth had a back-up plan for everything and the pre-made one for this is right here." He handed me the Emergency Preparedness Notebook.

I quickly took the book then shuttled the security guard, Al, and two other supervisors, Ray and Donnie, into an available private office. I asked Al to take a quick review of the book, while I turned my attention to the anxious guard, "Now tell me the facts."

He started, "My other guard spotted two guys with long hair who looked kind of…"

I reminded him judgmental statements were not needed, just the facts.

He qualified, "OK, let's say they looked like tree-huggers. They were sneaking down the back hill toward the stockpile dragging a big chain. And then we saw them cut a hole in the fence. You know, we have the property fenced completely except for the two manned gates."

"How long would it take them to get to the stockpile area?"

"Probably twenty minutes because they have to go through the creek," the guard stated.

I wanted to openly brainstorm with the others as we began making a quick plan. I stopped, pointed to Ray, one of the supervisors with us and asked, "Would you please get the Personnel Director and our company lawyer on the conference phone line so they can hear our discussion?"

We moved into the conference room with phone lines open and ready. I started writing on the office white board:

Our Goal
-to quickly disarm the situation, respectfully, and with low impact.

"Now, what do you see as their plan and goal?" Then I turned to the group and said, "Please, give me your ideas," and I started writing the responses:

-looks like they want to chain themselves to something
-probably try to stop the operation
-stop trucks
-try to cause trouble
-get us mad and stupid
-gain publicity

Then I said, "What should our plan be?"

Donnie responded, "Remove them."

I refuted, "No, that will be the police's job."

The security guard spouted, "Hurt them. Seth wanted to knock anyone down with the high pressure water hose from the water truck if this ever happened."

I said, "No, that is what they want, a scene, a lawsuit for 'harm.'"

Ray reacted, "Stop them!"

I again corrected, "No, it must be hands-off, we must out-smart them."

Donnie added again, "Embarrass them."

"No," I said once again, "then they will come back with a vengeance and the press will spin it."

I summarized, "we need to always keep our goal in mind and not get emotionally entangled in their intentions. Our action plan needs to get them to choose to get out-of-the way, and then we can isolate them until the police arrive. Now, look at the board notes, review our goals and let's stay away from theirs, and ask yourself what would MacGyver do?"

The Plan turned out like this:

Ray—Call the loader at the stockpile and tell him to start loading on the east end of the stockpile, which is out-of-the-way of normal traffic. Also, have someone move the extra bulldozer that's sitting near the main loading area to the stockpile's east side, so there is nothing in the main loading area. Leave the extra bulldozer running so it appears part of the process.

Donnie—Route the trucks temporarily to the east end but tell them to go slowly and watch for the people on the ground. Go down there and make sure no one goes near those people when they come out of the creek.

Security Guard—Lock down all the gates, and when *our friends* come out of the creek, assumedly heading to the stockpile, get on the bull horn and respectfully ask them to leave. Tell them this is private property, they are not legally trained, and they are in danger or could be a danger to others. Also, call the police in ten minutes.

I challenged, "Al, any ideas?"

Al came back, "I see in the guidebook that Seth has some ten foot high plastic fence with poles meant to trap someone. I can go get that with a couple guys. If they chain themselves to the bait dozer to stop the trucks, we can put the fence around them till the police arrive."

I reaffirmed, "Make sure neither the fence nor anyone touches them."

The personnel director shouted over the conference line, "Is someone filming everything?"

"Perfect," I said. "I will grab the training camera and someone to run it, and go down to the stockpile area to have an official conversation with them. Keep everyone else away who does not have a task; I want their interruption to be low impact."

Our lawyer inserted, "Sounds like a complete plan. I will be there in 20 minutes with a press release."

As everyone began to break out, I directed them, "Stay on channel 16 with your company radios."

By the time I arrived, the visitors were just coming out on the stockpile pad. As I watched, I thought about mice going to the cheese. They were running and dragging the log chain. When the loader man saw them, he started backing away, so they chained themselves to the idling, extra dozer, just as we planned. Al and a couple guys drove up in the mine rescue van and parked about 20 feet away. Al's team quickly un-spooled the plastic fence around the outside of the dozer and van, thus enclosing the two men. Al looked at the faces of the two intruders, who appeared to be in shock. This had obviously not gone the way they had planned. They were covered with creek mud and looked like they had just finished running a mid-summer marathon. Al set out a case of water from the van, two oxygen breathing apparatuses, and then stepped out of the immediate area.

Al's men zip-tied shut the plastic fence enclosure. I motioned everyone away and instructed the loader to take the trucks to the other end of the stockpile where they were to resume operations. With just the cameraman and film rolling, I came up to the fence, introduced myself, and asked if there was someone I could call for them, as I was worried about their personal health. They just sat there exhausted and in awe.

I hung a make-shift sign on the plastic fence: SEE THE TWO HELPLESS MICE; THEY TRIED BUT FAILED. We took pictures of our catch and then everyone left. About ten minutes later the state police showed up. We let them onto the property to collect the trespassers. The local TV crew, which had been mysteriously tipped off (not by us), remained outside the gate and visually blocked by a 'cooperating' delivery truck. Within 40 minutes of the initial intrusion onto the property, operations had resumed, *our friends* were leaving in a police car, and we had the only documentation of the event.

When Seth came outside of the mine and got off the elevator, I handed him the video camera. "Wow, Seth, you've missed out on a little action going on around here in the last 40 minutes or so. Here, this will explain everything, and give you the leverage of publicizing an embarrassing video if an anti-mining stunt is ever tried again," I assured.

The security guard came over to me and said, "That was impressive, we would have been calling an ambulance with Seth's plan."

Seth looked a little dumbfounded. He couldn't imagine what could possibly have happened in the short time he was out-of-pocket.

Al whispered, "Integrity usually triumphs blunt force, and it always builds respect and honor."

"Dirk," Al offered, "your leadership was stellar—you invited engagement, sincerely used the input, analyzed through multiple perspectives, steered toward a solution keeping our goals in focus, taught the logic and truth, designed a direct plan, delegated the responsibilities, stayed involved, but honored someone else with the trophy—the video of *our friends* and their predicament."

I responded, "I must admit, it turned out well. I don't know from where some of the ideas actually came, they just seemed to flow."

Al smiled and looked upward, "I do. He had some seeds to plant. Don't ever forget, when we follow His plan, He blesses our steps."

Note: The stories in this book have been written in the style of fiction, although most are completely true. But the story in this chapter of the two intruders may have been colored slightly. As I tell my wife with my hunting stories, 'All good adventures deserve to be embellished a little.'

II. OPERATIONS OVERVIEW

Chapter 7
Taurus #1 Mine

I had come to enjoy the rhythm of immersing in a different mine each week and the learning that surfaced as well. I was beginning to see things differently, as if I was looking through Al's lens. But on Mondays, the first day at a new site, during our drive time, I was the teacher. I prepped Al by telling him what I knew that would help give him perspective. I was eager for the Taurus #1 site, so as soon as Al was buckled up, I was like a horse out of the starting gate, eagerly sharing insights.

I knew Al would enjoy the Taurus #1 mine visit, so I was looking forward to it. I picked him up and started my review, "The superintendent is an ex-college football player so everything is about competition, but in a positive way. He sees competition as the driver within all of us. His favorite line is, 'It's not about competing against your teammate, because he is on your side. You can't win without him.'"

"I have also heard him tell his team, 'As the offense learns to block and the defense learns to tackle, we will each focus on the details of our game. Game day we show up united to win the game or in our case, survive the market. It's the coach's job to coordinate all the different agendas and to maximize the final performance.'"

Al couldn't hold back, "Those are perfect analogies. The main driver should not be to compete against our fellow employees; we should view them as internal clients since our achievements support and affect them. Many companies try to harness the competitive spirit by focusing it among the crews. It needs to be channeled positively in two different avenues. The first is toward the targeted process achievement. Start tracking performance and then chart the improvement percent over time. Once the process gets fairly refined, develop a benchmark goal. Channeling the competitive nature toward the benchmark goal and a continuous improvement percentage is always best. The second area of competition is directed to the market. Since we never know if today's performance keeps us in business, we should stress that our efforts are a continuous security journey. All we can do is inform our employees about market pressures and competitor's advances, track our progress, and focus on getting a little better every day. If we are truly committed to daily improvements, we can rely on the U.S. dollars motto, *In God We Trust.*"

I questioned, "If people ask you, 'When is *good* good enough?' What's the best answer?"

Al replied, "Our nature is to dislike change, but unfortunately no one has the promise of tomorrow. Who can predict the market and guarantee our future? It is a journey and only the strongest will survive. I love the fable popularized by Dan Montano:

Every morning in Africa, a gazelle wakes up.

It knows it must run faster than the fastest lion or it will be killed.

Every morning a lion wakes up.

It knows it must out run the slowest gazelle or it will starve to death.

It doesn't matter whether you are a lion or a gazelle:

When the sun comes up, you'd better be running.

I can picture the African plains looking peaceful and seemingly all the animals co-mingling. But there is another level going on—the battle for survival. The winners are the ones who perform the best, and that will be us."

I accepted the challenge to build a transformation plan. "We can build that plan and I firmly believe they will join us. There is too much at stake to lose; complacency is the breakfast of the losers."

Al added, "Good is the enemy of GREAT"

"All right, we are obviously saddled together," I continued. "I saved Taurus #1 Mine for last, on purpose. Al, you are going to enjoy the atmosphere. This operation has a mine and preparation plant, which is where all our mines send their coal to be cleaned. Taurus #1 Mine has been a solid performer but has always struggled to finish well. They have a new maintenance chief who will be a big help to them, as their equipment is older. The new chief is very strong on Preventative Maintenance (PM), so I am planning to use him to help set up a company-wide PM program."

As we pulled up on site, we saw a group of people eating breakfast around the grills. I motioned to Al, "There's the superintendent, the big guy in the middle." We headed over to join them and the ex-football player extended his massive hand.

"Hello, Mr. Hunt, my name is Tony Stephens. Let me welcome you to our home. Pardon our little party. It's an *appreciation feed* for the third shift magicians. These are the mechanics that patch things together so we can pay the bills from the day and second shift production tons. These guys are our superstars. Since I want to catch the entire crew as they come out, Dirk, how about you taking Mr. Hunt through the prep plant this morning and I will find you guys around lunchtime."

"That will work," I said.

We changed clothes, and Al suggested we start with the outside facilities. We looked at all the stockpiles, impoundments, and the large refuse storage area. During our climb to the top of the silos, we noticed a tour group of three, just ahead of us. As we approached I recognized them. They were a production foreman and his operators from the Lucky Star Mine.

I jokingly quizzed, "Are you guys lost? What are you doing here?"

The self-imposed spokesman came to their defense, "Dustin told us to come over to see how much rock we are sending outside, and not to come back until we have figured out how to reduce it."

The whole group laughed and someone said—"looks like our families are going to starve since we may never get our jobs back."

The spokesman said, "Seriously, Dustin thought it would be good for us to see the problem before we started working on the solution. We are a new Action Team set up to improve the product yield. We are blown away at the effect that trash, curtain, and wood are having on the coal cleaning process. We can stop almost all that. I've had people lecture that to me my whole career, but when you see it, it's different. Also the difference in separating various rock types has surprised us. Now we understand why the floor clays are so bad to try to wash out. We can definitely improve there too."

I was pleased to hear their sincerity and enthusiasm, "Remember, an ounce of prevention is better than a pound of cure. If you guys can figure out ways to reduce trash and rocks at the source, it would be huge for our security. In most cases, the cheapest prep plant is at the working face. We worked a *cost of loss calculation* for rock the other day. For every three inches of extra height from cutting more rock, it conservatively cost us $5.64/ton of coal sold. That's huge at the end of the day."

One of the miners interjected, "We will make you proud."

As we walked away, I looked at Al, "Dustin took your suggestion, what a commercial that was."

> **REACTIVE IS CONDITION STEERED AND SYMPTOM CONTROLLED. PRO-ACTIVE IS VALUE DRIVEN AND ROOT ADDRESSED.**

Al smiled, "I know it sounds like a broken record, but treat a person with respect and positively challenge them to raise the bar for a common gain, and they will perform. In most cases, just steering someone toward being proactive is all that is needed. In fact, look at that sign on the bulletin board: REACTIVE IS CONDITION STEERED, SYMPTOM CONTROLLED, AND PROACTIVE IS VALUE DRIVEN, ROOT ADDRESSED. Dirk, your people have the tools—we just need to tweak the process."

As Al surveyed the plant bulletin board, he was complimentary on its organization and the personalized compliments that were on the results graphs. He commented, "The fact that Tony took the time to editorialize a 'Thank You' for their cost savings help goes a long way in team building."

The remainder of the plant tour went very well. Al gave me a number of small efficiency suggestions, but in general, he shot me a thumbs up. We met Tony for lunch and he was anxious to talk.

"Rumor has it 'you got answers,' Mr. Hunt. That's good 'cause I have questions," Tony started.

"Call me Al," he said as the two shook hands. "I am flattered, and if my stories can help, I'm happy to share. To start with, your aggressive but humble introduction is impressive. And I like a lot of what I've seen so far. Let's tackle the problems. Where do we start?"

Tony led, "I am trying to build a team that self manages. I have heard you like the Management By Objectives (MBO) style and so do I. I would love to modernize that for the mines. Can you give me some specifics?"

I smiled, "Tony that's music to Al's ears."

Al warned, "You're going to get me wound up now. You're on the right track, Tony. Our management goal should be to build the boat and position the sail so the momentum continues propelling the boat forward. Our leadership side empowers and motivates. If the ark is built right, team success is fed internally and we, management, become scorekeepers. Management By Objective is an excellent framework and monitoring system. The vital link is to devise KPI's, Key Performance Indicators, and PI's, Performance Indicators, that tell the whole story. Giving people too much information or pounding them for results outside of their influence is counter-productive. As your teams dial into having the results steer their focus, you can fine tune their efforts by temporarily changing the priorities on certain indicators, as bottlenecks evolve and dissipate. I will send you an example of KPI and PI lists from a past company with which I worked (Appendix B.17 and B.18). I will caution you to make sure the objectives are set in a balanced manner. For example, always lead off with a safety KPI comment, to make sure priorities are never misread. Make sure that the gain in one area does not sacrifice in another. You need to pre-think about the ripple effect every time you monitor a specific result. Since the natural reaction is to report results in the most favorable and non-incriminating way, the initial numbers are usually just flushing out the loopholes. They are not telling the complete story. Once you get reporting guidelines refined, the focus on the desired output can be seen in the results. Here's an example:

I had the miner section bosses start tracking their Production Efficiency Rate (tons/up-time minute). The foremen figured out if they turned in all their downtime, their rate increased and they looked better. Previously they had not turned in the downtime, because it was easier to not write it down and the maintenance department commonly took it defensively. Thus, when no accountability was tied to the productivity rates, sloppy reporting was not penalized. Once the correct downtime was turned in, the only way to improve their efficiency rate was to actually reduce process losses. We saw production improvements of over 15% immediately AND we received a full list of downtime issues that we could pro-actively address. A win-win result."

Tony was awed, "That's us exactly. Our shift reports are very poor and the information sparse. But we are guilty of not having a follow-up indicator like *Production Efficiency Rate*. We've got to start that."

Al added, "Make sure you are ready to record, track, and follow up on the downtime before you ask for it. If you emphasize the importance of getting all the downtime, and it is not utilized and acted on, the workforce's commitment eventually will be lost. Human nature reminds us that if our effort today makes tomorrow better, chances are, we will comply. If you add a sincere pat on the back, there's even a better chance they will remain committed. From your cookout this morning, I sense you understand the payback of praise."

Tony stepped in, "What you celebrate, you reap, and this team is energized. Sometimes I think my lack of getting them focused on the right thing is our biggest problem. Your KPI and PI approach is enlightening, I'm going to think on that. As far as praising our people is concerned, I learned from my first superintendent, who used to say 'sincerely praising in public today reduces the frequency of private correction needed tomorrow.'"

Somehow the day had evaporated. Al grabbed a couple months of reports to review and I dropped him off back at the hotel.

†

When we returned to the mine the next morning, Tony was waiting for us with his new maintenance chief, Joe Fowler. After the introductions Tony took off at full speed, "Joe and I were up late last night talking about your ideas, Al. When we start pushing the downtime reporting, we believe the flood gates will open. We need an information handling system. Can you give us some advice?"

Al responded, "It starts with designing a good gathering vehicle. Every mine has them, but most are not designed with the level of detail needed. Your Shift Reports, that I reviewed last night, were no exception. Start with a list of Performance Indicators that feed the final results. Then build those measurement areas into the report. Not only are you getting the information, but more importantly, you are impressing upon the foreman the importance of specific factors. As you analyze the Performance Indicators, some will be more important at times than others, which will upgrade them to the Key Performance Indicator status. I suggest only having about seven KPI's at a time, two safety and five operational for each department. If you have too many, you will lose focus. Once all the data is gathered and reported, it can be analyzed, tracked, and the focus areas trended. Many companies track the data, but few turn it into helpful process improvement tools. In breaking apart from the normal, I suggest you add a data analyst position which will look for those trends and crew specifics. I will send you an example of the list of Trending Categories that might be evaluated (Appendix B.19). The downtime records accuracy is also a vital part of the process, stressing the good info in, yields the true story—helps us build better improvement plans. If the data is used correctly that information can point to problem repeaters (equipment and personnel), adjust Preventative Maintenance schedules, and fine-tune mini- and full-rebuild plans. I have even seen some aggressive companies' maintenance crews manage by developing a comprehensive equipment operating cost [defined as the specific equipment (parts/supply cost) + (maintenance time worked on the equipment x \$35/hour) + (delay-to-load downtime x \$100/minute)]. By reviewing each piece of equipment's operating costs, maintenance prioritizing plans can be made."

Joe was taking everything in and writing as fast as he could. "Those are good points but I want to take it further into reporting equipment problems. I just came from a small operation where the operator just verbally told the mechanics about a problem or potential issue, but we are too big here. We need a better system."

Al said, "I hate to suggest more paperwork, but that is the only way to not lose the operator's valuable input. If we lose it, we can't prioritize it, and it won't get done. Then we have a loss and the employees won't bother reporting it next time. This is the second part of the reporting process, and it's critically important."

Tony interjected, "If this is heading toward our operators filling out a daily report on potential or unfixed issues, well, we have tried it and *that dog won't hunt.*"

Al defended, "I used to think the same way. When I was a face boss, we were told, without an explanation, to have our people fill out a pre- and on-shift inspection checklist. Rather than hear the complaints and fight the rejections, I just asked each employee at shift end for their verbal complaints. Then I added a very condensed version of the complaints to my foreman report.

Years later I met up with a guy who was on one of my crews. He had quit and gone to work for Toyota. I asked him, 'What is it like over there?' He bragged, 'They treat everything we have to say as important and they really listen. Every employee keeps a small notebook and pen on their hip, *we are packin'*, and we have multiple checklists for our feedback. We are highly encouraged to look for potential losses and preventative clues, so we can take care of them. But if we can't fix them ourselves, we are to turn them in as a work request. All of our notes are turned in at shift-end so they can be logged and the work requests prioritized. That's how we make sure the communication is not lost. It keeps everyone standardized in how we do our job, and the checklists remind us of the detail that is critical. We also leave a carbon copy of our report in the machine or work area, so the next shift can get an immediate update. You guys ought to try this work request system at the mines. Your people will help you, if you explain why and then ask respectfully. When I was in the mines, a lot of people didn't take their inspections seriously. One of my Toyota bosses told us this example, 'If you were getting on a flight and you overheard two airplane mechanics talking, and one asked the other if he had made all the pre-flight checks, and he responded, "no, but I am sure that we're okay. After all, the plane limped in here from the last flight didn't it?" How would you feel? Would you board the plane?' Toyota teaches that the first show of respect must be a total commitment of everyone to prevention!"

Al continued, "I was dumbfounded. All those years I carried that inspection load on my back because I failed to ask for help. Now, I firmly believe empowering every employee is the key to greatness. We may buy their attendance, muscle, and compliance but excellence requires commitment, creativity, and loyalty—true gifts of the heart."

As we got ready to go underground, Joe directed our attention to the slogan

> **WE MAY BUY THEIR ATTENDANCE, MUSCLE, AND COMPLIANCE BUT EXCELLENCE REQUIRES COMMITMENT, CREATIVITY, AND LOYALTY—TRUE GIFTS OF THE HEART.**

at the mine slope, EQUIPMENT ALLOWED TO STAY BELOW "TOP CONDITION" COSTS US TWICE—ONCE TO REPAIR IT (which we will have to fix eventually) and AGAIN FOR THE LOSS IT CREATES.

"That's a motto I believe in," Joe exclaimed.

Al reassured, "It's a win-win motto, the challenge is tuning it to their WIIFM channel—music for their ears."

Joe looked puzzled. So I patted him on the back and said, "That's our employees' radio station—**W**hat's **I**n **I**t **F**or **M**e."

†

When we arrived at the bottom of the slope, we discovered that Tony already had brought the rail mantrip around, so we all got in and rode to the section.

As we walked up to the working face area, Tony turned to Al and said, "Let's see how good you are. The challenge is to find two cost-saving ideas and meet back here in an hour."

Al smirked and fired back, "The loser walks out?"

Tony teased, "This will be like tackling the punter."

Everyone split up, but I couldn't stand it, I followed Al from a distance. He took off immediately to the face area so he could watch the roof bolters and the loading crew.

After about 15 minutes of process time recording, he looked over at me and said, "The bottleneck is obvious. You can go tell Tony to start walking!"

Al spent the remaining 45 minutes mingling and talking to the face crew. It was an education just to watch him interact with people. He was a good listener. But I thought his greatest gift was helping people dig deep into their own experiences to generate proactive ideas. He always got a smile, their perspective, and an open ear to his teaching.

When Al had finished his last employee discussion, I asked him, "What is the key to getting people to open up?"

Al answered, "I'll use Mark Twain's explanation, 'I have never met a man that is not more senior to me in some area.' If you sincerely probe a man's mind, his heart will speak."

As everyone gathered back at the meeting place, Tony took inventory. "Joe, how about your two ideas?"

Joe reported, "I could only find one thing. Someone had run-over a box of bolting resin."

Tony agreed that was a loss, but the magnitude was low. He stressed it was important to mention the find, so as not to condone waste, but that our focus should be on a *bigger catch*. Then Tony locked onto Al, "Let's see what you found?"

Al opened his little *Columbo* notebook, and said "Your guys gave me eleven improvement ideas. Since the safe production enhancers carry the biggest payback, we'll call them the A's; we have seven A's."

"All right," Tony snapped, "Give me the best one."

Al was confident, and he had no trouble selecting his best, "A quick cycle-time check showed the two bolting crews were staying ahead of the continuous miner and cars by at least 25%. Since the bottleneck was the production crew, a couple common averages can be used. Industry averages reveal most continuous miners cut less than 30% of the total shift-time. So if we conservatively figure you are achieving that 30% of a 480 minute/shift, your average miner is only cutting 160 minutes/shift. By my time-study it was taking 60 seconds to cut an average car of coal (about 5 tons), and it was being loaded into the car in about 35 seconds. Those were common times, but the miner operator had a bad habit of only cutting when the car was under his boom. If you taught the principle of pre-cutting the coal while cars are changing out, 25 seconds/car could be saved. Over a 150 car shift, that is 62 minutes/shift potential savings. If we just achieved 40% of the bottleneck improvement, that would be 25 minutes saved. Thus, if we assume downtime cost us $100/minute (and that must be calculated for each operation and given economics), 25 minute/shift translates to $2,500/shift saved just by utilizing the pre-cutting technique."

Tony retracted, "I followed that, I think. But how can you make sure they pre-cut when we leave and aren't watching them?"

"Excellent question," Al answered, "because it is true that bad habits usually continue if there is no accountability for change. In this case, there is an easy solution. Have the cutting and conveyor motor hours reported from the continuous miner at the end of every shift. Their ratio will tell the tale of the pre-cutting compliance. This type of flow and bottleneck analysis is totally site-specific, but following up on the results is always worth the effort."

Tony hung his head and conceded defeat. "I'll start walking," he murmured.

Al came back, "I can't allow that, but I will take a pop when we get outside. My throat's a little dry. Remember, Tony, the only real losers are the ones that quit, and I don't see you as one of them."

> **SUCCESS IS EARNED IN THE TRENCHES, LEARNED THROUGH THE DETAIL, BUT CELEBRATED IN DOMINANCE.**

"Okay, you got it. And you're right, I'm not a quitter. I promise you, we will take your lessons and mature from them. Our guys know success is earned in the trenches, learned through the detail, but celebrated in dominance. I assure you, this is a team of survivors."

After we got outside and showered, we met with Tony for a wrap-up meeting. Al was encouraging and yet challenging on the work ahead. Tony seemed to receive it well, and promised to continue his focused track.

As I drove Al back to the hotel, I commented, "I can see how diligent you are about encouraging each superintendent in their managing and process style, but they are each so different. How are we going to build a corporate operating plan that allows for their individuality?"

Al smiled, "This is another excellent and insightful question. Most companies either avoid the challenge by accepting current performance or by adopting a suffocating program that does not respect the presiding general's strengths, passion, and plan. Over the next three weeks, you will see how it all will come together. I encourage you to do your part, write the list of foundational values. They will be essential for bringing all the pieces and people together.

III. RESTRUCTURING THE ASSETS

Chapter 8
Reallocating Facilities & Equipment

Waiting in the car outside Al's hotel, I had a sense that today was going to be different. To say I was a little apprehensive would be an understatement. Al and I were due to meet the Board first thing in the morning to discuss the future. I had so many notes from our past six weeks of mine visits, but I still could not see the common need or a core element on which to build a cohesive corporation plan. Al had assured me that he had a plan, but I had my doubts. It didn't seem like there was any continuity in management style. The challenges varied widely, and designing a macro operating system seemed to be impossible.

Al opened the car door to get in, and interrupting my fretting, said, "You look deep in thought."

"I am," I replied, "It was a good night for worrying and a bad night for sleeping. I've been trying to figure out what your plan is. We are a group of individual mines, not an autonomous organization. How can there be a single system?"

"In the beginning, there won't be. We will devise a base foundation, develop a process, and then provide a bag of tools and techniques for the operations. First we must know the parameters. Today we will ask the Board to define the business criteria, and then the strategizing begins. Perhaps I can help you see things a little more clearly by helping you shift your perspectives. You are getting lost in the management of issues, you are not focusing on the potential of leadership. GREAT companies are birthed from the foundation of values and matured through the execution of balanced process. We will get into that later. Let's just focus on the developmental plan right now."

> **GREAT COMPANIES ARE BIRTHED FROM THE FOUNDATION OF VALUES AND MATURED THROUGH THE EXECUTION OF BALANCED PROCESS.**

As we walked into the board room, there was a distinct aura of seriousness.

Before we could even sit down, Fred Miller challenged, "Al, I hope you've got a miracle up your sleeve because we sure need one. The market is tanking and costs are up."

Al met Fred's gaze, "I am confident we can sculpt a plan to not only survive but thrive. What I need is for the board to describe the landscape and economic goals."

"It's simple, make us a lot of money," Fred blurted out.

Al reacted, "That is the corporate-serving agenda that walked us into this situation. I thought we agreed to change and take a win-win approach."

"We did and we are," Jeff snapped. "I am sorry for our tone, but as you will find out shortly we got some bad news this morning. As for our goal, we are going to maintain the Integrity calling. The mission statement we gave you will not be compromised. We just have some more hurdles to add to the race. Let me ask Fred to review the Profit/Loss Results from the last two years."

Fred passed out the summary:

CORPORATE RESULTS BREAKDOWN		
	2011	**2012**
Broad Run	55%	51%
Taurus #1	19%	30%
Straight Ridge	20%	29%
Deep Hollow	26%	10%
Lucky Star	-18%	-5%
Lucky Road	-2%	-15%
	100%	100%

He expounded, "As you can see the Broad Run Mine has consistently brought in over half of our profit. Lucky Star showed the strongest improvement even though they still lost money. Lucky Road remains a disaster and is getting worse. The other three are solid, but Deep Hollow's problem is they have lost 30% of their sales price due to market dynamics. Since they produce steam coal versus the higher price metallurgical grade coals mined by the other operations, their future is tainted. It is not a rosy picture. I guess we are going to have to push more cost cutting."

Al stepped in, "Please hold off on the spending restriction approach. In a volume sensitive business, the efficiency focus pays higher dividends than the starving techniques."

Fred consented, "You might be right. Our productivity rates have fallen dramatically, since we started running our crews short and have restricted spending. Also, over the last two years we have cut out our equipment rebuild program to save short-term dollars and our downtime has exponentially risen." Then he added sarcastically, "So what magic wand are you going to use to reverse that trend?"

Marci Franco took the floor, "I hate to follow that report but I am afraid my news is worse. The bad news Mr. Page alluded to earlier was an audit we just received. We had requested a third party cost study on "government interference" to our business. The report projected cost increases due to higher taxation, permitting and legal requirements, and insurance increases of $6 Million/year. Mr. Hunt, we have to cover that in operational improvements, as we are highly leveraged with $33 Million in short-term debt already. The other two common ways to acquire funds are an equity raise, but the owners are neither interested in diluting ownership nor in reserve lease-back options. The lease-back option is a last choice, since the interest rates are high and our current collateral covenants may not allow it. I believe in the power of prayer, but we may be putting God in a corner."

Al replied, "He does not like to be in the corner, but I think He likes helping us get out of one. Truth is, He likes the relationship time whenever we give it to Him."

Jeff cleared his throat and said, "I know some of this sounds dismal but we still believe in our people. They have creative ideas, good work ethics, and resilience. Somehow there has to be a way to support and empower Integrity Coal to move from good to a surviving GREAT."

Everyone in the room stared at Al and me, for what seemed like an eternity.

Finally, Al said, "Dirk and I have an outside-the-box approach we'd like to suggest. It will take me a week to complete my individual operation reports that you had contracted me to do, and then another week for Dirk and me to work up our conceptual business plan. We will be ready to present in two weeks, and if I were you, I would be ready to say, 'YES! Let's go.'"

You could feel the Board's tension ease, but I wasn't sure my demise hadn't just been announced.

Marci stood and said, "I would like to sign-on to your passion, but the financial projections will have to lead to the approval discussion."

Al nodded and said, "fair enough. If we cannot build a self-sustaining plan, it will not work for the entire team."

At the end of the meeting, I felt drained. As we were driving back to the hotel, I looked at Al and said, "I hope you have an incredible plan because I am lost."

Al calmly smiled and said, "There's a Him-possible solution, we just have to find it, and we will. Hey, how about we pick up Nikki and the kids and go out for dinner. It's on me, my treat."

I knew Nikki would be game. "Let me call," I said. It turned out the kids had play practice at church, so it was just the three of us for dinner.

We had a nice meal. After our table was cleared away and we were enjoying after-dinner coffees, the conversation somehow turned to the subject of balancing time.

Nikki probed, "Al, how have you juggled your time between all your commitments? We have seen so many senior management families split and we don't want to follow suit."

Al shared, "I don't mind getting very personal here, but I want to be respectful of your beliefs. I am not trying to convince you guys to follow my lead. My wife and I have always felt strongly that we were called to carry our values openly in every facet of our lives. We have taken the position that to be servants means helping people achieve their potential and security in this life and the thereafter. So every time we have had a time commitment decision, our prayer was for wisdom in fulfilling that charge. During different seasons in our lives, God has steered us with a varied direction, but always in balance. We believe that as there is correct value balance in business, there must also be in our personal lives.

I have always subscribed to the thought that I am to wear four hats of responsibility simultaneously:

1) to my God: my personal spiritual walk, witness, and church family

2) to my family: my wife and then my children

3) to my career

4) to my hobbies/health

The hardest part is to stay sensitive and flexible enough to shift where and when He needs me to do so. For me, I have always felt God wanted me to keep all four facets of my life active, but to different degrees during different seasons. There is a great book called *Experiencing God* by H. & R. Blackaby and C. King that teaches about joining God in His work and plan for your life—not creating your own path. Often tough advice to find and follow, but rewarding and peaceful. I truly believe you will only be settled in your heart when you align with your calling. So my advice is, seek His direction first, and then be committed with the gifts given. My career calling was embraced by our whole family. They sacrificed in losing my time with them and in numerous home moves, but in the end it has worked for us. We have had some tough work and personal assignments, but the fruit we see in our six children's lives is just a small reminder of His faithfulness. We have been richly blessed."

"Enough about me, I have talked to the Board about how hard you have been working, Dirk, and the hours of your time that your family has sacrificed over the last six weeks. They wanted to show their appreciation for that and their vote of confidence in your leading the transformation. They asked me to give you this envelope. It's plane tickets and a one week vacation for your family to Florida. The caveat is you have to go next week, so you come back fully rested and ready to take on our challenge."

I looked at Nikki and vented a big sigh.

"I guess there's a few spoils of war," she said.

We smiled, hugged, and turned to Al, thanking him for the reward that I am sure he instigated.

Then I encountered a bit of a reality-check, "I can't leave during this time."

Al responded, "I have a week of write-up on the operations. You go sit on the beach and enjoy the gang. When we reconvene, the fireworks will start."

Knowing these gifts are not commonplace in our industry, Nikki and I decided to accept them with gratitude.

She looked at me and said, "If this is the fruit of integrity, I could learn to like it."

†

One Week Later…

My family and I were driving home from the airport when Al called. "The bad news is the Board wants to meet tomorrow to review our plan. The good news is I finished the operation write-ups early, so I have been crunching numbers on a new proposal and corporate structuring. Let's meet in the morning at 6:00 a.m. so we can be ready for their afternoon briefing. Oh yeah, welcome back to the corporate world!"

We both laughed, and I again wondered, what was it I was signing up for? As impossible as the assignments seemed, in my heart I was at peace. I reflected back on the medallion I saw hanging in Jeff Page's car two months earlier, HE HAS CHARTED YOUR DESTINY, BUT THE CHOICE IS YOURS. Oddly enough, the words felt comforting.

Our morning meeting was a blur, but since Al agreed to do the presentation, I was fine in being the silent but supportive partner.

During our drive over to the Board briefing Al gave me a stump speech on leadership and encouraged me to add to the presentation. I was ready, but I sensed Al was primed and loaded. As the Board assembled and were seated, Al energetically addressed the white board.

He began by listing the issues by mine location:

Broad Run [Superintendent Luke Couch]
+ strong cash value (solid performance)
- poor upside (stagnating management style)
- no synergy to other operations
- poor fit to Integrity Values

Deep Hollow [Superintendent Makirra Cole]
+ good equipment
+ excellent training agenda
- bad market
- poor geology

Lucky Road [Superintendent Seth Martin]
+ good equipment
- terrible management/workforce relationship
- union work practice issues

Lucky Star [Superintendent Dustin Sturgil]
+ improving performance
+ trust/respect being earned
- poor equipment
- high union cost

Straight Ridge [Superintendent Cody Myers]
+ strong performance
+ solid attitudes
- weak systems

Reallocating Facilities & Equipment

Taurus #1   [Superintendent Tony Stephens]
+ strengthening performance
+ healthy competitive spirit
- poor equipment

"Summarizing, I would say, every operation has pros/cons. I believe everyone and everything can be changed positively with unlimited time and money, but in our case, we have neither. After analyzing mining conditions, market effects, fixed costs, and team efficiency potentials, we recommend an immediate six step plan (Al distributed handouts to each of the board members):

> " EVERYONE AND EVERYTHING CAN BE CHANGED POSITIVELY WITH UNLIMITED TIME AND MONEY, BUT IN OUR CASE, WE HAVE NEITHER.

1) Sell Broad Run for an estimated $60 Million
   - The valuation was based on a 5 times multiple of their 2012 EBITDA earnings (EBITDA is defined as Earnings Before Income, Tax, Depreciation, and Amortization)
   - Since it produces a different grade of coal as compared to our other mines, it will not have a negative market effect in a competitor's hand
2) Shutdown Deep Hollow
   - Transfer the better equipment and personnel to the other mines
   - The poor geology and a weak steam market cast permanent investment concerns
3) Shutdown Lucky Road
   - Transfer the better equipment and personnel to the other mines
   - Union work practices would be difficult to quickly modify
4) Increase Lucky Star Capacity
   - Upgrade equipment
   - Change the operating structure and mining layout
   - Renegotiate some of the union costs and panel hiring rules
5) Increase Straight Ridge Capacity
   - Upgrade personnel and systems
   - Change the operating structure and mining layout
6) Increase Taurus #1 Capacity

- Upgrade equipment
- Change the operating structure and mining layout

Any reduction is bad news but in this case, market pressures, rising government charges, and escalating insurance costs are forcing us to make deep changes or we will lose everything. Even though two operations, Deep Hollow and Lucky Ridge, would be reduced, only 14% of the total workforce will be minimized. Let's look at the upside. The majority of the reduced-operation employees will be relocated to fill all open positions, add two more working sections, and all the remaining mines' sections will be upgraded from single-miner layouts to efficient super-sections. With respect to the equipment fleet, it will be upgraded by shuffling the best pieces to the remaining operations. The final upside from the plan change is that since the personnel, management, and workforce will be carefully screened and realigned, the resulting teams will be stronger.

You should have a *Restructuring Forecast* in your handouts (Appendix B.20). Detailed projections show a production increase of 18% with 14% less labor cost. This translates into a significant reduction in the cost per ton of 8.9%, which goes straight to the bottom line. The sale of Broad Run would be a stock sale, so the coal reserves, all personnel, retirement responsibilities, and equipment would transfer to the new purchasing company. Since it has been a solid performer in a niche market, it should not be a problem to find a suitor. It is hard to lose our top performer, but with limited upside due to the ingrained management style, their value to our entire program is better served by utilizing sale monies. The generated revenue would be allocated as follows:

+$60M	Sale Revenue
- $3M	Strong severance package for the reduced employees
- $2M	Donations to the community/local church projects
- $6M	Off-set the 'government interference' charges for one year
- $9M	Purchase needed equipment to complete the supersizing of all units and upgrade existing equipment.
- $7M	To be used for financing internal creative 'value adding investments'
-$33M	Liquidate Short Term Debit Obligations

Dirk and I strongly believe this plan will not only reduce our costs/ton by 8.9%, it will increase our sales by 20%. This will have a double positive in the bottom line financials. Our debt issue will be relieved, and it will also give us an upgraded equipment fleet and investment capital to achieve upside performance. We will be in a better position to not only survive but thrive. This plan maximizes

Reallocating Facilities & Equipment   87

our owners' investment, earns security for our employees, and continues to allow us to be a positive net asset to the community. It's a win-win-win."

Marci leaned forward, "Good presentation but let's back up and review your projections a little closer."

†

After about two hours of number crunching and discussion, the Board asked us to step-out, so they could privately caucus. As Al and I waited in the neighboring office, I asked him to explain the logic in selling off the most profitable operation.

Al explained, "Your reaction is typical for a senior manager, because you are analyzing through your perspective and are naturally driven toward the least turbulent approach, since you will have to carry it out, whereas an investor seeks the highest return with limited risk. Our solution yields the most stability and builds-in other avenues for operational upside. The best plans always have internal contingency opportunities, in order to balance out the unexpected, if and when it rears its head."

Jeff Page came out and invited us back into the room. He said, "Well done! Your mechanics are solid, planning thorough, and logistics reasonable. Exactly what I would have expected."

Marci and Fred both nodded in agreement as well.

Jeff continued, "Now, with the hard assets repositioned, let's refine the structure, design the process, sell the change, and implement the system. You have won our support, and we greatly appreciate your efforts. Now the hard work begins. Let's start the Journey. Tomorrow is a new day for Integrity Coal!"

III. RESTRUCTURING THE ASSETS

Chapter 9
Developing the Team

By now I was pretty accustomed to two things about Al: his directness and his optimization of our drive time. He was barely inside the car when he said, "Are you ready to start filling the boat?"

I perked up like a kid, whose teacher caught him by surprise with a provocative question.

Al continued, "This next phase of the transformation is ultra-critical, yet most companies mismanage and under-prioritize the human resource side of the business. Development of high-performance teams is a very important step in the creation of a GREAT organization. The prerequisites for building strong teams are a united mission combined with foundational values. The board supplied us with the mission and you are transcribing a list of foundational values. Is it ready yet?"

"Yes," I replied, "And I am really proud of it. There are nine foundational values that I have gleaned from our operations. Together, I think they make a statement of what we believe and can rally around. I am beginning to see the vision of what we can become if everyone pulls together."

Al smiled, "That's what I have been waiting for. When we can envision Integrity Coal on the pinnacle of success and take ownership of where we are going, we are off to the races. With conviction in our hearts, sincerity shows up and motivates. Now let's amp up the process. Great vision and values are powerless without the right team, so the key is in choosing the right personnel fit.

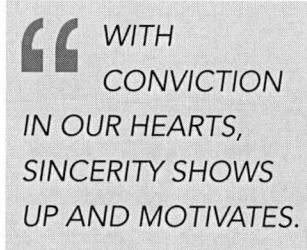

> WITH CONVICTION IN OUR HEARTS, SINCERITY SHOWS UP AND MOTIVATES.

Our company is filled with lots of good people, but our job now is to load the bus with the best, the ones that have the least baggage. The surviving companies are those that run light, lean, and flexible, but more importantly they operate efficiently and effectively. As we have stated before, it's not that some people can't change from old, negative, resistive attitudes, but in competitive business survival, we do not always have time to wait for their character to positively mature and their drive to evolve from compliant to committed. We all have issues, but some are so distracting that it weighs the team down. As the leaders, we are responsible for protecting the house! Whether we are designing a transformation like Integrity Coal, building up a brownfield, or starting a new greenfield, the individual selections are paramount. Too often we accept poor employment fits. It almost always turns into a lose-lose. The employee and employer both are frustrated and the breakup is inevitable. Worse yet, the safety and/or economics of the business is compromised, and everyone's job is put in jeopardy. A supervisor once told me, 'Skills and tactics we can teach, but attitude and character are what is brought to the table.' My advice is to seek the best, and they will help you earn the security we all are looking for. Eliminate those people who drain the energy and enthusiasm from the team. *Silencing the rooster* is always uncomfortable in the short term, but it is often necessary and rewarding in the medium and long-term. Warren Buffet offers his wisdom in a quote, 'In looking for your people, search for three qualities: Integrity, Intelligence, and Energy. And if they don't have the first one, the other two will kill you.' Cute but true.

> **ELIMINATE THOSE PEOPLE WHO DRAIN THE ENERGY AND ENTHUSIASM FROM THE TEAM.**

An individual's character is the jewel we seek. As we assess our people's character, I suggest we determine their position with respect to the following:

> **AN INDIVIDUAL'S CHARACTER IS THE JEWEL WE SEEK.**

1) Safety as an uncompromisable value

2) Respect for authority

3) Openness to change

4) Positive attitude

5) Creativity

6) High personal standards

7) Acceptance of our corporate values

Once we have limited the field to the strongest character fits, we will fine tune the search and placement depending on the operational needs. If an operation has not gone through a character-fits purging, it can be a healthy exercise. Usually a personnel reduction of between 2-10% can clean up a lot of value differences and improve the workplace environment dramatically. We need to always make sure reductions are handled fairly and consistently with our policies for all of our people. We have a responsibility to assemble the best team possible, one that is diverse, yet united and positive in procedure."

I responded, "In our case all the union-free operations have no employee handbooks, so there are no rules."

Al commented, "I hate to see companies operate with no written guidelines. Our employees always deserve to know the expectations, boundaries, and business format. Remember they are partners in our company. Let's make that an A Priority, to get a handbook written and in their hands as soon as possible."

Workforce Placement

Al continued, "The initial job is to delineate the required manning chart. Once the needs are listed, we can start the next line of selection. This is where it is helpful if a company has had an ongoing employee evaluation program and career development process."

I jumped in, "We have a good development program where we encourage cross training and have a subjective grading system on equipment skills on various pieces of equipment."

Al was pleased, "That's excellent, the career development process shows our investment and interest in each employee's future, and it telegraphs their commitment to the operation. During a selection process like this, the records give us valuable information on each person's skill sets and personal push for growth. It would be helpful if we had employee evaluations, but it is not uncommon to be without them. Moving forward, a solid evaluation process can help the committed employees to perfect performance over time, and it also weeds out the under-performers. A well balanced evaluation covers: work and safety records, attitude, cooperation, certifications, and individual improvement focus areas. It helps force two-way communication between management and the employee. Since we don't have an ongoing program, we will now have to develop one and fairly score every individual accordingly. The weighted criteria should include:

1) Technical skills (main, multi-equipment, certifications)

2) Work record

3) Teamwork/commitment

4) Seniority

Most labor contracts at union represented operations will over-prioritize the seniority time, but even that can be renegotiated in reductions such as ours. If we show the union our openness to keep more union members, they commonly will allow the seniority-weighting to be balanced against the other criteria, and we can come to a compromise."

I interrupted, "Do you mean we should consider relocating some union employees to surviving union-free operations?"

"I definitely mean that," Al answered. "As we have talked about before, the decision to unionize came from the past and should be honored. It was their right. The future will be based on how well we treat our people. Every site will always have a right to vote either way on their representation. The union-free status is an honor that management must be committed to maintaining by keeping everyone safe and treated fairly. I have always found it best to evaluate the entire workforce pool, and select the strongest employees based on: character, skill sets, work record, teamwork/commitment, and seniority. Then assemble the team by operation needs, team continuity, and employee preferences."

Managerial Build-Up

When it comes to developing the managerial staffing, he explained that we follow the same process as with the workforce. Al persisted in patiently explaining things to me, "Step one is to develop the organizational chart. We can start with a standard template, but we have to customize it. Every site has varying needs and a different operating style, strengths, and weaknesses. Because matching managers and teams is crucial, I have always been a fan of every manager taking an in-depth personality profile test, such as the Myers-Briggs. It specializes in highlighting correct position placement and interpersonal dynamics.

The results will help with employee placement to maximize skill set use, support personality combinations, and will weave the best teams. Complementary teams broaden the experience base and opinion scope. They are more beneficial than look-a-like groups. The diversity is healthy if the chemistry is right. For example, two over confident, type A personalities together equals a disaster. With the current downsizing, we have an opportunity to rebuild the steering wheel. Shame on us if we squander this chance. Even in situations of minimal change, management shuffling can refine skill set utilization and/or supportive personality matches. It can further fuel our goal of earning a win-win. The next cross-check on the management team is back to their individual character. We have to do our best to make sure that each manager is a perfect match to the corporate and operational values. How can a manager communicate and lead a team in a *change message* that they personally don't completely believe or are able to express? If they are not sincere, no one will follow. If we give authority to individuals with serious character flaw traits, we undercut the effectiveness of the team. Here's what we don't want in our managers:

Developing the Team

Unacceptable Managerial Character Traits

1. Arrogant
2. Close minded
3. Overly critical of others
4. Disrespectful
5. Insensitive
6. Indecisive
7. Dishonest
8. Blame throwing
9. Political/individual agenda driven

It is not that we will find the perfect person, because there are none, but the management group that is charged to carry out and empower the vision and plan, must be free of the critical character flaws. Without a doubt, this is one of the largest mistakes I have made through my transformations. I have been too tolerant and/or have not recognized these critical character issues. Our weakest link is commonly the detractor within our own walls. This is not an area to lower our standards. Even in the unusual situation where a manager is capable of quickly making a major style change, the workforce will probably be slow to forgive and forget. The perception usually is that their change is temporary and disingenuous. Trust can only be restored over time, which we commonly do not have.

The final stage is for the operation superintendent to refine the organizational chart structure to fit the groups' talents and then fill in the names. General staffing goals are to keep reporting lines as simple and flat as possible, yet broad enough to cover the needed cross-checks and offer future succession planning. Flat organizational charts help in communication, empowerment, and the delegation of accountability to all levels."

I challenged Al, "What are the management team groupings you would recommend in our situations?"

Al thought for a few moments. "First of all, I would assemble the strongest management team at the operation of highest potential, not necessarily the site of the largest problem. This provides the best return and security. Let me ask you, who do you see as the strongest three superintendent choices?"

> **I WOULD ASSEMBLE THE STRONGEST MANAGEMENT TEAM AT THE OPERATION OF HIGHEST POTENTIAL, NOT NECESSARILY THE SITE OF THE LARGEST PROBLEM.**

"I feel most comfortable with Cody, Dustin and Tony," I replied. "Although Makirra is a close second, she is a little more passive than I like. I do think her confidence will improve over time, though."

"I agree," Al added. "She will be ready down the road." Al moved over to a nearby whiteboard and started writing. "I think these are some natural fits:

	Style	Strength	Weakness
Team A			
Cody: Supt.	Encourager	+People Skills, Empowerment	−Standards, Discipline
Makirra: Asst.	Teacher	+Training, Process Improvement	−Hands-on, Inspiring
Team B			
Dustin: Supt.	Director	+Open-minded, Prioritization	−Process, Follow-up
Pete: Asst.	Refiner	+Systems, Prevention	−Balance, Creativity
Team C			
Tony: Supt.	Coach	+Positive Competiveness,	−Detail, Planner
Joe: Asst.	Mechanic	+Perfectionist, Standards	−Non-visionary, Weak Communicator

These are some initial, confidential suggestions I would make to you. Let's get some personality profiles done, and you gather the input and suggestions from each of your three superintendent choices. I would also like to ask each of the managers to write you a letter answering four questions:

1) What specific changes would you like to see incorporated in the company?

2) What are your strongest three personal assets?

3) What are your two weakest personal assets, and what are you doing to improve them.

4) If you had to list some foundational values of a strong secure company, what would they be?

Their answers will give us further insights into their character and personal expectations."

"Are we going to bring any management in from the outside?" I asked.

"If possible, I would rather build from within. Outsiders are usually distrusted and their motives and commitment questioned. The only time I break that rule is if we need specific help very quickly. But I don't see that in our case."

"Good," I replied, "I think we can assemble a strong team with the players we have. We can make the personnel decisions when we get all the information, and then ink the organizational charts."

I continued, "I agree with your management pairings and individual critique. But I am wondering, what should we do with Seth Martin? I don't see him fitting in with the new management style."

Al shook his head in agreement, "You're right. He's not a good fit. We cannot allow his adversarial style to pollute the progressive build-up of our teams. He has chosen his own destiny and alienated himself. I would offer him to Luke at Broad Run. Their styles are similar. Since that operation will be sold as a separate unit, he will not negatively affect our future. And as far as his father-in-law, Fred Miller will just have to accept the decision—welcome to senior management. Sometimes our role is to be the interference and to protect our workforce, but it is always to do the right thing, and earn the trust of our team."

III. RESTRUCTURING THE ASSETS

Chapter 10
Operating Style Shift

A l took the lead, and I listened intently. The more he explained, the more excited I felt, and the more I believed in the potential transformation. "Today, you and I are going to shift gears. We are going to start building the operating style of our new house. Profit Coal was a normal company with the standard disconnect between the corporate owners, management, and the workforce. As we have drawn a new line in the sand, renamed our company, mapped the mission and values, and are restructuring the operations, we must agree on the management style. We have seen various styles work to different degrees, but if we are going to engage and empower our entire team, I'm recommending the *servant leadership* style. Other management styles, even on their best day, peak at about 80% effectiveness. Servant leadership, by earning a deeper degree of trust, takes us into the 80-95% effectiveness range. It opens hearts and that is where change starts—from within. It is the most empowering style and will accent each of your manager's strengths while building teamwork. The basic premise is that the entire senior management and support departments work for the frontline. Think about the organizational chart being flipped upside down.

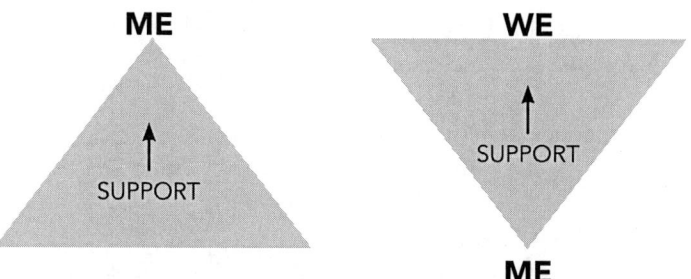

Flip the ME to obtain the WE. The concept is that everyone is working toward a bigger purpose and to have a wider influence. This will be foreign to most of our managers. In the beginning, they will see servant leadership as a loss of power, instead of a broader sharing of ownership and empowerment. It will make them nervous and uncomfortable at first, but there is far more reward, personally and corporately, in sowing for a greater harvest than carving a single trophy. We have to teach our managers to build and arm the soldiers, rather than mounting the charge on their own. We are clients of the production group. Our job is to serve and support their needs. Once, a young manager told me he was never going to wear a shirt with his name on it. He thought it was degrading. I looked him in the eye and said, 'to serve is an honor and by its perfection, authority will be earned.'

> **TO SERVE IS AN HONOR AND BY ITS PERFECTION, AUTHORITY WILL BE EARNED.**

I hoped to shift his perspective from a narrow focus to a broader one—from Me to We. Being part of a larger purpose, something everyone can rally around and believe in is highly motivating and essential to the kind of transformation we are seeking. This type of management system will require a different support structure. As we will see shortly, gathering input and following up on improvement plans will be the core focus, and the first line and middle management groups will need help. We'll need to create a new position, called the Process Coordinator (PC). This person will be assigned to each superintendent. They will replace the assistant superintendent position but with a very defined responsibility. The PC's task focus and priorities will evolve as the overall plan matures. I can provide a breakdown of the responsibilities and supporting functions (Appendix B.21). The personnel selection for the PC is very important. Their style should be a strong complement to the superintendent. The PC's technical strengths should accent the projects at perspective operations. They should have the capabilities to be considered the superintendent's successor. Between the superintendent and the PC, 24/7 operation follow-up coverage should be possible without wearing out either party. Honoring the need for personal time to maintain balance must be built into the managerial staffing plan. Commonly in industry, senior management is forced to choose between their home responsibilities and work. All kinds of negative consequences evolve from that mandate, including the workaholic tendencies that have become an accepted trait of those positions. We have a moral responsibility to break that cycle and to honor the family."

> **HUMILITY IS NOT THINKING LESS OF ONESELF, BUT IT'S THINKING OF OTHERS FIRST AND OF YOURSELF LESS OFTEN.**

"I am so glad to hear you say that," I sighed. "Throughout my career I have seen so many casualties within the family unit for those very reasons."

Al continued, "The change to servant leadership will be easy for some and very difficult for others. Our society views servanthood as a weak character trait, but the truth is that it takes a more secure person to show humility. I like the following definition: 'Humility is not thinking less of oneself, but it's thinking of others first and of yourself less often.' Keeping the emphasis on the team motive is well-served by servant leadership.

In contrast, short-term personal gains commonly drive the more dictatorial management styles. I wear a bracelet on my wrist that says, 'I AM SECOND,' which reminds me, it's not all about me. Our human nature is selfishly driven, but that can be tempered or transformed if WE is put before ME. Servant leadership is counter to the way our world has evolved, especially in business. It's a very different philosophy."

Al drew a little matrix on his paper:

	Servant Leadership	World Teachings
Personal Focus →	To serve & support	Take care of self first
Values →	Strong moral principles	Be neutral & tolerant to all

"This illustrates my point. It is imperative we don't underestimate the radical change this management style is from the past and our current social climate. The character of the messenger, our managers, needs to be aligned with our philosophy or principles/values. The cultivation of the employee buy-in and the vision transfer begins with communication.

We have to speak the crew's language sincerely, see through their eyes, and earn their trust. Trust is earned if they can answer 'yes' to the following five questions:

1) Are you telling me the truth?

2) Will you listen to me?

3) Do you understand me?

4) Do you care about me?

5) Will you help me?

Once we gain their trust and start the ball rolling, and the team is steering toward solutions, we will see crew cooperation improve. Then that will start to bleed out to the other crews and even to support groups. That lateral inter-departmental teamwork is where we will yield the major gains. As we surge forward, some of the players will not be willing to adapt to this cooperative style. It is up to us to ascertain if each individual is willing to work under the serving approach. If they are not, it needs to be dealt with immediately and firmly.

Support Departments, which set-up and supply the production crews, need to be regularly audited to ensure they are keeping:

1) A *client attitude* toward the production department

2) Operationally close and involved with the sites and personnel needs

3) Paperwork that is required from the field minimized

4) Results and trends reported to the operations for their systems refinement

Before we can start asking our employees to embrace this type of change we must lead by example. Our management presentation has to consistently reflect this operational change as we introduce the new MVP (Mission, Value, Process) plan to our people."

I agreed that this type of leadership would be received the best. And the new senior management teams that we paired would naturally flow well with this style. "What would be the best way to kick off all the changes?" I asked.

Al leaned forward, "Good question, but we are not there yet. First of all, you need to complete the management organizational charts, with all the feeding input and superintendent approvals. When can you have those finished?"

"Personality profiles and the management questionnaires are scheduled for this week, so we should be ready in two weeks. I am going to involve an outside industrial psychologist in the organizational chart meetings with the superintendents. I figure their non-biased opinions on personality pairing will be very helpful."

"Excellent," Al responded. "Organizing or selecting the most effective management team is worth the extra time and effort, and utilizing diverse perspectives strengthens our decisions. In the next two weeks, I will formulate the teachings on servant leadership, why and how to sell change, and continue working on the finale, *the process*."

"I have been meaning to ask you about that. We are obviously building toward the process. Can you give me a sneak preview? What is its introduction timeframe?"

Al answered, "Since part of the process depends on the list of values that you are compiling, it is still being customized. I have seen numerous corporate transformation failures. One of the most common causes is because the process is not personalized for the individual operation. We will not make that mistake. For your own edification, I will send you a list of the other major mistakes which I have seen companies make when introducing change (Appendix B.22). To your second question, our timing for introducing the process depends on how fast we master the foundation values. Usually it takes about six months before the foundation is solidified enough to start building upon it. Starting too early risks the long term growth goals, and we won't make that mistake either. Dirk, over the next two weeks, can you detail the foundational values and be ready to share them? Also, can you delineate the needed operations changes and sketch out the workforce needs?"

"Yes, yes, and yes," I affirmed. "I'm looking forward to that. I want to start painting the picture of what Integrity's success will look like in our leadership's mind. I want them to envision as it will be, not as it was, so we create a growth expectation, support it, reward it, and celebrate it."

"You are getting it, Dirk. Self-prophetically, we need to declare the victories. When we infect our managers with the dream, they can lead the multitudes. As Dr. Martin Luther King announced, 'I have a dream…' Our job will be to cast the vision and illuminate the path. Our mission can and will energize not only our people but the entire community. Sounds like we will be ready for a Management Meeting in two weeks.

I responded, "Yes Sir."

Al followed, "I'll get a hold of the Board and ask them to be there to present the Mission Statement. At the end of the Managers Meeting we can break out into groups to finalize the hourly employee evaluations. With those evaluations, we can complete a numerical employee ranking, make fair decisions, and fill-in the manning charts. Reducing the workforce by 14% is not a positive outcome, but in light of the market pressures, it's a necessary one. After we have explained the complete corporate transformation, I believe our management group will be able to progressively and positively carry out the reorganization."

"Dirk, I want to congratulate you on stepping into the leadership role," Al beamed. "Your passion is effervescent and sincere. Your heart, the sincere concern for the people, is showing."

"Thank you, Al. This means a lot coming from you. I was sharing with my wife last night, how energized I was. Nikki said she had been praying for God's wisdom and timing for us. I am not sure I understand about the *God intervention* but I do feel we are doing the right thing.

Al offered, "God chooses to carry out His plans through His people for His people. If we get up every day and look where He is working around us, and join Him, our works are anointed. We will feel the peace in our hearts and the passion will be visible in our actions. That is the calling on which we should all focus. Then one day, we will hear, 'I am pleased, thou good and faithful servant.'"

"Is that where you got the *Servant Leadership* title from?"

Al answered, "That's where all our successful principles originate. To help teach them, biblical parables are offered to give us day-to-day examples of the fruit reaped from sowing God's word and values."

I confided, "That's also what I feel your stories do for me. They show the effect of the value application. But I must admit, your stories usually seem to carry a parallel and deeper meaning. I get the feeling it's not just about our workplace, is it?"

Al encouraged, "Be sensitive to those parallel lessons. In many cases, He is using those times to direct us. God teaches us through living-life-lessons, but He gives us the choice to apply them personally. I have seen choice defined as *a heart/mind negotiation*. I like that concept, because it reminds us that the outcome is completely up to us. Since He is a gentleman, God will never force a decision on us. But He will make His wisdom and ways available should we choose to let Him lead."

†

Two weeks later…

The Managers Meeting was finally here. Al and I had rehearsed the format plans and points so many times I was technically ready, but admittedly a little apprehensive. I could tell Al was excited about the event, and he was confident it would be received well. Al had requested that I invite the managers and their spouses or significant others, but I must admit, I was hesitant. He kept saying it was going to be a complete mindset change, and all the influencers needed to be present. With the expanded invitee list, we were expecting over two hundred. The local hotel was our only option for a meeting room that was large enough.

As everyone filed into the conference hall, there was an air of excitement and yet uncertainty floating about. Al had everything choreographed to the smallest degree, but all the presenters only knew their own area of responsibility, so we were all a little in the dark. When everyone was seated, the lights were dimmed. All eyes were focused on the stage, whose curtain was closed. Fred Miller stepped out from behind the curtain to the podium. The stage lights were brought up, and the curtain retracted. Fred welcomed everyone, and introduced himself as the founding owner of Profit Coal Company. He then gave a short history of the past 16 years.

Fred shared his appreciation for the loyalty and commitment from so many, but also said that times had changed, and unfortunately tough decisions needed to be made. He shared that due to health reasons, he had been stepping back over the last two years and now he would limit his involvement to being a passive investor. Then Fred introduced Marci Franco.

Operating Style Shift 103

Marci explained her role as the chairwoman from one of the long-standing company investor groups. She talked about the challenging coal market, effects of global economic issues, and recent government cost increases. As dismal as some of the facts were, she also conveyed a sense of hope. She emphasized that if the leadership group truly believed, we could not only weather the storm, but could *lead the field*. And that is what it will take for a good company to grow to be GREAT. Marci walked over to center stage where the 4ft x 4ft Profit Coal Entrance Sign had been positioned. As the lights were being dimmed, she declared, "A lot of sweat and hard work got us here, but if we are to continue to provide security for 500 plus families, we all must change. The rock we thought we were counting on for our daily bill payments, children's schooling, and our retirement is sinking. Then she asked, "The question is 'are you willing to change for your family and the team?' "

With that, the lights went out, and a small flame ignited at the bottom of the wooden Profit Coal sign. An eerie silence fell over the crowd and we were all filled with the feeling of helplessness as we watched the sign slowly burn. It was like someone was destroying everything we had worked and lived for, and all that we could do was to watch. From the left side of the stage, through the smoke, Jeff Page stepped out. Dressed in military fatigues, laced up boots, and a hard hat under his arm, he started his address, "How this story ends, is up to you. Past experience in similar circumstances has shown that most people and organizations quit, because it gets tough. Some tried and failed, because they doubted and partially complied. But a few soared. Why? Because they were committed. We have to decide how serious we are. If you feel this analogy is not relevant to you, or you can't see through the smoke, you aren't the leader our 500 plus families need. You aren't the supporter this community must have, and you aren't the builder Integrity Coal requires to transform or to achieve its noble goals."

As Jeff completed his stanza, a bright light pierced through the smoldering sign's smoke. It was an iridescent yellow/orange glow that cut through the haze and illuminated a large sign that read, Integrity Coal. Jeff's tone was solemn but passionate as he spoke again. "If you are willing to leave the past, step out and apart from the pack, lead your crew or unit, and build a united empowered team, WE WILL SUCCEED. There is a place in the market for World Class Excellence, and we can fulfill that calling.

To do so, we need a clear united Mission; '*Integrity Coal was founded to be a positive contributor, influence, and supporter to our community. We are committed to earning security for all of our partners, and to unifying resources and people in building a first class organization with a character of true integrity. In using our endowed gifts, we aim to be a blessing.*'

We intend to:
- Focus on the foundational values that built this organization
- Prune a few detractors that will not subscribe to our values and mission
- Ask for the Lord's favor, wisdom, and protection

Restructure the mine sites to fully utilize:
- Our inspired leadership team
- Our elite workforce
- Our strongest equipment
- An investment of $9 Million in new and upgraded equipment
- A progressive growth into efficient super-unit layouts
- Special project investments from a pool of $7 Million

The financial investors, represented by Fred Miller, Marci Franco, and me, are ready to leverage our positions to support this vision. If you can commit to your role in this journey, we invite you to join us now, up here on stage."

There was no hesitation; the seats emptied. With the stage packed, Jeff Page stood up on a chair and emotionally thanked everyone for their response.

He declared, "The commitment we make today will reap a foothold into tomorrow's security." And then he closed the morning session with a prayer.

I stood there completely mentally drained but ready to serve the cause. Nikki leaned over to me and whispered, "it is for this day you were formed, and I am proud to be your helpmate." I could see a tear in her eye, as we clutched hands in solidarity.

As everyone was filing out for the lunch break, my eye contact with Al told me we were right on schedule and in-step with his plan. When I finally made my way over to Al, I said, "So what other emotional roller coasters do you have planned?"

> **HELPING PEOPLE SEE REALITY AND GENERATE PASSION TOWARD THEIR INVOLVEMENT IN A SOLUTION, IS WHAT VISIONARY LEADERSHIP IS ALL ABOUT.**

He grinned and said, "I imagine that was a little uncomfortable for some people, but if we don't pull this transformation off, the emotion in the next kind of meeting will be negative and down three octaves. Helping people see reality and generate passion toward their involvement in a solution, is what visionary leadership is all about. With that, let's get our group to that next step.

IV. PROCESS DEVELOPMENT AND PRESENTATION

Chapter 11
Building the Foundation

After lunch I sensed, and I'm certain others did too, a strong and expectant spirit in the room. You could feel the thirst for direction. Al took the stage and introduced himself as a friend of the team. He explained that he had committed to the Integrity family and to helping us through what he called our rebirth.

Al explained, "The journey you are electing to take will have many roads. Some of them will be addressed over the next two days, others will be explored on the fly. Before we start on the technical plan, we want to solidify our foundation values and management style. It is imperative our style speaks and tells the same story to our people. The direction must be given through servant leadership. To best explain this, I have asked a good friend of mine to join us today. His name is Mr. Steve Harrop. Mr. Harrop runs a large, very successful organization and I have been honored to have him as my mentor for the last five years. He is greatly respected for his work ethic, management skills, professional knowledge, but most of all, his *servant's heart*. He leads by example, and the results are out of this world. Please give a warm welcome to Mr. Steve Harrop."

Through the clapping, Steve politely cleared his throat at the microphone and the crowd quieted. He orated a challenging message on earning respect and trust through service. He dwelled on the fact that people buy into a plan only after they buy into the leader's character. That buy-in must start with communication, which leads to respect and trust. "Our society has grown into one that expects immediate results. There is no tolerance for things that take time, and the *developing trust*

> **PEOPLE BUY INTO A PLAN ONLY AFTER THEY BUY INTO THE LEADER'S CHARACTER. THAT BUY-IN MUST START WITH COMMUNICATION, WHICH LEADS TO RESPECT AND TRUST.**

concept is being lost. Couple this with the workforce's distorted and deteriorated perception of authority figures, and it's no wonder why the desire for leadership is in low demand and not initially well received. As an example of the lack of mentoring guidance, just look at the degraded role of the father in our homes. Some sectors of our communities report fewer than 30% of our kids have a live-in father. We have to reverse the trend, and step up to provide the direction. Through service, example, work ethic, relational engagement, and unity, we must radiate a better and stronger example of character to those around us. In so doing, we will find our circle of influence is much wider than we would have initially thought possible." Steve reminded us that we would be the catalyst by which Integrity would grow. Then he got personal, "Each one of you were uniquely designed to serve in a manner different from anyone else. I would encourage you to consider the service style you operate under best. Here's a clue, how would each of you fill in this sentence? The most impacting servant leader I have ever seen or been mentored by is _____. Your answer will probably steer you toward a style you relate to and respect the most. This may very well be the area of strength from which you should operate. Serving from your giftings commonly helps optimize your impact. The people you lead will carefully analyze your motives and *listen* to your actions. Your words will be tested with fire. If your position is stamped 'sincere' and 'honorable,' they will follow. Take this opportunity to influence and help your people attain their potential and destiny." He closed by saying, "You have been given a rare business opportunity to start with a clean slate, and I pray you passionately serve and lead your people wisely. I look forward to hearing of Integrity's success and I appreciate the opportunity to share with you today. Thank you."

Al genuinely thanked and hugged his friend.

After the brief but ample supper hour, Al got right down to business. "The next discussion topic is our mining plan. To present this, we have our new Operations Manager, Dirk Brothers."

After an appreciative round of applause, I began, "Because of the market changes and cost escalations, we proactively developed a general plan. Over the next two days, we will outline the attack."

Reorganizing the Operations

During the next four hours, I explained how we were going to condense our six current operations into three upgraded sites. The logistics of all the facility-changes were reviewed. I also re-emphasized what Al and Steve had shared about servant leadership. "This operating and management style will become the signature for Integrity Coal Company." I acknowledged that servant leadership may be a new concept and that we would be patient in its growth toward perfection but that we would also be intolerant of anyone who did not work hard to embrace it. "Respect for each other, will be our trade-mark."

> **SERVANT LEADERSHIP MAY BE A NEW CONCEPT AND WE WILL BE PATIENT IN ITS GROWTH TOWARD PERFECTION BUT WE WILL BE INTOLERANT OF ANYONE WHO DOES NOT EMBRACE IT.**

We took a five minute break while the spouses and significant others were excused and passed out the new managerial organization charts. As everybody looked them over, I explained the reasoning for the personnel re-alignment. We then began the hourly employee performance evaluations. The evaluation and workforce manning process was long. We worked until 10 p.m. and were relieved that all the charts were complete. I made a request before adjourning for the night. "We would like each superintendent to ask their management group to suggest names for their new consolidated operations. Please take five or ten minutes in your groups to brainstorm. Sleep on your ideas if needed, but supervisors, be ready—the new names will be announced during tomorrow morning's session. Good night everyone!"

T

As we assembled the next morning, there was a noticeable air of anticipation. To take advantage of this, I asked each superintendent to share on their name change. I explained the importance of a new start and a fresh push on the momentum flywheel. To set the stage, I used a John Maxwell quote, "momentum is the most powerful change agent." Stepping down, I said, "Now let's see what you have!"

Cody led off by saying he and his partner, Makirra, sorted through a lot of good suggestions, and decided on the Majestic Mine. "We intend to set our people's aspirations high and help the team attain them," he proclaimed.

"That is a great strategy since your team's natural style is development," I responded.

Dustin took the floor next. "We have decided to change our name from Lucky Star to Destiny. Our position will be to control our future and security through good ideas, a passion for excellence, and prioritized hard work." With a grin he then announced, "And we plan on having some fun along the way."

Chuckles filled the room as Dustin made way for Tony.

Tony ended strongly. "Our team was named Taurus #1, a cosmic counterfeit. Our new logo is Champion. We will excel through personal and team achievement."

I closed the morning session by encouraging the entire team of the potential ahead and that we should always appreciate the board and our investors for hanging with us. Everybody appeared upbeat, and the expectancy level seemed quite contagious.

✝

Returning from lunch, Al reviewed the transformation plan.

Al started, "Before we go macro to make sure everyone sees the whole picture, let's review the immediate events. After today's meeting, the human resource departments will promptly and professionally handle all the personnel changes, and the correct manning and relocation assignments will be completed by this Wednesday. Each operation will develop their own specific reorganizing agenda to get to the desired mine layout as quickly as practical. All the supporting equipment additions and relocations are already underway and should be in place within the next two months. Those are the important physical changes.

Now, let's talk about the organizational transformation. This is where we must be in sync. Many companies try to implement wholesale change without addressing the operation, culture, and attitude. We, the leaders, must humbly, yet confidently lead this change. Our people need to see a united front. They need to understand the structural layout we are going to use." Al turned to the marker board and drew an illustration.

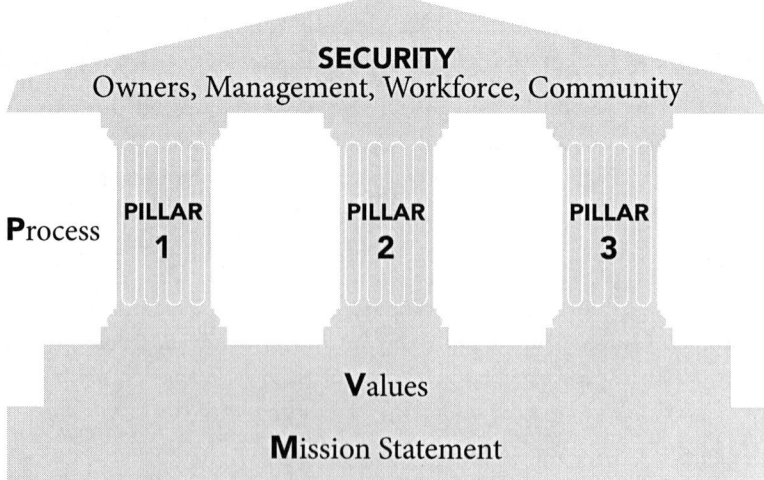

Al explained, "I refer to it as the MVP (**M**ission-**V**alues-**P**rocess) Transformation Plan. I want to point out on the drawing that the security earned must be based on the MV foundation and supported by multiple pillars. One pillar can be used, but the security earned will be limited. Too many pillars will spread us too widely. I would expect the process of our overall transformation to take about two years. During the first phase, which will be six-months, we will introduce and solidify the Mission and Values. We will focus on the I, II, III Process Pillars in the last year and a half. The transformation that will take place is going to be exciting. For it to be successful, we all need to envision what we are building. Let's direct our attention to the first phase. We have reviewed the Mission Statement already, but we need you to reinforce it with your people. This is why we are taking the time to explain the new operating plan and style to everyone at one time. Most companies introduce change in a *shotgun start format* with just part of the management. This sends mixed signals, as some groups are forging ahead with the new agenda and others are lagging behind in the old culture. After today's presentation with the management team, we will do another company-wide presentation with everyone this Thursday. We will always honor the leaders by introducing change to them first."

Al gave me the microphone, "Your crews will revere your opinion highly. To them you are the breath of the Company. If you keep our Mission honored and in focus, your people will support it. Now that we agree on what the mission is and where we are going, we need to talk about our values. After reviewing all our strengths and the management input letters you turned in last week, I summarized our values into a list of nine:

> " SAFETY IS THE UNCOMPROMISABLE VALUE. IT IS A BASIC REQUIREMENT IN EVERY DECISION, IT'S NOT A CHOICE

A Values List

1. **Safety** is the uncompromisable value. It is a basic requirement in every decision, it's not a choice. Since most people believe they are bulletproof, and that accidents won't happen to them, commonly it is more successful to view safety as a team requirement and a mental commitment.

2. **Prevention** is the belief that eliminating all types of losses, injury, violations, downtime, rework, and waste results in high efficiency and eventually security (The tenets are more fully explained in Appendix B.23).

3. **Teamwork** is achievable when everyone is committed to the common goal of operational security. We all have to focus on ways to improve efficiency in our area, and that includes outside our immediate department.

4. **Mutual Respect** is the building block for relationships and trust. It is showing sincere appreciation for each other and valuing everyone as a key part of the

110 BUILDING INTEGRITY

team. Utilizing employee input is a strong sign of respect and fosters the best ideas, buy-in, and morale. Our differences can be a strength, if we honor and respect each other and value diversity. Truly, the quote, "it is level at the foot of the cross" reminds us that no one is superior to another.

5. **Communication** is the vital link between all members of the team and the coordinated movement from today to our victories of tomorrow (A detailed Corporate Communication Plan is offered in Appendix B.24).

6. **Training** is an important facet of individual and business development. It is not only a key to employee empowerment, but it is also critical for intelligent decision making and process refinement (A comprehensive training layout is included on Appendix B.27).

7. **Accountability** is the acceptance of responsibility for our actions and circle of influence. We are charged to continue expanding our influence area and responsibility scope.

8. **Continuous Process Improvement** challenges each of us to keep looking for the most efficient (safest and most productive) way possible. One must realize it's a multi-priority journey, not a single-factor destination. The continuous refining of Best Practices (BPs) earns security.

9. **Reverence** is the action of honoring our God for our opportunities, giftings, protection, and His wisdom. We will respect each other's definition of God, but we will not apologize and be trampled for our forefathers beliefs. We, at Integrity Coal, will make a moral statement and be an example to our families and in the community. We will proudly let these values permeate every facet of our lives.

UNITY

The applause spontaneously built, and within a couple minutes, everyone was standing. You could almost see the empowerment released, and you could unmistakably sense the vision had been transferred.

Jeff Page came over to the microphone and said, "I feel an anointing has been unleashed and He is approving of our values commitment."

The other two board members also came on stage to offer their support. Marci reread the Mission Statement and said, "I believe this team is catching the dream and is ready to share it with our people. Please know your investors will be supporting your efforts financially and in prayer. I will close by stating our state's motto, *In Him all things are possible*. He promised it and He will help us do it."

Again, the emotional applause erupted.

Al took over and humbly said, "I am not going to try to follow that. I am just going to join the train. We have a great opportunity to build personal family security, earn a return for our investors, and help support the community. As we shared, start with the mission, and then agree on values—that will be our first phase. We will not proceed to the Process Phase until we have transformed our new culture through these nine foundational values. Biblically there are promises made, "if a house is built on a firm foundation it will stand. If seed is sown in fertile ground, it will bear fruit." The values Dirk collected from your past can be the cornerstones for the future, if we all accept them. There is a lot of hard work ahead to refine this values list, but I firmly believe with the resolve seen today, we will reign. And when it gets tough, He will be expecting a call!"

IV. PROCESS DEVELOPMENT AND PRESENTATION

Chapter 12
Selling the Change

As everyone filed back into the room, Al welcomed the tiring crowd and announced that we had reached the last segment of the weekend meeting. You could feel a little emotional release from the group. This had been a business meeting different than any I had ever experienced.

Al in his typical, inspiring way said, "We have shared the foundation of our plan, now we need to solidify how you are going to sell it. Maybe this is going to sound a little abrupt, but there is no middle of the road in our next phase. If you cannot sincerely take our plan to your people, let's part company now. Too many companies enter a transformation soft and undefined. When we ask someone to change habits and attitude, we must first convince them it is worth that effort. I am going to write the word

> *WHEN WE ASK SOMEONE TO CHANGE HABITS AND ATTITUDE, WE MUST FIRST CONVINCE THEM IT IS WORTH THAT EFFORT.*

CHANGE

in bold letters on the white board, because I want everyone to visually see it as a formidable challenge.

Please respect the fact that most people will run from change, but it is in fact change that will separate us from the pack and earn our survival. Some workforce groups feel security can be negotiated; the truth is, security is only saved for the *leader of the field*.

There are ten hurdles with respect to change that must be conquered:

Change Hurdles

1. Is change really needed?

Dale Carnegie said, 'A man changed against his will, is of the same opinion still.' No one carries the influence and respect of your people like you do. No one can usher in change like the immediate supervisor. We, as a whole body, need each of you to infect your circle of influence. You must sell the need for change and then the plan to accomplish it. We will not proceed to step three, Process, until we are unified under steps one, Mission, and two, Values. Senior management will have a role to introduce, explain, teach, and support, but the implementation and follow-up will be yours. It will take the entire team to maximize our potential. If the market continues to deflate, it will take everything we have. The good news is that most of the industry will not bind together to reach their best. We are climbing a peak that few trek; one that only teams ever reach the summit.

It is imperative the entire team see the need for change. The hold-outs must be handled quickly, discretely, and professionally. I know that sounds cruel, but total transformation does not need those distractions. Distractions also come from situations we have allowed in the past, and we need to preventively seek to eliminate those. I am reminded of another quote appropriate for this discussion, 'Only freed from past burdens can we take advantage of the present.' It is our job as leaders to purge the closet of distractions.

> **LET'S KEEP JOB SECURITY AS THE FOCAL POINT.**

Once we set the table, we need to continue to serve the facts of the market, competition, and economic drivers. We need to educate our people about the issues and engage in a discussion of solutions. The greatest innovator is necessity, and there should be no one more incented than we are. If we can't get our people to accept change and begin tracking toward success (mentally and physically), then we must not have explained it correctly. Some will question our motives, but if we lay out the facts correctly, then the change we are asking for should obviously be beneficial to all of us. The most common statement heard when closure notices are handed out is, 'We did not realize it was so serious.' Let's make sure the severity is communicated. Our duty is to present the honest truth and help steer proactively toward solutions; our people are smart enough to see the need and their personal gain. I have seen CEO's give stump speeches that included goals that did not relate to the people. Distrust is then bred into the plan's motives. Let's keep job security as the focal point.

2. Change is naturally resisted.

The word change could be defined as crossing a paradigm, or described as a black cat looking in a mirror while under a ladder. Why is it bad? Is it the fear of the unknown? The belief that *status quo* is safer? The fact is that we are all naturally resistant to change to some degree. Thus when we introduce the subject of change, we must be respectful yet confident, slow yet methodical, understanding yet full of conviction. Your demeanor in the discussion will be a huge determining factor in our teams' acceptance. Individuals will generally respond from one of two perspectives. The first perspective is one that projects that there is no realistic choice. This person will only leave their current state if you can prove to them that *no change* means melt down and their loss. The fact that life is a dynamic event, not a static state, petrifies them. They will never get close enough to the cliff to envision the flight or see the prize below. They will only move if they think the mountain they are standing on is going to crumble. If you push them off into change, they are so bound internally, the result may be ugly.

The second viewpoint is one that will weigh the benefits. The individual will change or let go of their position only if the expected future state is considerably better. They need assurance that the pain is worth the gain. They will calculate the investment needed and the expected return. They will also analyze where they will be if they invest in change-efforts and it fails. This person needs help measuring all the unknowns. They will lead the cliff jump only after they complete their equation. Both perspectives must be covered in your presentations. Most companies fail to personally address these variables, thus the employees never join the team.

3. Resistance to accountability is a safer position.

Because of poor management in all of our past, most of us are initially hesitant in accepting accountability. We have so often seen people get blamed for things out of their control. The natural defense is to avoid responsibility and just passively participate. Yet, we all realize nothing is achieved without action, an event of change. A plan is a group of supporting actions formulated to achieve an outcome. Even though everyone may agree on the desired outcome, few want to be accountable for the total plan. As leaders we must assure people that the plan is solid AND the team needs them to guarantee their part. Most people can be convinced to accept accountability for their commitment to their position or roles, as long as they are not responsible for the final outcome of things they cannot control. As management, our jobs will be to design the system and roles to honor and respect those concerns. The results will be that numerous actions conducted by highly accountable tasked individuals meshed together will yield success. Once success is felt and confidence secured, individuals will begin crossing the boundaries of previously entrenched roles and a team will be formed. It is those teams that produce the GREAT results and voluntarily accept accountability for the outcome. Expressed another way, to conquer individual resistance, management must build a plan that slowly incorporates accountability in parts, so that the system emerges with

> **WE ALL REALIZE NOTHING IS ACHIEVED WITHOUT ACTION, AN EVENT OF CHANGE.**

outcome buy-in from all, when it matures. If you remember our earlier discussion of how individual efficiencies leads to team effectiveness, you can see the parallel.

4. People are prone to the lazy and negative, minimum-compliance position.

While I agree we all have our bad days, I will not agree to accept this characteristic. We must draw a line that this position is a violation of progress. When this trait rears its head, it must be addressed quickly and firmly. Negativism must be exposed as counter-productive to the quest of earning security, an enemy of the state.

5. Changing personally for the team has lost its patriotic appeal.

The honor to protect a united house has been commonly replaced by selfish motives. Never before has society been so splintered. It shows in our businesses, politics, faith, and allegiances. We must rally behind the common values we share, and march toward a clear goal. The transformation plan may start by gaining supporters as they view their personal wins, but it must eventually evolve to the patriotic victory, a team win. There is power in numbers and what we can achieve together.

6. Change will cause other problems.

This is the nature of progress. As one bottleneck is solved, another will be encountered further on down the line. Each time we push the problem to the next level, we progress. Management's goal should be to celebrate achievement, so the momentum is not lost. If people feel the appreciation and see the benefits of their efforts, the rolling ball eventually will be self-sustaining. Our job will be to anticipate upcoming obstacles and preventively lead our people in addressing them.

7. Limitations can't be eliminated.

Some obstacles will definitely appear onerous, but creativity can mitigate most. It may test a group's problem solving abilities, although that also will add a buy-in factor when it's conquered. In fact, I would usually take the second best idea that came from a committee, rather than my own idea that may have even been a little better. I love this saying, 'Challenge a group to find the solution and you can get a commitment to the victory.'

8. Diversity in generations can't be overcome.

This is another *can't* that we will not accept. Granted, the differing perspectives of the generations are a challenge, but the solution is simple. Sideline the differences, work skills, and ethics, and center on the common goal: job security is earned through efficiency. Keeping security in focus, we then can work on the preferences and habits of the workforce. Having a number of schedules at the same facility is an example of reaching across the aisle. Different age groups commonly prefer different schedules. If efficiency and employee satisfaction are

Selling the Change

shared goals, this solution is a double win-win, even if it means changing a sacred past scheduling practice.

9. Short term programs will fade away.

Because of past change failures, our management staff and workforce will be cautious about embracing change. It must be shown that the current need requires a different approach. Senior management must be seen as sold out to the new plan and employees convinced that their buy-in is sincerely needed, for the long haul.

10. Employee empowerment is a fad that will go away.

> *EMPOWERMENT IS THE STRONGEST TECHNOLOGY OF THIS CENTURY, YET MANY COMPANIES ARE SLOW TO EMBRACE IT.*

Empowerment is the strongest technology of this century, yet many companies are slow to embrace it. The workforce is an easy sell, as they want to be involved. The first line management is the tougher sell. They resist because they feel it is a loss of power personally and most are unfamiliar with this style. Everyone must see the change to this operating style as permanent and it must be incorporated into every facet of the business. The doubters will have to be proven wrong over time, or removed quickly if they don't soften within a reasonable time frame.

As we navigate our way through these hurdles, the successful team becomes more unified. The next stage builds on that direction, and commitment intensifies. Leadership will set the pace by how we handle the following:

1) Our presentation. How do we communicate and cast the vision? This first step will be to change a person's perspective of the future. Great leaders sell potential.

2) Managerial respect. People don't have to agree with all your beliefs, but the respect for your character is paramount. They have to see your commitment to them. 'People don't care how much you know until they know how much you care.'

> *PEOPLE DON'T CARE HOW MUCH YOU KNOW UNTIL THEY KNOW HOW MUCH YOU CARE.*

3) Timing. How well we lay out the planned steps is extremely important. Proverbs reminds us, 'Action and heart without wisdom will leave us frustrated and beat down.'

4) Workplace attitude. Management must take responsibility for improving the workplace environment. With these changes, attitudes evolve and the potential and altitude lifts.

5) Customization and flexibility. Every transformation must be uniquely designed and refined. 'It's like driving a battleship through a mine field; you analyze the hazards, chart the course, and keep your hand on the wheel, and stay ready to alter the route. But no one must doubt that we are going to eventually emerge in clear water.'

6) The use of successful building blocks from the past. I always recommend starting with a familiar platform from their past and expand on the successes.

7) Complacency. We all can fall into this state. I am going to pass out a sheet of Complacency Definitions (Appendix B.28). I challenge you to visit these with your crew often and discuss the pitfalls. Here is a staggering definition of complacency. Complacency is the result of operating without detail and goals. Maybe that is only piercing to those of us who have some OCD (Obsessive Compulsive Disorder) tendencies. If so, I will verbally encourage my fellow afflicted; long live the achievers!

We have covered many questions and apprehensions preventing change. We have warned about issues and obstacles blocking passage, but we will need to proactively address these points. Our future depends upon it. As leaders, we have over 500 families in our company that are depending on us to lead them through the mine field. We can't let them down.

Once people do commit to change, we must be there to encourage leaving behind the broken habits. A list of the reasons for not breaking habits is the second hand-out (Appendix B.29). Remember, our people will initially engage to a certain level. That is why the early project order is so critical to ensure a strong start. When we show legitimate progress, we will earn their continued support. As we evolve to the next stage, we will elevate our techniques and intensity. At each level of accomplishment, it will be exciting to realize and celebrate this leadership group's influence in facilitating the earning of security for the employees' families, and indirectly to our community. Potential we are given, security we will earn," Al concluded.

As I thanked Al for his words, I was overwhelmed by the enthusiasm throughout the auditorium. I reiterated the challenges before us and time tables outlined over the previous two days. Not wanting to deflate the momentum Al generated, I profoundly added, "WE are all advancing into an unknown, but shoulder to shoulder, I have confidence our common goal will be achieved. Change commonly requires the sacrificing of self, for the team gain of much, and in the end I am sure it will liberate our future."

I closed the meeting, thanked everyone for their attendance, and challenged the entire team to be a positive catalyst in the change process.

IV. PROCESS DEVELOPMENT AND PRESENTATION

Chapter 13
Integrity Process

With the weekend meeting wrapped up, Al and I returned to the routine. I picked him up at his hotel and we launched into conversation like there had never been a pause. "Everyone is energized to a level I have never seen. Usually the management group is guardedly optimistic. This time they seemed to be engaged."

"We took the time to treat them as equal business partners, Dirk. We explained why change had to happen to earn the common goal of security or we would all lose. They decided the pain was worth the gain. Let's set up superintendent/employee meetings at each of the operations. I will help you work up the presentation, but I think it is best for you and the mine superintendent to be the presenters. A local change agent is always best. Also, let's inform your three superintendents we will meet every month to review their progress on the Foundational Values. I'll reiterate though, we will not proceed to Process until the Mission Statement and Foundational Values are ingrained in the team. I expect to see fruit from their servant leadership, and we will need that platform to build from."

"How will we know when we can proceed to the next step?" I asked.

"I will work up an extensive audit that we will start conducting after month three. When the entire group achieves a plus 90%, we will proceed to Process."

I cut my eyes over at him and asked again, "Can you explain Process to me?"

"Let's hold off until time gets closer. I want everyone to stay focused on perfecting the task at hand."

"Okay, no distractions, right," I conceded. Somehow I knew that was coming. "You mentioned earlier you have used the Integrity Process at other industrial facilities. I can see how everything we have done is general to people and process. The examples may be different but the principles and goals are the same. Al, as you have said, people are people and process is process. And everyone wants to win and be secure. Another technique I can see you are using is *divide and conquer*. You have broken a lot of our big issues into smaller pieces, then prioritized and finally delegated responsibility. Before everyone even realizes it, the whole elephant is eaten, one bite at a time!"

†

Four Months Later…

Four months into our journey, we facilitated the third Foundational Values Progress Review with the superintendents. I was hoping our progress would be good enough for Al to let us advance to Process.

After discussing numerous accomplishments, Al began, "I am seeing a lot of *excellence* and a little bit of *average*. Let's start with personnel. Earlier, I had asked you to identify the managers who were still playing neutral to our plan."

"We let three go after the first month because it was obvious their people skills and respect was not coming around." I explained. "That was a huge wake-up call to everyone, so it has been pretty good since."

Al snapped back, "Pretty good is not what we are building. I can be a little more patient with workforce transformation, but our leadership must show strong, value-centered character now."

"Honestly," I said, "We have another four who we have met with twice and progress is very slow."

"My suggestion," Al responded, "is to let them go and promote four others from within. Then recall four more from the first reduction. Are there any distractors at the workforce level?"

"We conducted performance reviews last month like you asked. We had 28 of the 400 hourly who received weighted scores below 70%. The HR department reviewed the scoring and felt the weighting was fair. We have put those 28 on probation for the next two months. Our goal is to strengthen them, but they have to show a desire to improve."

Al agreed, "Be fair but firm. Remember we committed to our families that we would protect the house. How did the last operation's Foundation Values Audit come back?"

"Here's the tally," I said, handing him the reports:

Integrity Process

Destiny Mine 84% | Cody (Supt.)/Makirra (PC)
- \+ excellent bulletin boards, detailed charts with notes
- \+ strong weekly communications meetings and follow-up
- \+ super morale and feedback
- \+ interactive training received well
- − some complacency toward continuous improvement

Majestic Mine 79% | Dustin (Supt.)/Pete (PC)
- \+ many proactive Kaizens submitted and completed
- \+ strong prevention commitment and action plans
- \+ good Key Performance Indicator accountability
- − improved labor relations but not great

Champion Mine 82% | Tony (Supt)/Joe (PC)
- \+ big improvement in maintenance support (teamwork)
- \+ continued strong safety allegiance, loss-studies thriving
- \+ excellent response to surveys and performance evaluations
- − light in technical and business training

Al commented, "No surprises there. What's your plan?"

"I was going to ask you."

Al corrected, "I am here to help, but it's your show."

"Okay, I thought I would look at the management staffing and see if I could swap a few around to strengthen Dustin's labor-relations weakness."

"Good plan," Al remarked. "Just don't send someone with a bad attitude or character to somewhere else. Sometimes a few face changes are good."

"I was also going to have Makirra moonlight a little with Tony, to help him with the training programs. Cody can work through his issues in the next few months."

"I think you are right in principle," Al responded, "but I think you can raise your expectations higher. I have been looking at your numbers. Granted you are in the middle of an internal rebuild and your accidents and violations are down 25% and your productivity numbers improved 21%; that's good, but not great. I think they have another gear. If you remember the graph we talked about a few weeks ago, building a solid foundation takes a little more time in order to see the big pay-offs, but I believe we are on the road to GREAT. When I hear Cody is getting 50 to 60 good idea Kaizens completed every month, he's not at Dustin's plus 100 rate, but his people are engaged. It's an exciting day BUT you have to keep expecting their best. Be a cheerleader and show appreciation for their efforts, but be a driver to excellence as well."

"I am in awe over the progress, and I agree I have not pushed them to their potential. I have an idea to stir up a little friendly competition that should raise the stakes. What is your view on incentives?"

"Incentives are strong motivators and have a place in the right season," Al answered. "There are two hazards with incentives. First, if a situation unfolds where you later must ratchet back the payout provision, due to unforeseen changes, negative attitudes can come forward. Even if the business logic can be explained clearly, trust is destroyed. The second incentive pitfall is when bad months outweigh the good months, we pay incentive monies on good months and lose money on the bad months. This can create bigger losses to the bottom line. I have seen companies doom themselves financially from these actions. Let's hold off a while until we get some stability, then I will help you develop an incentive package to present to the board. A good incentive plan will be multi-faceted and have an incentive share, but will not be seen as an employee entitlement program."

†

Two Months Later...

"I have been so looking forward to this call, Al. I am proud to report we have everyone above the 90% threshold and we are ready for Process," Dirk said excitedly.

"Super!" Al responded energetically. "Let's set up a day class to lay out the principles. The superintendents and their immediate staff should be invited. By the way, you never did tell me your competition idea."

"It is working really well. We took the five business Key Performance Indicators you gave me last month and added the Foundational Values Audit score as a sixth. Each mine is charting their progress month-to-month. Not against each other, but against their own past record!"

"I love it!" Al beamed. "What is the prize?"

"I told them it would be good, but that they had to trust me. It may be stretching my influence, but we'll see."

Al remarked, "Motivating a person to improve their position in life and have a positive influence on others will always be the right thing to do. Follow your heart, keep preaching balanced improvement and everyone's a winner."

Finally, the long awaited Process Meeting was at hand. There was quite a buzz stirring around this next *mystery phase*.

Al opened up, "You have done an incredible job of teaching efficiency. You have helped your people weigh through the decision of buying-in. Your management team has decided to flip the triangle from ME to WE. We asked you to sell prevention as a proactive tool to earn security. We asked you to empower your crew and work toward total accountability. The platform your team stands on is 34% higher in safety and productivity than we were six months ago. That precedent is just a fraction of where we can go. With the enacting of our plan, we have received $9 Million in new equipment, paid off our $33 Million debt, donated $2 Million for community improvements, and the Board has approved $7 Million for special investments. Remember, that plan was set in motion before we asked your teams to show a commitment to the transformation plan. Notice how we committed and delivered, and then we asked them to join the program. Now that your teams have signed on, the throttle is to the floor. We have to be very careful not to abuse the trust and respect that has been developed. The next building phase will lift us to another level, but before we go there I want to review some history in our backgrounds. Some of the negative management lessons in the past may have tainted your views on certain operating techniques or tools, and in other cases there are examples of imbalance that we don't need to repeat. An example of this was a pre-1980's common phrase, 'production volume makes up for all the sins.' MSHA, the federal regulatory group, responded with tough laws to reign-in industry and the unions flourished to protect and bring balance.

In the 1980's and 1990's, safety emphasis improved, but the attack on reducing cost purged every area. Most of the industrial engineering efficiency groups were reduced to save administrative labor. Productivity did not drop off though, since the workforce was extremely experienced. The early 2000's came and market pressures were relentless. Many companies erroneously tried to save their way to a profit. Most of the surviving companies have now redirected focus back to efficiency. With a lot of inexperienced labor, we have to get back to the basics. We have to develop processes from which to grow. Our overall transformation plan is the MVP Plan. You have taken us through the **M**ission Statement and **V**alues introduction. I encourage you to keep up the commitment in those areas. Senior management will continue periodic Foundational Value Audits to make sure value commitments are not dropped, but our split-focus will be to also add to our arsenal.

> *INTEGRITY PROCESS IS BASED AROUND WHAT WE CALL THE PRINCIPLES OF PROCESS.*

Now I want to introduce you to the last part of Integrity Process. It is going to be the bundling of common management techniques, many of which you may have heard of or are currently using. The big difference is in the way they are fused together and refined. Many companies introduce a decent plan yet fail to gain input and buy-in. Then, they utilize poor implementation practices and do not modify the final procedures to maximize their potential. Everyone leaves frustrated, and results fall short. I am here to offer an alternative. Integrity Process is carefully designed to the specific situation and based around what I call the Principles of Process.

Step One is to Gather information.

We need employee input, condition notes, equipment information, operation reports, analysis results, Kaizen ideas, meeting suggestions, and survey comments.

Problem: How do we assimilate and collect all the data?

    a. We commonly mean well, but we get sloppy and miss some and/or are so overwhelmed we don't get the detail.

    b. The lack of consistent follow-up to the collected data convinces people their input is not important, so attention to detail degrades over time.

Solution: Develop specific gathering tools and train everyone how to report the information. Then set up a data collection system and provide a check-and-balance plan to assure everything is tracked.

Step Two is to Refine the process.

Almost every piece of information gathered suggests a change, repair, or preventative measure.

Problem: How do we prioritize, organize, and make the changes?

    a. We always try to get everything fixed completely, but reality happens and we fall short. Our people see this as a lack of commitment, so they lose faith and drift.

    b. When suggestions cross departmental lines or have multiple facets, they get lost and improvements are not seen.

Solution: Devise improvement systems that will prioritize, assign responsible parties, and will propagate follow-up until complete.

Step Three is to Monitor results.

Any positive change usually results in some good and a little bad.

Integrity Process

Problem: If we do not measure all the infinite change-points, the next round of refinement will be lost. Results monitoring will also reveal the next bottleneck.

> **ANY POSITIVE CHANGE USUALLY RESULTS IN SOME GOOD AND A LITTLE BAD.**

a. We drop the detailed monitoring and track general trends. With so many variables, the small refinement follow-up needs are marginalized.

b. Our people do not feel their efforts are noticed or appreciated so they disengage.

Solution: Set up a data analysis system to track and trend macro and micro performance results, and report in a useable manner. Progress should be measured against percentage of improvement from the past and variances to the various outputs.

The handout I am circulating (Appendix B.30) reviews the Integrity Process Basics. Now here is an interesting twist: Step 1, 2, and 3 are perpetual. It is like a wheel in motion. We Gather info, Refine process, Monitor results, then we decide on the next line of improvements needed and start again: Gather, Refine, Monitor (GRM). The GRM Principle never stops because continuous process improvement is what?"

Someone in the back yelled out, "A foundational value!"

Al smiled, "Perfect answer! We have to sell an operating plan that is consistent with our values and promotes progress toward what?"

"Security!" This answer came from the front.

"Spot on!" Al assured. "I like the wheel analogy because it is so true. As long as the wheel is moving, it stands up. When it slows or stops, it falls over. It is all about forward motion and we call it progress. If it goes in reverse, we slide back and eventually it steers to a stall and falls over. Moral of the story—we either advance our process or we fall and backslide. Idling is not an outcome state of where we want to be. We could build the same analogy in our personal lives also."

Al continued, "The second twist to Integrity Process is that we are only going to initially address a limited number of techniques. Those techniques will be carefully selected to compliment and complete the specific process. Our starting position will be to select a tool bag of programs that we feel comfortable with and which will address our issues. The reason for the dialing down in focus is that we need to be responsive to a smaller scope first. I would rather that we put out a fire completely before we move on, rather than chase flames and get burned by the hottest coals or the flame-ups behind us. After lunch, I will lay out three separate Process Pillars. Those pillars will be the tool bags for our transformation. They will gel the numerous programs and management techniques into a system leading us to success."

IV. PROCESS DEVELOPMENT AND PRESENTATION

Chapter 14
Building the Process Pillars

After lunch everyone filed back in and hastily took a seat. Al continued to explain the challenge. "You know your operations history, conditions, hot buttons, workforce, management strengths, and weaknesses better than anyone else. We need you to select the Process Pillar that best fits your need. Where is your *return on effort* going to be the best? Initially, we want low hanging fruit and momentum. I am here to help each one of your operations maximize improvement, but I am not above fueling the fire. I understand there is a competition for the *top dog*."

Tony spoke up, "There is no race. I don't even see a serious competitor. The Champion Mine will live up to its name. We are ready to claim our pillar and go to work!"

"I'll let you crow a couple of times, but in the morning we plan to pluck a few feathers!" Dustin rebuked.

I looked at Cody to see if he had a response. He smirked and said, "The hunt's just begun and my dog is coming out of the box!"

Al resumed the floor, "Now that everyone has marked their corners, let's discuss your pillar choices. Each pillar will be made up of:

Gathering Tools

Refining Procedures

Monitoring Systems

The pillar provides security only when GRM is continuous and supported by all. When we utilize it as the backbone of our transformation, our entire teams will see Integrity Process as the means to the end—our path to earn security."

Al picked up the marker and headed to the whiteboard. He started to talk and write:

PROCESS PILLAR I

Gathering Tools
(information)

Refining Procedures
(process)

Monitoring Systems
(results)

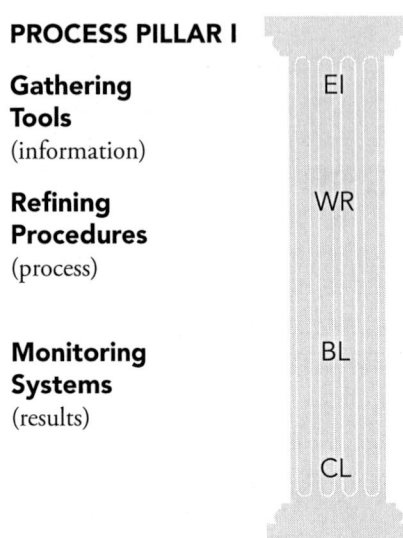

Employee Inspection: every employee will turn in a daily checklist and comment note on their area

Work Requests: repairs or preventative measures are prioritized, responsibilities assigned, completion checked, and progress tracked

Backlogs: outstanding WRs are monitored for completion, time to finish, and repeating trends

Cost of Loss: failed items or losses are evaluated in total economic terms and publicized

Al explained, "This can be an extremely strong pillar. When an operation fully grasps the potential of every employee looking hard to find preventative measures in order to avert losses, the sky is the limit. We need everyone to think like an owner, look and listen like an inspector, and be part of the solution. The major hurdle with this pillar is the *fear of lists*. We have beat-up the messenger so many times in the past that job survival has meant passing the blame or just not reporting issues. The only way to counter *the fear* is to convince the workforce it's a new day with a new management style. This only works if they can see a high integrity approach. Building respect first, by being committed to the communicated plan and responding to Kaizen ideas, shows management has committed to the transformation process. Then and only then, will the workforce start looking deeper and in more detail. We all must take equal responsibility for ours' and the teams' future.

One of the advantages of a detailed checklist is that it helps us remember to check every detail. And with the excessive *cost of loss*, none of us are good enough to remember everything. It's a new age of accountability and penalties, our inspections and follow-up must be to a 'super degree.' Another advantage of *listing* is that it serves as a teaching tool for the new employees who may still be learning the ropes. A third asset of the expansive lists is that they work as a great communication tool when we are briefing the next crew. If problems were not permanently fixed on shift, when employee inspection lists are turned in, the open jobs would then be prioritized by the foreman and logged as a Work Request.

Building the Process Pillars

I have seen many well-intentioned companies start similar programs and fail to track the progress. If you start losing ground or a project slips through the cracks, creditability decays the gathering process. Likewise, even if a resulting Work Request (WR) is completed, we often need a later follow-up check on the repair. This has been built into the recommended management system. It's flow chart is being circulated now" (Appendix B.31).

"This looks extremely effective," Makirra remarked. "I can now see why we had to perfect the Foundational Values first and earn the platform to be able to ask for their help. But, Al, will you be providing us copies of the employee inspection checklists?"

Al answered, "Good try, Makirra, but that's a very important part of the Pillar that you and all the team leaders/supervisors must work through. You need to develop those lists with your people's input. With respect to the Work Request numbers you will be receiving, I will give you a clue of the probable trend you will see, which might be helpful:

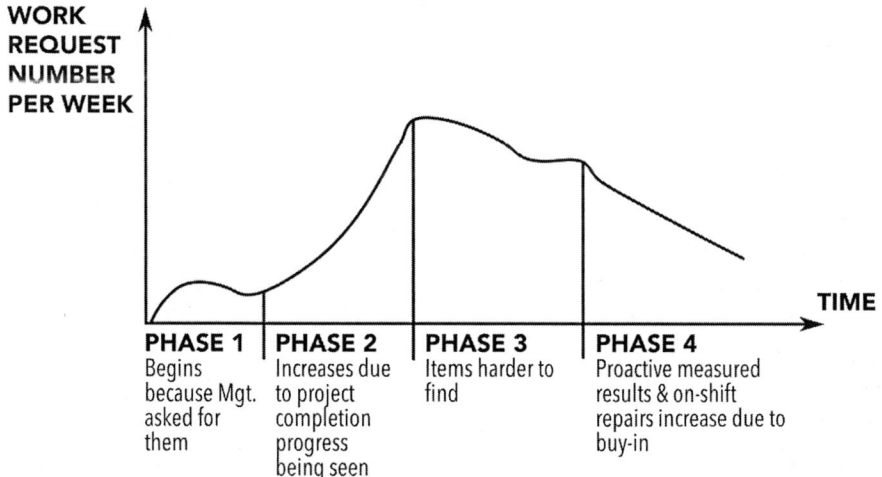

Phase 2 is the critical one to survive through with your maintenance staff. They see the number of Work Requests escalating so fast, that they can quickly get overwhelmed. Keep encouraging them to push through this phase. Phase 3, of course, is pretty straight-forward. Phase 4 is the self-managing pay off. The first monitoring system of this Pillar, Backlogs, is important in making sure the maintenance backlog is not growing outside of the evolution stage (Phase 2 in the above graph). If the backlog number of projects or 'days to repair' is growing, that might be the trigger to reprioritize a maintenance time-blitz. The second monitoring system is to continue calculating the cost of loss. Our people understand dollars, and thus we should all realize the cost of loss and its effect on our future. If a visitor came to your operation and asked an operator the cost per minute of downtime, would the operator know? If not, how can they prioritize and make correct decisions? In the past, owners believed they could just hire the smartest superintendents who would then give all the orders. Nowadays, we realize an empowered and accountable workforce can do a far better job. We have some reprogramming to do, but it's very feasible. And it's fun to keep score when everyone pulls together. I know some of my stories and teachings are repeats from prior discussions, but they reinforce points I am especially trying to drive home.

PROCESS PILLAR II

Gathering Tools (information)

- **ES** — **Efficiency Survey:** an on-shift interview with an employee probing for input, ideas, or suggestions to improve safety and productivity
- **PS** — **Process Study:** a data gathering and motion study of each job and its effect on flow
- **AT** — **Action Team:** a group of employees selected to work on a specific issue

Refining Procedures (process)

- **BP** — **Best Practices:** the agreed upon, most efficient way to do a job and/or process
- **PP** — **Prevention Projects:** highlighted improvement projects
- **WR** — **Work Requests:** repairs or preventative measures which are prioritized, responsibilities assigned, completion checked, and progress tracked

Monitoring Systems (results)

- **EA** — **Efficiency Audits:** an on-shift study (motion, input, and observation) on the compliance to BP's (job and process)
- **ROI** — **Return on Investment:** the calculated result of an improvement project
- **BL** — **Backlogs:** outstanding WR projects are monitored for completion and time to finish

This pillar is designed to continually update our Best Practices proactively through input and observation. As we saw in the first pillar, if the workforce and first line management believes in our motives and we respect them in our treatment of their input, their buy-in will be earned. This will empower the refining progresses. It is also important that we train a *client service concept* into our employees. We need them to look around and find things that could be

Building the Process Pillars 131

done to strengthen safe output (efficiency), even if it's outside their area. This maturation is a trait of greatness. If everyone raises the standard of expectation, everyone's families win.

Are you starting to see how Pillar II accomplishes the same GRM repeating strategy, just with a different sets of tools?

We **G**ather information-by survey, study, and Action Teams.

We **R**efine process-by evolving Best Practices, developing Prevention Projects, and completing Work Requests.

We **M**onitor results-by visual/verbal audits, measuring results, and then continuing GRM over and over again.

If you choose this one, let me know and I can send you some blank Prevention Project Forms (Appendix B.32) and supporting Action Plan Forms to standardize the procedure (Appendix B.33)."

Al joked, "And here we go to see what's behind door #3!"

PROCESS PILLAR III

Gathering Tools (information)

- **SR** — **Shift Report:** any report that conveys production/output and/or downtime information
- **LI** — **Loss Investigation:** a study & recommendations pertaining to a loss (injury, violation, downtime, rework, or waste) or near miss
- **RA** — **Risk Assessment:** a study and recommendations pertaining to a potential loss

Refining Procedures (process)

- **FM** — **Failure Maintenance:** repair of the damaged item
- **PM** — **Preventative Maintenance:** pro-active action to eliminate or push-out a loss
- **WR** — **Work Requests:** repairs or preventative measures which are prioritized, responsibilities assigned, completion checked, and progress tracked

Monitoring Systems (results)

- **DT** — **Downtime:** delay caused by a loss
- **PI** — **Performance Indicators:** performance measurement that tracks progress
- **OC** — **Operating Cost:** cost calculated per each piece of equipment, it is the cost of the downtime and cost of the repair parts/supplies and cost of maintenance repair time
- **BL** — **Backlogs:** outstanding PM and WR projects are monitored for completion and time to finish

"The third pillar obviously has the same repeating GRM plan, but is driven by a more analytical monitoring system. The focus on the shift report can be a strong problem reporting tool and a tremendous efficiency teaching instrument. By emphasizing specific Performance Indicators, flow inhibitors can be highlighted and addressed. One of the keys to the downtime reporting is correctly identifying the event root cause, not just the symptom. The circulating handout shows some examples (Appendix B.34). In many cases, asking WHY five times sends you to the root.

The Risk Assessments, RA's, and Loss Investigations, LI's, are similar in steps, with the RA's being pre-incident and most of the LI's post-incident. The LI's will evolve over 3 Levels.

Level 1-investigate all medically treatable injuries and order violations (base level).

Level 2-investigate all reported injuries, S&S violations/orders, and downtime over 30 minutes (after 4 months).

Level 3-investigate all reported injuries, all violations, downtime over 15 minutes, equipment damage over $10,000, rework costing +4 man-hours, noted waste issues, and reported near misses.

We should get to Level 3 within the first year if a progressing focus is maintained. This pillar requires an extensive amount of training to build effective analysis teams, but the results will be huge and will pro-actively protect against losses. After the information is gathered, the refining process addresses the suggestions. Just as Best Practices continued evolving in Process Pillar II, the Preventative Maintenance, PM, module continues to be expanded. The scope of its potential is expansive (Appendix B.35). Further clarity is gained by knowing the total operating cost of each piece of equipment, and then a tailor-made PM plan can be sharpened even further. The individual cost history will allow major and competent rebuilds to be based first on operating cost, then on tonnage history, and lastly on equipment age.

Let's take a meeting break and then huddle to discuss your pillar preference. Please keep in mind that you will want to select a pillar that gives you:

1. The best return for your time and money

2. The one your team is passionate about. Passion indicates your giftings and destiny. It is those journeys that commonly bear the most fruit in our lives."

Building the Process Pillars 133

> **PASSION INDICATES YOUR GIFTINGS AND DESTINY. IT IS THOSE JOURNEYS THAT COMMONLY BEAR THE MOST FRUIT IN OUR LIVES.**

After the superintendent meeting break, I brought each of the superintendents forward to announce their choice.

Cody led off. "We liked the first two pillars the best, but we chose Process Pillar I. The main reason is that we have started a weak version already and are seeing decent results. The biggest difference we have seen is the attitude of our people and I think that has come from the values-focus in our communication and training programs. The other reason for Pillar I is that it will require strong inspection teaching and Makirra is especially good at that.

Tony followed, "The Champion Mine picks Process Pillar III. Since Joe is a maintenance legend, we are going with our asset. Plus, we tried the employee checklists and time studies under the previous *blame game management*, and let's just say that those scars are too fresh. Joe and I have some maintenance and downtime reduction ideas that are sure winners."

Dustin stepped forward, "This worked out perfectly, since we want to go with Process Pillar II. We still have some distrust issues, but I think this pillar's approach can turn that weakness into our signature strength."

I complimented the groups on their choices and logic. I also pre-set a monthly Accountability Meeting with this same group to review their Pillar progress and Foundational Value Audit Results. I then asked Al to come up and close the meeting.

Al cleared his throat, "I am really impressed with the commitment I am seeing and the early results. I will share a fitting quote, 'Expectation determines the potential, perseverance earns achievement, and follow-up protects against decay.' I caution you all to frequently evaluate your team's progress and assess their growth. Let's not lose what your teams have worked so hard to achieve. I will send Dirk an assessment sheet (Appendix B.36) that each operation should complete quarterly, then redirection can be personally outlined for each site. With respect to the Process Procedure, I am pleased with the aired reasoning shared on your pillar choices. The gravity of the importance of our leadership decisions should never be taken lightly. Many people rely on our wisdom to custom-make the plan to protect our house. I would always encourage you to analyze the facts, gain input

> **SOMETIMES, OUR GUIDANCE COMES IN THE SIMPLEST OF INDICATORS.**

from your team, lift it up in prayer, and then follow your heart. Sometimes, our guidance comes in the simplest of indicators. The passion you are carrying toward our Mission Statement must be obvious to all. In fact, here's a $100 bill for anyone who can repeat it perfectly. But if you miss it, you owe me $20!"

We could see everyone rehearsing mentally, but no one came forward. I couldn't stand it any longer, so I let it go, "I will take your $100 and buy some flowers for my gals at home!" I said.

Al smirked, "I am proud of your prioritized retention, but I must admit the lack of others knowing the Mission Statement disappoints me. How can you lead on a platform you cannot recite? Honestly, the repetition of the Mission Statement at your operations should be so prominent that you have it memorized. And, Dirk, nice try on the money, but we wouldn't want anyone to think you have insider foreknowledge of the question or something, so I think we'll have to just donate your winnings to a Christmas charity!"

Laughter could be heard through the group.

"Changing subjects," Al continued, "I will give you a chance to redeem yourself. As we previously announced during the corporate restructuring meeting, provisions were made to earmark $7 Million for special investments. That was a vote of confidence that your teams would come up with Kaizen ideas which would report a strong Return on Investment (ROI). The board asked me to play banker over those funds. Starting next week those monies are available, since we closed the sale of our previously owned Broad Run Mine. The procedure will be: everyone will start with a $1 Million credit to invest. There is another $1 Million allotment if someone can show a decent return on an expanded project list, and a $3 Million sum if someone can show a very strong Return on Investment (ROI). I will attend your monthly Accountability Meeting in three months to analyze your results and decide on the future appropriations."

V. MONITORING AND MATURATION

Chapter 15
Progress Reports and Creep

A light breakfast and coffee at the small café next to the lobby of Al's hotel was a nice deviation from the standard straight drive into work. Nikki and I had driven separate vehicles to accommodate Nikki's return home.

"Al, Nikki and I would like to thank you for taking the time to meet with us. We really need something or someone to help us. As great as everything is going at work, our family life is beginning to hurt. You always preach balance but honestly—well, we're starting to fall apart. Do we have to pick one or the other? Are we being selfish?

Nikki added, "Dirk and I feel strongly that the Lord has directed us to bloom in this season with these tasks at hand, but we feel torn in different directions."

Al responded, "Assuring balance is an important part of the maturation process. I commend you guys for noticing the budding issue and addressing it. First and foremost, you have to agree upon the long-term priorities. Quite awhile back, my wife and I started up what we now refer to as a periodic priority-setting session. In our case, we also believe God has a calling on our lives and we are continuously seeking His direction. As we go through different seasons, we may temporarily prioritize our time differently, but never can we allow our hearts' balance to change. During concentrated, short-term projects, such as a work transformation project, the Lord has always graced my wife and I with the perseverance to make it through them. The trials have taught us to trust Him even to a deeper degree. We have always considered these intense career projects as our family's ministry, since everyone sacrifices. For my family, we set our spiritual walk first, then family and careers, and hobbies/health fourth. We then commit to work hard to complete our prioritized list of goals within each of the four areas. I am not going to say that focusing on a multi-faceted agenda is easy, but I believe

> **ASSURING BALANCE IS AN IMPORTANT PART OF THE MATURATION PROCESS.**

the Lord anoints our steps and gives us the wisdom to succeed and stay balanced. I don't worry about tomorrow, when I keep my motives on His service. The peace He gives me is one that goes beyond all understanding.

With respect to your *how-to* question, I strongly believe time is a gift and it should be invested wisely. I will take responsibility for how I spend every minute. In many cases I actually calculate the time taken versus the reward, to prioritize their ranking. It's a disciplined approach but it keeps my eyes on the main target. I don't allow myself to say, 'I did not have time,' I say, 'I did not get to it yet.' The challenge is to improve our personal efficiencies so that we gain time to achieve more of our prioritized *to-do* list. I'll be happy to send you a copy of my monthly check-list that I use to fill out as I self-monitor my own progress (Appendix B.37). From this list, I am continuously working to improve. This commitment to improve also works as an example to the others who will be watching you. In many cases, that is the best mentoring one can receive."

"Al, I understand the diligence part and that the monthly Progress Test is a good idea—one I will plan to incorporate, but how do I know when I am ready for the next step in my walk? This *trusting God* is new to me."

Al answered, "Dirk, your heart and relationship is what God seeks. When you set your motives around Him, He will direct your path. I would ask you to read about Joseph's story (Genesis 37-46) and then we will talk later. I really believe God is going to use these current economic challenges to deeply touch a lot of people through your leadership. You can be a *lighthouse in the storm*."

"Speaking of leadership, we have that three-month follow-up meeting with the managers in half an hour," I reminded him.

"That's right, Dirk, so we better go—Nikki, keep your prayers up. They're working."

She smiled and bid us a confirming good-bye.

☨

My first order of business at the meeting was to have everyone read the Mission Statement and Values List from the wall sign. "I apologize if that sounds childish", I told them, "but we have to get these principles in our spirit." Then I had the superintendents review their most recent Foundational Values Audit with the group. The progress seen in the team building was astounding. I was truly understanding why it was so important to lay the foundation and build the organizational structure before we started Process. Now we had the mutual respect working for us, not undermining the vision. I continued to encourage the specific discussion about the Pillar techniques, as I could see the superintendents were learning from each other. As we drew that section of the meeting to a close, I stated, "As we continue illuminating the vision of security in our people, we as leaders, must also be right there with the plan. It is during these times they will be the most moldable. Be a master of momentum and keep the positive alive. Be mindful of the information sharing and agenda pace, yet keep the throttle maximized. These are the times only you know your team's potential for progress. This time will not only be inspirational, productive, and enlightening, but it is proving to be the turning point of our future. I am so proud of everyone's achievement. Let's move on now to the Process Pillar status review."

Cody led off, "We have seen a huge success already in violation reductions from our Employee Inspections. As the inspection information is turned into prioritized work requests, the plan has been easier to address. We tried the inspection program a couple of years ago and it flopped because the tracking system was not in place. We are excited because this time people are already seeing the gains. As we build confidence in the process and work hard to bring the backlogs down, the prevention results will result in lower injuries, less downtime, reduced rework, and eliminated waste. We will begin posting all the positive trends and keep everyone informed of the successes. I see this as a strong springboard into even more detailed inspections."

I encouraged Cody with some statistics, "The Majestic Mine has reduced their violations by 29% in the last three months. That's a proactive attack on loss. When we wait for regulatory agencies to indirectly manage our operations through compliance violations, we are reactive. Being on the front end allows us to solve the problem at the root, set our own priorities, and also use the fine-monies for the future by not paying for yesterday's mistakes." I reaffirmed his excellence and complimented his focus forward.

"How about your progress Dustin?"

Dustin answered, "In working with Pillar II we have seen a big improvement in our operating efficiencies due to a push on Best Practices. Safety habits and operating skills on the production crews have been targeted. The supportive non-productive positions have also been addressed. We have been able to reduce three extra people from the outby areas, since work efficiency has improved, and we've been able to move them to the production face. This has provided help when production crews are short on manpower. It helps flow."

Al couldn't stand it. "That's music to my ears!" he exclaimed.

"I thought you would like that," Dustin added. "Our team also has come up with a new design to improve the current belt scrapers. It will require less maintenance, reduced beltline shoveling, which we consider rework, and will result in fewer violations. That's a triple win."

> **HANDS-ON TRAINING OF BEST PRACTICES YIELDS BIG GAINS IN SAFETY AND PRODUCTIVITY ALIKE.**

I applauded, "Very good, keep it up. I would even encourage you to step up the operator skills training. If you need to add a trainer position, I will approve that right now. Hands-on training of Best Practices yields big gains in safety and productivity alike."

"Now Tony, can you give us an update?"

"With pleasure Sir," Tony responded. "We put the heat on the *value of every minute* like Al preached. As we looked for our largest potential, it was the eight hours on third shift. Conventional thinking was that this had to be for maintenance. We challenged the paradigm and got out-of-the-box. Joe chaired a group that studied the maintenance requirements on third shift and they came up with the criteria that we needed—four man-shifts per night to stay ahead of the Work Request backlogs and Preventative Maintenance schedules. We set a goal of picking up four hours of new production every night without losing any support work. The result: we call it *Swarm Maintenance*. We increased the current maintenance staffing from three to six and added another man to the dusting/prep crew on two trial sections. Then we trained and set up everyone on third shift to have a maintenance responsibility along with their normal functions. Some nights we have longer jobs, like belt moves, but others, when things are caught up, we have loaded coal up to six hours. But in all cases, day shift has to be ready for a push-button start. The first month of Swarm Maintenance we only averaged 91 minutes of extra production per night, but this month we are at 320 minutes per night and climbing. We also closely monitor the production and maintenance Performance Indicators from the day shift crews, to make sure we are not robbing from them. Our guys have done GREAT. Yes, we added four people per unit, but the Return-on-Investment (ROI) has been very high. We would like to take the Swarm concept to the other section if our project ROI has earned us further investment monies."

Al stepped in, "OK, I see where you are heading. Let's say you earn an extra allotment, what would be your plans?"

Tony spouted back, "We figure it costs us about a half a million dollars per section to staff and support Swarm, so our third section would chew up half a million and the remaining $2.5 Million we would invest in rebuilding our roof bolter components. Those components would be changed out on the highest operating cost machines first. We picked roof bolters as the focus equipment, since they have the biggest effect on our productivity. They are our bottleneck."

Progress Reports and Creep

"Sounds like you guys did your homework," Al responded, "with the intention of bringing home the biggest investment allotment. Let's see how the others did with their $1 Million purses."

Cody responded, "We have been frugal with those monies and have not turned them loose yet. We have a committee that will decide on the best Kaizens Investment Projects and then we will move forward. We have a lot of ideas, but we are cautiously evaluating them."

I came back, "Cody, this is not where we want you to be conservative. Those dollars were entrusted to you to earn a return. If you are not going to use your gifts, you risk losing them to someone else who will put them to work. *Analysis Paralysis* sends a very bad message to creativity and innovation. We desperately need your people's ideas, and the best encouragement you can give them is for them to see us investing in those ideas and getting them done. Please push your committee into a faster turn-around. Paper ideas do not pay the bills, their results do."

> **ANALYSIS PARALYSIS SENDS A VERY BAD MESSAGE TO CREATIVITY AND INNOVATION.**

Cody followed, "Point well taken, we will step it up."

"I will consent victory to Tony's team," said Dustin, "for the big monies, but we want the second prize of another million. Our Action Team was assigned the task of increasing the plant yield of our coal. In our attempt to do that, we came up with a nine-point action plan. It included installing ash analyzers, tripping chutes, a parallel beltline, and the retraining of our miner operators on ways to selectively cut without impeding production rates. The Performance Indicators on plant yield and cost show us we have reduced rock by two inches in our mining height and improved the yield, which equals to a savings of over $4/ton."

"Impressive," Al said. "What would you do with another million?"

Dustin was ready, "We have a growing safety concern in our water pumping system. We are legal, but preventatively, we could be better. For that investment we could automate the pumps and provide a back-up system. The return would be less potential high water issues and lower downtime due to saturated floor conditions. Aesthetic improvements would also be gained in the process."

"I like your thought process and priorities," Al replied. "We will grant your team the extra $1 Million investment and the Champion Mine will earn the big allotment. I do hope you both realize the Board expects a monthly evaluation on the ROI rate and progress updates, though. And if those ROI rates drop below 30%, the remaining investment monies will probably be retracted, unless they have a safety component."

Tony and Dustin nodded their heads in agreement and Tony said, "We understand business accountability, we will make you proud!"

"I know you all will," Al commented. "We have a GREAT thing started here, and a lot of people will gain when we pull it off. But it's going to take us driving every potential path we can find and anticipating the obstacles that will face us. As we have discussed, every improvement action will result in a countering, reactive effect, sometimes immediate, but most of the time in the near term. That is why continuous refinement is a mandate and is forward-focused. I assume that every positive action has a negative, creeping reaction—a counter to good. I call it CREEP. So every time we create good, I protectively look for ways to preventatively guard the ground we have taken. I will send you some examples of CREEP that are commonly seen (Appendix B.38). A similar list with different specifics could be developed for any process oriented industry. Let's stay on the attack. The quest of continuous process improvement is a worthy offensive position, but the sense of accomplishment along the way is the heartfelt motivation that should energize your next move. I challenge you to expand your expectation:

> **I PROTECTIVELY LOOK FOR WAYS TO PREVENTIVELY GUARD THE GROUND WE HAVE TAKEN.**

Good is achieved by a solid plan and aspiration, GREAT is achieved by the refining of the plan and perspiration!

Let's use that as a close to a very progressive meeting," Al concluded.

I stood up and said, "With all the positive results we are seeing at the three-month point on the Process Phase, I think we are ready to schedule a Celebration Banquet. In three months, on our one-year anniversary of introducing Integrity Process, we will plan a special evening. All employees and their families will be invited. It will be a good time of reflection and an opportunity to continue expressing our appreciation for the teamwork and commitment. Keep your progress swelling. I will go ahead and leak a rumor that there will be some winners crowned at the special evening's celebration."

As Tony was heading out the door, I hurried to catch up, "Congratulations on the top investment honors."

"Thank you," Tony said, "It's our pleasure to be an asset and part of the overall team."

"You played your cards perfectly on the investment monies. It was almost like you knew what was going to happen," I added.

Tony smiled, "I did. I read The Book."

V. MONITORING AND MATURATION

Chapter 16
The True Winner: Earning Balanced Security

The date was finally arriving for the employees' Celebration Banquet. Al and I had been working to ready all the meeting plans and Power Point slides. I teased Al that there would be no whiteboard, but he assured me his illustrations could be put into a slide show. I again gigged him, "Are your comments going to be laced with their normal dual meanings or are you going to stay simple?"

He smirked, "Dirk, everything in life can be handled at face value, or alternatively taken deeper. Level one is good but deeper challenges reward greater returns."

I added, "It is like what you are teaching with the mine investment projects. We are rewarded by our efforts and returns."

Al followed, "'To whom much is given, much is expected.' We are all gifted with different strengths, but as we bring them to the table of service, it is their level of diligence and perseverance that determines the reward. I truly believe if our motives are correct, the fruit of our labor will be honored and multiplied."

> **I TRULY BELIEVE IF OUR MOTIVES ARE CORRECT, THE FRUIT OF OUR LABOR WILL BE HONORED AND MULTIPLIED.**

"By the way," I countered, "When I was telling Nikki about the investment projects, she said you swiped that *payback race* from the biblical Talents Parable."

Al admitted, "I sure did. All of our strongest business principles can be traced back to The Source. And I am not bashful to say, God is my source. Politically, that statement might not be accepted well, but I believe politic's biggest problem is the lack of standing on strong infallible principles."

I admitted, "You have drug me a long way over this last year since we started working together, but every time I think I have it figured out, you stretch me again."

"Remember, it's a journey and we all have so much to learn," Al responded. "There are many forks in the road to decipher. People spend their lives waiting for a *burning bush* experience, but for me it's that faint small voice in my spirit. If you set your direction to serve others, He will equip you with the vision and tools."

I questioned, "Is that why you asked me to read the Joseph Story?"

"Yes," Al replied, "What did you gather from it?"

"I saw it being a story of obedience. Joseph lived a life of values not commonly accepted, but ones he never betrayed. He was open about his convictions, even though most of society rejected him. Although Joseph lived through some dark days and unfair accusations, in the end his efforts were rewarded. He actually was elevated in status and authority because of his values and service. I guess that's the model we can follow, right?"

Al assured, "That's what He promised, and what I call integrity's return. Why would everyone not use that strategy in every facet of our life?"

"It must be because people don't see the plan and know how it is going to end," I explained. "Why would someone worry about destiny when it's already been worked out?"

"Good question Dirk, I guess they are not the first people to roam around the desert looking for the *promised land*. Let's go share some direction."

†

With all the families invited, we had over 1,200 people in attendance and the atmosphere was electric. I knew the general script, but Al was promising some surprises. I was looking forward to their unfolding!

Al welcomed the crowds and made a few encouraging remarks about the strong progress over the last year. He reminded everyone about the Perception Survey that was mailed out a month prior, and that it was to be collected at the end of the evening. Al emphasized the importance of their opinion and viewpoints. "We are committed to you, and will work hard to support our mutual goal of security."

Al passionately stated, "The level of our future opportunities is shouldered

The True Winner: Earning Balanced Security

on the expectations we have had and the character we have refined. As we reflect on those drivers, I want us to visit the meaning of our namesake. Last month when we sent out the invite to tonight's event, we challenged the kids to define integrity and send in their responses. We

> **THE LEVEL OF OUR FUTURE OPPORTUNITIES IS SHOULDERED ON THE EXPECTATIONS WE HAVE HAD AND THE CHARACTER WE HAVE REFINED.**

would like to share three in particular. The first is from Milly McFarland. She is eight years old and her father works at the Majestic Mine."

Little Milly came forward, bashfully stood at the microphone, and addressed the crowd. "Integrity is the place my daddy works. It's a place where a bunch of people work together to take care of their families. And it works because they let everyone give something to the team. My dad is a mechanic and I am really proud of him. He keeps equipment running for the workers to safely mine the coal. It takes everyone sharing their best. Integrity pays our bills and honors our loyalty. Thank you."

The crowd gave her a warm round of applause.

Al came back and commented, "It's that trust we must all be committed to never lose. One of our greatest assets is the team we forge."

Then Al introduced the second young person, "This is Lori Sturgil. She is the teenage daughter of the Destiny Mine's superintendent."

Lori read her definition, "Integrity is the standard by which we serve. Being true to one's morals, values, and beliefs. Knowing you have been faithful to yourself despite life's temptations to change you. It is a character choice made by the heart and shown through your hands. It's to commit your best with no visible reward, but it feels good inside, so you ought to try it." And then she flashed a big smile.

I led the hand clap and then continued, "Our final contributor to share their meaning of our company name is Baylor Alexander."

Al offered, "He is the son of our lead accountant and is a new engineer who has recently joined our company."

Baylor proceeded, "I define Integrity as the self-directed alignment between one's values, calling, and conduct. It is a stance of unselfish belief and service to others that requires a deep level of sincerity and authenticity. It is a heart driven lifestyle that is infectious to those around you. The pay-off is in seeing people positively influenced, sharing their giftings, and fulfilling their destiny."

Al followed, "Excellent and all encompassing! All three definitions were strong. Their different perspectives challenge our understanding. The important point is to be true to the values of the team, and that keeps our foundation solid. With that said, let's review our progress."

I came up and went through the charting for the Key Performance Indicators, Foundations Value Audit Scores, and the number of Kaizen Ideas completed. A huge success! Every category showed improvements from 21% to 45% over the last year. The individual mine's improvement percentages were also reviewed. Numbers revealed the Majestic and Destiny Mine tied for the lead with a combined average of 32% improvement. We had each operation member come forward and receive a winner's envelope for their accomplishments. Next, we showed the current results of the Investment Projects and crowned the Champion Mine KING for their high ROI returns. They were also presented with an appreciation check. I lavishly congratulated everyone for their year of achievement and summarized by saying, "we did not only persevere the market, but we earned another year of security for all our families and partners. It has taken this whole room of supporters to pull it off. Let's give each other a show of appreciation." I led them in a strong round of applause.

> **WE CHALLENGED EVERYONE TO STRAP ON A CODE OF INTEGRITY AND COMMIT TO A QUEST OF CONTINUOUS IMPROVEMENT VERSUS STAGNANT STALE COMPLACENCY.**

As Jeff Page came to the podium, a banner was lowered, center stage. The banner read, **A CELEBRATION OF CHOICE**. He began, "One year ago, we asked each employee to embrace and commit to a Mission Statement. It was a commitment to a unified focus on security. We asked you to step away from past practice and help us create a preventative approach to our future. It took a decision of choice. We challenged everyone to strap on a code of integrity and commit to a quest of continuous improvement versus stagnant stale complacency. You, the families of Integrity Coal Company chose well. We reorganized, built on mutual foundational values, and began a process that is earning a GREAT status. That standing is our best assurance of economic security. It's the marriage of partners' talents that provided the fuel, a technical plan of transformation which offered a spark, but it is the continuous drive for excellence that is the catalyst for the future. When we met a year ago in our last corporate meeting, we asked you to look through the smoke of our past and envision a bright tomorrow. I asked you to believe in something that you could not touch or see, and it required faith. I promised you rewards for that choice. Some of our family decided not to commit to the change, and unfortunately they are no longer with us. Our heart was and is, that each of you choose to join the Integrity Family and unite in one vision. Tonight, we celebrate your choice and accomplishments. And we want to continue to share in some of

The True Winner: Earning Balanced Security

the fruit of your labor."

With that, a couple thousand balloons and a blinding flurry of confetti dropped from the ceiling of the large conference room.

Jeff energized the room further by announcing, "every balloon has an individual number inside that is redeemable for a children's prize at the end of the evening!" To convey it mildly, the kids were ecstatic, and their anticipation was peaking.

After a brief break, Al resumed the meeting. He started, "I hate to douse the atmosphere with business, but we do have two more points on the agenda. The first is a short glimpse into the next phase of our business plan. As all the employees know, the last six months have been focused on introducing one of three Process Pillars to their operation. That Process Pillar has provided the structural framework to continue our improvement after the foundational values were laid. Each operation chose a pillar that would assure quick return and maximize momentum. To usher in our next wave of efficiency gains, we are going to ask each operation to add another Process Pillar to their arsenal. Then after another six months, we are going to incorporate the third Pillar into each site. Next year at this annual celebration time, we will again review our progress. And yes kids, if your dads and moms continue the efficiency improvements, the board promises another pile of presents to drop from the sky!"

That announcement brought cheers from all the kids.

Al added, "How's that for employee accountability back to their family? This may even be better than peer pressure."

That got a vibrant round of laughter.

As I relieved Al at the microphone, the group quieted down. I explained, "To help the introduction of each new pillar, the Process Coordinator that had worked with each of the specific pillars over the last six months, will be temporarily transferred to the next operation. This should help in the training and logistics needed to ensure the new pillar has a smooth acceptance. It is very important that all three Process Pillars are eventually incorporated into our operating plan, helping us achieve the needed balance. In order to further understand Integrity Process, please refer to the slide visual on the screen (Appendix B.39). In support of our unified teamwork and to keep all the families rewarded and incentivized, beyond a consistent paycheck, the next slide (Appendix B.40) illustrates the new employee SHARE PLAN that the Board has approved. For purposes of keeping the meeting rolling along, we'll defer the detailed explanation of the last two slides until next week when we will set up crew meetings at each site. We wanted to take these couple minutes to communicate the developing operations plan layout, so everyone continues to see our direction and how we are intending to SHARE the spoils of the war on security." That brought another round of appreciation applause.

As the clapping subsided, I was getting ready to shift to the last part of our meeting, when I noticed Al carrying my little six-year-old boy over to the podium. I was stunned, but yielded to Al's surprise, as the two approached the microphone.

Al said, "I would like to introduce Colt Brothers to everyone tonight. Colt came over to me a few minutes ago and asked if he could add something like the other kids did at the beginning of the celebration. I am going out on a limb and taking a chance that will be all right."

An encouragement of applause emerged from the crowd, framing the bronzed moment.

Colt took the microphone and with a quivering, nervous little voice started out, "I want to thank everybody for working with my daddy to make things better for all of us. I also want to thank Mr. Al for believing in him and helping him. Mr. Al promised me that if I kept praying for my daddy's heart and wisdom, God would help him to lead everyone to a secure destiny. My mommy says that means a great future. So I have been praying every night, because we all know God keeps His promises. Mr. Al told my daddy to teach me about what was happening at work, so every night he tells me stories of how great everyone is doing. I've been keeping track of which mine is doing the best in different areas and I am happy for all the different winners tonight, but I have been thinking…we should always try hard and do our best, but isn't the GREATEST GOAL of Integrity to *fill our wagons* with as many of our friends as possible and get across the finish line together?"

You could have heard a pin drop, even the little kids were quiet with a sense of reverence.

I tried to return to the stage, but I had a check in my spirit. It was as though the silence was being preserved for personal reflection.

Jeff Page finally made it up front. He began, "It's times like this we realize that being humble and allowing our hearts to be touched may be the lesson of the moment. As little, but mighty, Colt proclaimed, our filling of the wagons must always rank at the top of our focus. Achieving the influence, or platform, to help each other make the right choices is a weighty calling, but one we have been equipped to handle.

Each of you has the choice, to continue the quest to strengthen your character's integrity. You will define your moral fiber and attitude, and they will be the seeds that are scattered. Each one of us will be responsible for all the seeds we sow. We will also be accountable for the indecision in our lives. Remember, not taking a stand or avoiding a choice, is a 'NO' DECISION.

The True Winner: Earning Balanced Security 147

Each of you has the choice as to what to do with the giftings you have been given. If you invest them for good, your works will be honored and your voice heard. Reflecting back on the last year, your efforts have obviously been blessed. Now, I challenge you to continue paying forward to others. That type of service is what fills the wagon."

> **I CHALLENGE YOU TO CONTINUE PAYING FORWARD TO OTHERS. THAT TYPE OF SERVICE IS WHAT FILLS THE WAGON.**

I thanked Mr. Page before he left the stage and then—I took my turn. "Al always prides himself in having all the surprises. So I was determined to *best him*. In our last managers meeting, Al introduced us to Mr. Steve Harrop. Al said he had been mentoring under him for the last five years. Since I was struggling with some interpersonal questions, I figured I would seek out my teacher's teacher. I had been so impressed with Mr. Harrop's peaceful confidence, I figured he could help me as well. I not only found that he helped me with a lot of my questions, but I found he was also shepherding another 600 families, of which my family has now been added. Rev. Harrop, or Pastor Steve as many have come to refer to him, helped me see the full chest of treasures that rewards a character of integrity. It was then I realized our seven *benefits of integrity* had been manifested in the stories we had been living over the last year.

UNITY

WISDOM

GUIDANCE

COUNSEL

BENEFITS OF INTEGRITY

MOTIVATION

KNOWLEDGE

ENCOURAGEMENT

When we commit to values of integrity, others benefit and we personally grow. But it has not always been easy. Some days, I thought we had been alone. In actuality, He was protecting and carrying us. Pastor taught me that when we give to others, as His Word teaches, we allow Him to join us. I wanted to share Pastor Steve with you tonight, so I asked him to join us. Let's give him a warm welcome."

After a healthy round of applause, I asked Pastor Steve, "Now you can make this relatively short, right?"

Pastor Steve responded, "You are asking a long winded preacher to be short?" Everyone laughed.

Pastor continued, "That might be as big of a miracle as the parting of the Red Sea, or the Integrity-ites finding the promised land." He got a bunch of smiles on that one. "All joking aside," Pastor encouraged, "You guys are living a modern-day-miracle. With over half of the coal industry underwater or at least in a desert, you are the survivors. You chose to unite behind a strong set of values toward one purpose. Never forget where you came from, but stay fixed on the mission at hand. I can only reinforce the lessons you have shared tonight by saying, congratulations to you *good and faithful servants*. I would encourage you men and women of Integrity, to read Proverbs 11 for guidance in your individual life's calling. In closing, my prayer is that each of you would accept His protection, provision, and wisdom AND that you share it with another. And remember, He has respectfully invited you to call Him and make a reservation, so for those who have not decided yet, He will *leave the light on for you* if you want to join Him.

Amen, and thanks for investing your time in the building of integrity."

To continue equipping the Integrity Process developers, the author is working on the next volume in the Integrity Series. The second book is called REFINING INTEGRITY and is in the process of being developed. It will expound on the detailed mechanics of Pillar Processes and Value Enhancement (the Table of Contents is offered on B.42). Further information on supporting material for the Integrity Series, Integrity Process, and contact information can be obtained though **www.IntegrityDevelopment.us**

Appendix A
Notable Quotes

These quotes were gathered from the previous text and offered as a review. They are general in application and are supportive to any career involving people and process. Unless referenced otherwise, these quotes were taken from the author's experiences or paraphrased from life's lessons.

INTRODUCTION

We are all endowed with a basket of strengths that are unique, and when matured, each one of us can be a positive influence to the world around us. Accepting that challenge to perfect *our basket* is the initial step.

Integrity Process is a high value, win-win approach to business that centers around the belief *integrity of character will yield integrity in process*. It is an employee empowered process that provides return to the investor, offers security for employees and their families, and illuminates a positive influence toward the community. The result is a true win-win-win outcome.

OBJECTIVES

The amount of effort exerted and follow-up applied, determines the reward. Let's be committed to helping someone else reach the potential they were designed to become.

CHAPTER 1

He has charted your destiny, but the choice is yours.

If we do not react decisively to the industry change besieging us, we will be left behind. The faster and more efficiently we retool, the further ahead in the pack we will start.

Take care of the team first, as there will be times they carry you.

If we unite together, we can out-perform the field.

The giants in our land are real obstacles, but it is our choice on what we choose to focus. Some consider obstacles to be those frightful things seen when they take their eyes off the goal. Our camp, though, will decide to pursue the prize.

Every operation is different in history, conditions, management personality, timing, equipment constraints, skill and talent levels, scheduling, and workforce make-up. An outsider can mess-up an operating plan if everyone is not onboard and the plan is not completely customized.

Many companies push for the *flash in the pan* results. In the long run, it splinters the company, misses the creative input of the employee base, loses buy-in, and the GREAT status is never achieved.

The corporate agenda of "short-term profit" does not completely translate to the employees' needs for a secure job.

Motive diversity across all the layers of the organization is usually the turbulence—but bridge that, and there is a win-win for those willing to change. A divided house will not stand.

The values we support are those we live and promote. We honor what defines us.

Good is achieved by a solid plan and aspiration; GREAT is achieved by the refining of the plan and perspiration, but we have to earn that level to start refinement. That's the second book of the journey.

We must view and treat our employees as equal business partners and work toward a larger common goal.

Communicating the driving economics sensitizes them to the challenges ahead. If they understand the WHY and HOW, we engage, empower, and energize the team in one direction.

When we improve the safety and productivity, and therefore economic performance, investors see profit and employees see safe job conditions and employment opportunities. The result—security is earned.

When business deals a crisis, successful companies use it as fuel, a catalyst for change, and view it as an opportunity. Let's be a GREAT company, first class, a united contributor, with high integrity.

Integrity is a strong word with a lot of responsibility; don't go there unless you are sold-out 100% to its mission. It is a position and lifestyle, which once announced, will invite close judgment. If you make a mistake of the heart, the sale is over. If you hold to your values, the team can be impenetrable.

CHAPTER 2

Most people cannot get out of their own world long enough to think of another's perspective.

Optimum performance is achieved when every detail is delineated and executed, and that is achieved when communication successfully threads all parts together.

Repetition is an important key in making a new procedure a habit.

Repetition via visual signage is free, and it subconsciously keeps the advertising constant and the desired behavior in-focus.

It's like preparing the ground, there is a time to plow and then a time to sow. Get those right, and there is a harvest.

If the foundation is not laid correctly and timely, we labor in vain.

If a lesson is important enough to share, the intelligent ones will write it down and reuse it.

Convince them that your focus is on the process, not people and names. Show them you are willing to get in and understand their world, and give them the assurance their input will be considered—then they will join in the solution.

Studying cycle and individual process times are vital in bottleneck reduction, but they have to be done in a way not to demoralize the workforce.

Once you have lived their world, shown humility, and earned their trust, they will share information because they believe it will add value.

We spend 80% of our time with 20% of the people and commonly a disproportionate number of them are the disgruntled ones. People-investment is always good, but with limited time you are charged to get the most out of every minute.

Compliant is doing something because we are told to do it. Committed is doing something because we believe and want to do it.

We are charged to *protect the house*.

Studies have shown weeding out the negative not only protects the positive, it promotes creativity, and encourages growth and retention of the strongest.

Dropping your expectations temporarily for a few, shows inconsistency. It's a delicate fine line.

If we continue accepting lower standards and attitudes, GREAT will not be achieved.

Their loyalty must be earned, as they first will need to believe in the cause, then the leader, and finally the program.

By keeping safety your lead-off issue, you are re-enforcing to your team that it is an uncompromisable core value.

Efficiency is defined as Maximized Safety balanced with Optimum Productivity.

We have to get in the habit of teaching efficiency: The balanced attack to the *earning of security*.

Since we have all been taught that over 50% of our communication is through non-verbal means and the first impression carries heavy weight, falling in to help someone as we communicate is extremely effective.

People don't remember how long you worked with them, but they do remember you were humble enough to help. Don't forget, they are constantly reading your heart.

Begin every meeting with an end-in-mind. (Stephen Covey)

General cost reduction programs are okay, but specific prioritized attacks will yield more immediate results.

Speak their language through their eyes.

Our people are listening to their filtered channel, WIIFM—**What's In It For Me**.

Getting people off their own agenda to listen to what you have to say is always a challenge.

Most people don't listen to understand, they listen to reply. (Dale Carnegie)

Do an excellent job of praising your people in public and disciplining in private.

Offer the sincere specific praise for one situation and then cordially encourage them on another project.

Appendix A 153

Once you earn their respect and trust, and they are listening to WIIFM, you will have an opportunity to lead them across the rainbow.

The ownership buy-in felt among your people is a testament that they are sharing in the business accountability. Our job is to tool them, lay-out the plan, and help them maximize their potential.

Morale is a barometer of engagement.

Attitude is a daily choice.

Reading outside your normal environment continues to sharpen your sword, as scripture shares, "iron sharpens iron." Keep in mind that my studying favorites are a reflection of my heart and my values, you must find your own.

You have to choose for yourself, "whom and what you will serve."

CHAPTER 3

We should use productivity tracking as a positive accountability tool and as a method to teach improvements, not to instill fear.

If you want to lead the field, you have to be willing to break from the old paradigms.

Being a student of the environment and adaptable to change, keeps you from being one of the extinct dinosaurs.

Some companies are so resistant to change they die without accepting the new book.

An interactive industrial process is more like a game of chess rather than checkers. Every process change cascades a new line of limiting factors and opportunities. The faster those challenges are dealt with, the greater the chance of survival.

As we monitor, they will manage, and we all win.

The heart of ensuring effective output is to address the correct Key Performance Indicators, and then to make sure smart, hard work gets rewarded in earned security.

Teach them the Key Performance Indicators to manage by and the process clues to look for.

The best teams are those that pull together and understand the dynamics of their load.

The closer and more often you monitor, the better the results.

Sometimes by feeding the lion, we can focus and direct its attack.

The way we treat people and handle trials broadcasts our character and values. Our mouth speaks our heart's response.

A one-man army does not win many wars. It pays to enlist the troops.

Most of the time, the default should be on the longer lasting and better performing part. Buying poorer quality supplies can have intangible effects on employee morale and in many cases can be linked to injuries and violations.

The right and best practices yield top safety and productivity performance together.

There is usually low hanging fruit that gets the progress momentum moving the fastest.

Our people want to be communicated with and involved.

Our employees understand dollars, so arming them with the cost of our losses helps them relate to the WHY we need to change and the information to prioritize which areas to change first.

I am going to treat you like an equal business partner, because you are, and then proceed to explain the performance effects to the bottom line.

Total economics determines our future, BUT safety failures are also factored in because they have huge costs. More importantly, we all have a moral responsibility for being our brother's keeper.

People always perform better when they feel they are sincerely valued and their ideas are considered.

Multiple inputs are always better than one perspective.

None of us is smarter than all of us.

Make sure you are looking at the right numbers, and remember it's the total performance at the end of the game that counts.

Management builds the atmosphere and employees copy the attitude.

Negative atmosphere yields low personal efficiency and thus a failing team effectiveness—the result being: operations economically fold and families go hungry. A lose-lose.

It is better to lead wisely, than to rule sternly.

It is better to gently lead the team or a flock, than to beat them with a stick. If you guide people through respect, you will earn their best.

CHAPTER 4

Business and operations cost-teaching enlightens the mind to better make decisions. I firmly believe that those foundations, problem solving, and loss prevention techniques can proactively address actual and potential issues.

Having a strong training element also allows us to hire for character, and then we can train the skills our way. That gives us better employees in the long run.

A loss is an injury, violation, downtime, rework or waste.

We believe each of those five losses is the symptom of a failure.

Prevention accomplished, yields security.

Maximizing process is about protecting flow. Even the best time studies do not show the complete effect of flow disruption or capture the momentum gains seen in a good shift.

Strengthening or eliminating the true weak link is the only thing that will release the flow.

When you see a result in variance of more than 10%, a process study and improvement must be made.

Step one is to open our people's eyes and plow the ground. Then when the ideas appear, seeds are planted, and finally everyone will work together to reap the harvest.

Technology can accelerate change, but it does not cause it. (Jim Collins)

Being sensitive to employees' needs, while correctly staffing the operation is a formable challenge, but it is one we need to take on.

The search for excellence is a journey not a destination.

Your attitude is the banner of your values and character.

The level of loss you accept is the inverse of the success and security you will earn and enjoy.

Stand on the principle that reducing production volumes drives up the fixed cost ratio, which increases the cost/ton. In most cases we need to protect our production volumes and resist any detractors to efficiency.

The incurred downtime effect would be dollars lost compared to the purchasing nickels saved.

Common cost cutting techniques in a tight economic market are counter-productive to progressive value added decision making.

Never let reactive policies dictate or alter your principles. Policies should always support sound principle.

Value-driven decisions hold up to the test of time.

Staying principle-centered is the right way to operate. (Stephen Covey)

CHAPTER 5

When you do the right thing, the right people notice.

Behold the turtle, he makes progress only when he sticks his neck out. (James Conant)

Openly re-evaluating our course regularly is critical, not only due to financial implications, but sometimes because the goals change.

Sometimes our greatest obstacles to solutions are our own paradigms.

People who don't make mistakes end up working for people who do. (John Maxwell)

Creativity could be defined as a vision unshrouded by limitations of the past.

In many cases, it is management's role to make sure to point out the improvement needs and then step back and let our people invent.

I would estimate potential productivity gains of 5% to 30% are available if we did better at designing our equipment in line with our operator's preferences.

Walls will come down as management steps forward first and shows sincere appreciation.

To manage is to direct and coordinate a process or plan, to lead is to empower the heart.

I let them know I am willing to get into the transformation trenches with them.

The joint plan was better because it included a diversity of viewpoints that balanced the approach. And it achieved buy-in and acceptance of all the groups.

Our enemy was the *at risk behavior* not the individuals.

Many good ideas were shouted, some heard, and yet few done.

The biggest motivation seems to be completing the A-priority list and then publicizing the progress.

As you build success on the easier initial projects, your people gain self-confidence and become ready to handle the tougher loss challenges.

Most major victories must first be set-up in the hearts and minds of the people, and then they will flow into the field situations. We, the leaders, must choreograph these victories.

No direction, no plan, and low expectation, so—chaos ruled.

Safety commitment – the ultimate show of respect to each other and our families.

A ship does not sail on yesterday's wind. We need a new vision and plan, but without the right Senior Team, it is rudderless.

The change-process leadership cannot be delegated or hired out.

The rallying leader must be able to sell the common goal of security, before the people sign-on to the mission, value, and plan.

If you choose the *committed transformation*, then you have truly chosen an operation life change. The potential security earned is huge, and it will be a dynamic, breathing, evolving operating style.

Holding to your values and altering your course as new rocks appear, will be the duties of management.

The gamble with the committed path is that if you don't stay involved and sincere, the workforce will feel betrayed, and ground will be lost.

If you choose the compliant transformation approach, then you have chosen an operation based on requirements and rules. Its longevity relies on enforcement and is usually fear-controlled.

In business, a successful company strives to synergistically increase value using available resources like investors' money, employees' giftings, community support, and our natural resources.

The challenge is to achieve the commitment from everyone, along with all their resources, and get them working together.

We will need that energy and persuasion to win out peoples' hearts, but when we do, and we will, a GREAT Company will be born.

CHAPTER 6

Don't ever feel hesitant to ask for help, all that says is that you have either tackled a project that is stretching you beyond your experience/skill set—and that's admirable—and/or you are sharing ownership to empower someone else's help.

To whom much is given, much is expected is a biblical quote reminding us that God has gifted us to in turn *pay it forward*.

Accepting the calling to be a value influencer or mentor is a very high honor.

Integrity of character will produce integrity in process, and both are required for a GREAT Company.

Your character will set the standard. Leading by example with respect to values, will be critical.

We will earn commitment and we will succeed through everyone's contribution.

It is truly satisfying to help people maximize their potential and unite with others to weave the common thread of security.

I realize He wants to share knowledge and timing into our lives. But we have to choose to enter into that type of relationship with Him.

Meet people where they are, but stand on strong principles. They may not like or agree with you, but a common direction will be respected and supported.

Leaders are sold out to their beliefs, are totally committed, and are loved AND hated. If you lead because you think everyone will appreciate it, you picked the wrong profession.

Your resolve to leadership must come from your passion to influence positive change, even if some do not appreciate it.

Improving tomorrow requires forgiving and often forgetting the past, and the leadership must help that transition by taking the first step.

It may not be your fault that you are in the hole, but it is your fault if you stay and wallow in it.

Look at a grievance as a grudge symptom. Usually the complaint is just a vehicle to vent frustration.

Leadership must rise above the pettiness, and build for a greater connection—we need to earn their buy-in by asking for their input.

Attitude is a reflection of the atmosphere.

You get the standard that you expect and inspect.

Our actions communicate our true message, and our people are always listening for inconsistencies.

Our autopsies of a loss should be centered around the root cause and preventative counter measures, not the blame.

I prefer to teach that I will take responsibility for the first mistake, but we all must pay the tuition.

Over 85% of losses are behavior oriented, but if we lash-out after them upfront, the situation usually gets adversarial. If we look for all the contributing factors first, operator admittance usually comes out.

We must communicate and follow up on our expectations.

I was always taught to try to travel alternative paths to increase exposure for learning and follow-up opportunities. It helps to keep you sharp and deters mentally drifting.

Integrity usually triumphs blunt force, and it always builds respect and honor.

CHAPTER 7

It's the coach's job to coordinate all the different agendas and to maximize the final performance.

The main driver should not be to compete against our fellow employees; we should view them as internal clients since our achievements support and affect them.

Channeling the competitive nature toward the benchmark goal and continuous improvement percentage is always best.

All we can do is inform our employees about market pressures and competitor's advances, track our progress, and focus on getting a little better every day.

Complacency is the breakfast of the losers.

Good is the enemy of Great...

Remember an ounce of prevention is better than a pound of cure.

Reactive is condition steered and symptom controlled. Pro-active is value driven and root addressed.

Our management goal should be to build the boat and position the sail so the momentum continues propelling the boat forward.

If the ark is built right, team success is fed internally and we, management, become scorekeepers.

The vital link is to devise KPI's, Key Performance Indicators, and PI's, Performance Indicators, that tell the whole story.

Giving people too much information or pounding them for results outside of their influence is counter-productive.

Make sure you are ready to record, track, and follow-up on the downtime before you ask for it. If you emphasize the importance of getting all the downtime, and it is not utilized and acted on, the workforce's commitment eventually will be lost.

Human nature reminds us that if our effort today makes tomorrow better, chances are, we will comply. If you add a sincere pat on the back, there's even a better chance they will remain committed.

What you celebrate, you reap.

Sincerely praising in public today reduces the frequency of private correction needed tomorrow.

The first show of respect must be a total commitment of everyone to prevention.

Empowering every employee is the key to greatness.

We may buy their attendance, muscle, and compliance but excellence requires commitment, creativity, and loyalty—true gifts of the heart.

Equipment allowed to stay below "top condition" costs us twice—once to repair it (which we will have to fix eventually) and again for the loss it creates.

The challenge is tuning in to their WIIFM channel—music for their ears.

Success is earned in the trenches, learned through the detail, but celebrated in dominance.

Most companies either avoid the challenge by accepting current performance or by adopting a suffocating program that does not respect the presiding general's strengths, passion, and plan.

CHAPTER 8

GREAT companies are birthed from the foundation of values and matured through the execution of balanced process.

In a volume sensitive business, the efficiency focus pays higher dividends than the starving techniques.

There's a Him-possible solution. We just have to find it, and we will.

We were called to carry our values openly in every facet of our lives.

We have taken the position that to be servants means helping people achieve their potential and security in this life and the thereafter.

Just as there is correct value balance in business, there must also be in our personal lives.

Everyone and everything can be changed positively with unlimited time and money, but in our case, we have neither.

With hard assets repositioned, let's refine structure, design the process, sell the change, and implement the system.

CHAPTER 9

Most companies mismanage and under-prioritize the human resource side of the business. Development of high performance teams is a very important step in the creation of a GREAT organization.

With conviction in our hearts, sincerity shows up and motivates.

Great vision and values are powerless without the right team, so the key is in choosing the right personnel fit.

Our company is filled with lots of good people, but our job now is to load the bus with the best, ones who have the least baggage.

The surviving companies are those that run light, lean, and flexible, but more importantly are efficient and effective.

We do not always have time for their character to positively mature and their drive to evolve from compliant to committed.

Skills and tactics we can teach, but attitude and character are what is brought to the table.

Eliminate those people who drain the energy and enthusiasm from the team.

In looking for your people, search for three qualities: Integrity, Intelligence, and Energy. And if they don't have the first one, the other two will kill you. (Warren Buffet)

An individual's character is the *jewel we seek.*

Our employees always deserve to know the expectations, boundaries, and business format. Remember, they are our copartners in our company.

The career development process shows our investment and interest in each employee's future, and it telegraphs their commitment to the operation.

A solid evaluation process can help the committed employees to perfect their performance over time, and it also weeds out the under-performers.

A well-balanced evaluation covers: work and safety records, attitude, cooperation, certifications, and individual improvement focus areas.

Experience has shown that individuals with maintenance backgrounds are commonly better in-tune with taking care of their equipment as compared to run-and-gun operators.

Complimentary teams broaden the experience base and opinion scope. They are more beneficial than look-a-like groups. The diversity is healthy if the chemistry is right.

Each manager must be a perfect match to the corporate and operational values. How can a manager communicate and lead a team in a 'change message' they personally don't completely believe.

Our weakest link is commonly the detractor within our own walls.

Flat organizational charts help in communication, empowerment, and the delegation of accountability to all levels.

I would assemble the strongest management team at the operation of highest potential, not necessarily the site of the largest problem.

CHAPTER 10

If we are going to build our ark to travel at max speed, I'm recommending the *servant leadership* style.

The basic premise is that the entire senior management and support departments work for the frontline.

The concept is that everyone is working toward a bigger purpose and to have a wider influence. This will be foreign to most of our managers.

There is far more reward, personally and corporately, in sowing for a greater harvest than carving a single trophy.

We must teach our managers to build and arm the soldiers, rather than mounting the charge on their own.

To serve is an honor and by its perfection, authority will be earned.

Senior management is forced to choose between their home responsibilities and work. All kinds of negative consequences evolve from that mandate, including the workaholic tendencies that have become an accepted trait of those positions. We have a moral responsibility to break that cycle and to honor the family.

Our society views servanthood as a weak character trait, but the truth is that it takes a more secure person to show humility.

Humility is not thinking less of oneself, but it's thinking of others first and of yourself less often.

Lateral inter-departmental teamwork is where we will yield the major gains.

I have seen numerous corporate transformation failures. One of the most common causes is because the process is not personalized for the individual operation.

We need to declare the victories. When we infect our managers with the dream, they can lead the multitudes. As Dr. Martin Luther King announced, "I have a dream…"

God chooses to carry out His plans through His people for His people. If we get up every day and look where He is working around us, and join Him, our works are anointed.

If the leadership group truly believed, we could not only weather the storm, but could *lead the field*—a good company could grow to be GREAT.

How this story ends, is up to you. Most people and organizations quit, because it gets tough. Some tried and failed, because they doubted and complied. But a few soared. Why? Because they were committed.

There is a place in the market for World Class Excellence, and we can fulfill that calling.

The commitment we make today will reap a foothold into tomorrow's security.

Helping people see reality and generate passion toward their involvement in a solution, is what visionary leadership is all about.

CHAPTER 11

People buy into a plan only after they buy into the leader's character. That buy-in must start with communication, which leads to respect and trust.

The people you lead will carefully analyze your motives and *listen* to your actions. Your words will be tested with fire. If your position is stamped "sincere" and "honorable," they will follow. Take this opportunity to influence and help your people attain their potential and destiny.

Servant leadership may be a new concept and we will be patient in its growth toward perfection but we will be intolerant of anyone who does not embrace it.

Respect of each other, will be our trademark.

Momentum is the most powerful change agent. (John Maxwell)

We intend to set our people's aspirations high and help the team attain them.

Our position will be to control our future and security through good ideas, a passion for excellence, and prioritized hard work.

We will excel through personal and team achievement.

Your crews will revere your opinion highly. To them you are the breath of the Company. If you keep the Mission honored and in focus, your people will support it.

Safety is the uncompromisable value. It is a basic requirement in every decision, it's not a choice.

Prevention is the belief that eliminating all types of losses, injury, violations, downtime, rework, and waste, results in high efficiency and eventually security.

Teamwork is achievable when everyone is committed to the common goal of operational security.

Mutual Respect is the building block for relationships and trust. It is showing sincere appreciation for each other and valuing everyone as a key part of the team. Utilizing employee input is a strong sign of respect and fosters the best ideas, buy-in, and morale.

Communication is the vital link between all members of the team and the coordinated movement from today to our victories of tomorrow.

Training is an important facet of individual and business development. It is not only a key to employee empowerment, but it's also critical for intelligent decision making and process refinement.

Accountability is the acceptance of responsibility for your actions and circle of influence.

Continuous Process Improvement challenges each of us to keep looking for the most efficient (safest and productive) way possible.

Reverence is the action of honoring our God for our opportunities, giftings, protection, and His wisdom.

In Him all things are possible. He promised it and He will help us do it.

If a house is built on a firm foundation it will stand. If seed is sown in fertile ground, it will bear fruit.

We will reign. And when it gets tough, He will be expecting a call.

CHAPTER 12

When we ask someone to change habits and attitude, we must first convince them it is worth that effort.

Most people will run from change, but it is in fact change that will separate us from the pack and earn our survival.

Some workforce groups feel security can be negotiated; the truth is, security is only saved for the leader of the field.

A man changed against his will, is of the same opinion still. (Dale Carnegie)

No one can usher in change like the immediate supervisor.

Senior management will have a role to introduce, explain, teach, and support, but the implementation and follow-up will be yours.

We are climbing a peak that few trek; one that only teams ever reach the summit.

Only freed from past burdens can we take advantage of the present. It is our job as leaders to purge the closet of distractions.

The greatest innovator is necessity, and there should be no one more incented than we are. If we can't get our people to accept change and begin tracking toward success (mentally and physically), we must not have explained it correctly.

Some will question our motives, but if we lay out the facts correctly, then the change we are asking for should obviously be beneficial to all of us.

Our duty is to present the honest truth and help steer pro-actively toward solutions; our people are smart enough to see the need and their personal gain.

Let's keep job security as the focal point.

The fact is that we are all naturally resistant to change, to some degree.

When we introduce the subject of change, we must be respectful yet confident, slow yet methodical, understanding yet full of conviction. Your demeanor in the discussion will be a huge determining factor in our teams' acceptance.

Some will never get close enough to the cliff to envision the flight or see the prize below.

Some need assurance that the pain is worth the gain. They will calculate the investment needed and the expected return.

They will also analyze where they will be if they invest in change-efforts and it fails. This person needs help measuring all the unknowns.

Most companies fail to personally address these variables, thus the employees never join the team.

We all realize nothing is achieved without action, an event of change.

Most people can be convinced to accept accountability for their commitment to their position or roles, as long as they are not responsible for the final outcome of things they cannot control.

The results will show that numerous actions conducted by highly accountable, tasked individuals meshed together will produce success.

Once success is felt and confidence secured, individuals will begin crossing the boundaries of previously entrenched roles and a team will be formed. It is those teams that produce the GREAT results and voluntarily accept accountability for the outcome.

To conquer resistance, management must build a plan that slowly incorporates accountability in parts, so that the system emerges with outcome buy-in from all when it matures.

Negativism must be exposed as counter-productive to the quest of earning security, an enemy of the state.

We must rally behind the common values we share, and march toward a clear goal.

Each time we push the problem to the next level, we progress.

If people feel the appreciation and see the benefits of their efforts, the rolling ball eventually will be self-sustaining. Our job will be to anticipate upcoming obstacles and preventively lead our people in addressing them.

I would usually take the second best idea that came from a committee, rather than my own idea that may have been even a little better.

Challenge a group to find the solution and you can get a commitment to the victory.

Sideline the differences, work skills, and ethics, and center on the common goal: job security is earned through efficiency.

Empowerment is the strongest technology of this century, yet many companies are slow to embrace it.

People don't have to agree with all your beliefs, but the respect for your character is paramount. They have to see your commitment to them.

People don't care how much you know until they know how much you care.

The first step will be to change a person's perspective of the future. Great leaders sell potential.

Action and heart without wisdom will leave us frustrated and beat down.

Management must take responsibility for improving the workplace environment. With these changes, attitudes evolve and the potential and altitude lifts.

I always recommend starting with a familiar platform from their past and expand on the successes.

Potential we are given, security we will earn.

Change commonly requires the sacrificing of self, for the team gain of much, and in the end I am sure it will liberate our future.

CHAPTER 13

We will not proceed until the Mission Statement and Foundational Values are ingrained in the team.

I expect to see fruit from their servant leadership, and we will need that platform to build from.

Another technique I can see you are using is *divide and conquer*. You have broken a lot of our big issues into small pieces, then prioritized and finally delegated responsibility. Before everyone even realizes it, the whole elephant is eaten, one bite at a time!

I am seeing a lot of *excellence* and a little bit of *average*.

Pretty good is not what we are building. I can be a little more patient with workforce transformation, but our leadership must show strong, value-centered character now.

Remember we committed to our families that we would protect the house.

Be a cheerleader and show appreciation for the efforts, but be a driver to excellence as well.

Incentives are strong motivators and have a place in the right season.

A good incentive plan will be multi-faceted and have an incentive share, but will not be seen as an employee entitlement program.

Motivating a person to improve their position in life and have a positive influence on others will always be the right thing to do.

Follow your heart, keep preaching balanced improvement and everyone's a winner.

We have to be very careful not to abuse the trust and respect that has been developed.

Many companies erroneously tried to save their way to a profit. Most of the surviving companies have now redirected focus back to efficiency.

Integrity Process is based around what we call the Principles of Process. Step One is to Gather information. Step Two is to Refine the process. Step Three is to Monitor results.

Any positive change usually results in some good and a little bad.

We have to sell an operating plan that is consistent with our values and promotes progress.

As long as the wheel is moving, it stands up. When it slows or stops, it falls over. It is all about forward motion and we call it progress. If it goes in reverse, we slide back and eventually it steers to a stall and falls over. Moral of the story—we either advance our process or we fall and backslide. Idling is not an outcome state of where we want to be.

CHAPTER 14

Each pillar will be made up of: Gathering Tools, Refining Procedures, Monitoring Systems. The pillar provides security only when GRM is continuous and supported by all. When we utilize it as the backbone of our transformation, our entire teams will see Integrity Process as the means to the end—our path to earn security.

When an operation fully grasps the potential of every employee looking hard to find preventative measures to avert losses, the sky is the limit.

We need everyone to think like an owner, look and listen like an inspector, and be a part of the solution.

Building respect first, by being committed to the communicated plan and responding to Kaizen ideas, shows management has committed to the transformation process. Then and only then, will the workforce start looking deeper and in more detail.

We realize an empowered accountable workforce can do a far better job. We have some reprogramming to do, but it's very feasible. And it's fun to keep score when everyone pulls together.

If the workforce and first line management believes in our motives and we respect them in our treatment of their input, their buy-in will be earned. This will empower the refining progresses.

It is also important that we train a *client service concept* into our employees. We need them to look around and find things that could be done to strengthen safe output (efficiency), even if it's outside *their area*. This motivation is a trait of GREATNESS.

If everyone raises the standard of expectation, everyone's families win.

Passion indicates your giftings and destiny. It is those journeys that commonly bear the most fruit in our lives.

The gravity of the importance of our leadership decisions should never be taken lightly. Many people rely on our wisdom to custom make the plan to help protect our house.

I would always encourage you to analyze the facts, gain input from your team, lift it up in prayer, and then follow your heart.

Sometimes, our guidance comes in the simplest of indicators.

CHAPTER 15

Assuring balance is an important part of the maturation process.

As we go through different seasons, we may temporarily prioritize our time differently, but never can we allow our hearts' balance to change.

I am not going to say that focusing on a multi-faceted agenda is easy, but I believe the Lord anoints our steps and gives us the wisdom to succeed and stay balanced.

I don't worry about tomorrow when I keep my motives on His service. The peace He gives me is one that goes beyond all understanding.

I strongly believe time is a gift and it should be invested wisely. I will take responsibility for how I spend every minute. In many cases I actually calculate the time taken versus the reward, to prioritize their ranking. It's a disciplined approach but it keeps my eyes on the main target.

The challenge is to improve our personal efficiencies so that we gain time to achieve more of our prioritized *to-do* list.

Your heart and relationship is what God seeks. When you set your motives around Him, He will direct your path.

I really believe God is going to use these current economic challenges to deeply touch a lot of people through your leadership.

As we continue illuminating the vision of security in our people, we as leaders, must also be right there with the plan. It is during these times they will be the most moldable.

Our people understand dollars, and thus we should all realize the cost of loss and its effect on our future.

Be a master of momentum and keep the positive alive. Be mindful of the information sharing and agenda pace, yet keep the throttle maximized.

As we build confidence in the process and work hard to bring the backlogs down, the prevention results will result in lower injuries, less downtime, reduced rework, and eliminated waste.

Being on the front end allows us to solve the problem at the root, set our own priorities, and also use the money from losses for the future by not paying for yesterday's mistakes.

Hands-on training of Best Practices yields big gains in Safety and Productivity alike.

If you are not going to use your gifts, you risk losing them to someone else who will put them to work.

Analysis paralysis sends a very bad message to creativity and innovation.

We desperately need your people's ideas, and the best encouragement you can give them is for them to see us investing in those ideas and getting them done.

We have a GREAT thing started here, and a lot of people will gain when we pull it off. But it's going to take us driving every potential path we can find and anticipating the obstacles that will face us.

The quest of continuous process improvement is a worthy adversary, but the sense of accomplishment along the way is a heartfelt motivation that energizes our next move.

Every improvement action will result in a countering, reactive effect, sometimes immediate, but most of the time in arrears. That is why continuous refinement is a mandate and is forward-focused.

Good is achieved by a solid plan and aspiration, GREAT is achieved by the refining of the plan and perspiration!

I protectively look for ways to preventatively guard the ground we have taken.

CHAPTER 16

Everything in life can be handled at face value, or alternatively taken deeper. Level one is good but deeper challenges reward greater things.

We are all gifted with different strengths, but as we bring them to the table of service, it is their level of diligence and perseverance that determines the reward.

I truly believe if our motives are correct, the fruit of our labor will be honored and multiplied.

All of our strongest business principles can be traced back to The SOURCE.

And I am not bashful to say God is my source. Politically that statement might not be accepted well, but I believe politics' biggest problem is its lack of standing on strong infallible principle.

If you stay sensitive to the calling, He will help you excel at all four facets (spiritual, family, career, and hobbies/health) together.

People spend their lives waiting for a burning bush experience, but for me, it's that faint small voice in my spirit.

If you set your direction to serve others, He will equip you with the vision and tools.

The level of our future opportunities is shouldered on the expectations we have had and the character we have refined.

Integrity is a place my daddy works. It's a place where a bunch of people work together to take care of their families. And it works because they let everyone give something to the team.

Integrity pays our bills and honors our loyalty.

Integrity is the standard by which we serve. Being true to one's morals, values, and beliefs. Knowing you have been faithful to yourself despite life's temptations to change you. It is a character choice made by the heart and shown through your hands. It's to commit your best with no visible reward, but it feels good inside, so you ought to try it.

I define Integrity as the self-directed alignment between one's values, calling, and conduct. It is a stance of unselfish belief and service to others that requires a deep level of sincerity and authenticity. It is a heart driven lifestyle that is infectious to those around you. The pay-off is in seeing people positively influenced, sharing their giftings, and fulfilling their destiny.

The important point is to be true to the values of the team that keeps our foundation solid, and from which all is built.

We asked each employee to embrace and commit to a Mission Statement. It was a commitment to a unified focus on security. We asked you to step away from past practice and help us create a preventative approach to our future.

We challenged everyone to strap on a code of integrity and commit to a quest of continuous improvement versus stagnant stale complacency.

We reorganized, built on mutual foundational values, and began a process that is earning a GREAT status. That standing is our best assurance of economic security.

It's the marriage of partners' talents that provided the fuel, a technical plan of transformation which offered a spark, but it is the continuous drive for excellence that is the catalyst for the future.

I asked you to believe in something that you could not touch or see, and it required faith. I promised you rewards for that choice. Our heart is that each of you choose to join the Integrity Family and unite in one vision.

We should always try hard and do our best, but isn't the GREATEST GOAL of Integrity to fill our wagons with as many of our friends as possible and get across the finish line together?

Achieving the influence, or platform, to help each other make the right choices is a weighty calling, but one we have been equipped to handle.

Each of you has the choice, to continue the quest to strengthen your character's integrity. You will define your moral fiber and attitude, and they will be the seeds that are scattered.

Each one of us will be responsible for all the seeds we sow. We will also be accountable for the indecision in our lives. Remember, not taking a stand or avoiding a choice, is a 'NO' DECISION.

I challenge you to continue paying forward to others. That type of service is what fills the wagon.

Some days, I thought we had been alone. In actuality, He was protecting and carrying us. When we give to others, as His word teaches, we allow Him to join us.

My prayer is that each of you would accept His protection, provision, and wisdom AND that you share it with another. And remember, He has respectfully invited you to call Him and make a reservation, so for those who have not decided yet, He will *leave the light on for you* if you want to join Him. Amen.

Note: To assist your review of the 'Notable Quotes' a recorded CD or downloadable MP3 clip can be obtained from **www.IntegrityDevelopment.us/purchase**

Appendix B
Support Resources

APPENDIX B.01

SUGGESTED READING LIST & BIBLIOGRAPHY

1. Bennett, Dr. James. *The Loss Prevention System.* Bibliojunky, 1997.
2. Blackaby, H. & R. and C. King. *Experiencing God.* B&H Publishing, 2008.
3. Carnegie, Dale. *How to Win Friends and Influence People.* Pocket Books, 1981.
4. Collins, Jim. *Good to Great.* Harper Collins Publishers, 2001.
5. Covey, Stephen. *Principle Centered Leadership.* Simon & Schuster, 1990.
6. Deming, Dr. W. E. *Out of Crisis.* MIT Center of Advanced Engineering, 2000.
7. Dennis, Pascal. *Andy and Me.* Productivity Press, 2005.
8. God. *The Holy Bible.*
9. Goldratt, Eliyahu. *The Goal: A Process of Ongoing Improvement.* North River Press, 2012.
10. Harvey, Eric. & Al Lucia. *Walk the Talk.* Performance Publishing, 1995.
11. Hunter, James C. *The Servant.* Prima Publishing, 1998.
12. Lawson, Ken. *Successful Negotiating.* New Holland, 2010.
13. Liker, Jeffery. *The Toyota Way.* McGraw-Hill, 2004.
14. Mann, David. *Creating a Lean Culture.* Productivity Press, 2010.
15. Maxwell, John. *The 360° Leader.* Nelson Study Books, 2005.
16. Peters, Tom and Robert Waterman, Jr. *In Search of Excellence.* Harper & Row Publishers, 1982.
17. Robbins, Anthony. *Awaken the Giant Within.* Free Press, 1991.
18. Warren, Rick. *The Purpose Driven Life.* Zondervan, 2002.
19. Zigler, Zig. *Over the Top.* Thomas Nelson, 1997.

Note: The selected bibliography is a list of resources and suggested readings. A best effort has been made to cite referenced works; if some credits were missed, apologies are offered. In some cases, the original source of a quote has been lost and the quote itself altered through evolutions of paraphrasing. For the most part, the content of this book is based on the author's experience and expertise, but includes the influence of many teachers.

PROPERTY EVALUATION CATEGORIES

Primary

Secondary

I. FINANCIAL

Primary	Secondary
1) Employee Liabilities (Retiree Medical/Pension/Black Lung/Work Comp.)	1) Subsidence Liabilities
2) Environmental Liabilities (Water/Reclamation/Seals)	2) Workman's Compensation Rate
3) Financial Liabilities to Creditors	3) Mine Inventory Cost/Credit
4) Bonds	4) Depreciation
5) Royalties (Coal & Surface)	5) Insurance Policies
6) Equipment & Property Leases	6) Transferable Tax Credits
7) Cost Statements/Cash Flow/Profit Records	7) Receivables & History
8) Purchase Price & Terms	8) Operation Reputation/Focus
9) Advanced Minimums (Past/Future/Recoup.)	9) Warehouse Inventory
10) Litigation (Past & Pending)	10) Closing Fund
	11) Asset or Stock Sale
	12) Vendor Term Agreements

II. SALES

Primary	Secondary
1) Current Contracts (Price, Term, Quality, & Specs)	1) Reject Spec. Levels
2) Future Market Expectation (Medium & Long Term)	2) Premiums/Penalty & History
3) Transportation Costs & Carriers	3) Outsourcing Potentials
4) Synergetic Value to Current Properties	4) Storage Capabilities
5) Market Specifications vs. Mine Specifications	5) Washabilities
	6) Local Competition
	7) Local Sales Opportunities (Transp. Adv.)
	8) List of Clients (Past & Current)

III. RESERVES/ENGINEERING

Primary	Secondary
1) Current Quality & Quantity in Classification	1) Defined Operation Boundaries
2) Current & Future Quality ISOPAC Review (Thickness/Sulfur/Btu/Ash/Chlorine/Met. Specs.)	2) Coal & Surface Ownership
3) Current & Future Conditions Map (Overburden/Immediate Floor & Grade/ Immediate & Main Roof/Old Works/Sandstone/Water/Faults)- HAZARDS MAP	3) Coal Channel Sample/Cores/Strat. Columns
	4) Level of Quality Confidence
	5) Define Neighboring Coal Ownership & Potentials
	6) Adverse Property
4) Level of Geological Confidence	7) Lease Terms & Assumability
5) Permit Maps	8) Delineate All Coal Seams
	9) Parting History
	10) Roof History (Current & Adjacent Operations)
	11) Previous Mining
	12) Oil/Gas Right & Drilling History
	13) Local Restrictions
	14) Permit Renewal Issues & Timing
	15) Mining Notices
	16) Drilling Program
	17) Level of Operational Involvement from Eng.
	18) Outstanding Permitting & Ops Plan Status

PROPERTY EVALUATION CATEGORIES (CONT.)

Primary

Secondary

IV. MINE OPERATIONS
1) Major Projects/Upgrades (Current/Future)
2) Projected Capital Expenditures (Current/Future)
3) Production Rates (Past/Present)
4) Mine Plan Timing & Concerns
5) Safety Record (Injuries/Violations) & Restrictions
6) Potential Regulatory Changes Effects

1) Production Methods & Number of Units
2) Equipment Condition
3) Downtime (Level/Majors)
4) Coal Cutting Conditions
5) Roof Drilling Conditions
6) Roof Support System
7) Reclaimable Supplies (HV/Track/Belt Systems/...)
8) Power Cost
9) Unusual Operating Cost
10) Rebuild Schedule
11) Total Asset List
12) Ventilation Problems & Future Shaft Plans
13) Production Limiters (Belts/Plant/Gas/Skips/ Freshwater/Discharge Water/Power/Conditions)
14) Seal Discharges
15) Local Services/Supply Support

V. PREPARATION
1) Yield
2) Refuse Area
3) Major Projects/Upgrades
4) Common Shipping Delays (Truck/Rail/Barge)
5) Plant Efficiency (Areas of Improvement)

1) Slurry Impoundment
2) Raw Coal Blending
3) Rail Sidings
4) Cost Per Ton (Past/Projected)
5) Flow Chart
6) Sampling System
7) Dry Screen Potentials
8) In-line Ash Analyzer System
9) Major Rebuilds
10) Trucking Cost & Issues
11) Surface Layout Maps

VI. HUMAN RESOURCES
1) Workforce Quality
2) Management Quality
3) Benefit Costs
4) Labor Rate & Salaries
5) Workforce Hiring Demographics

1) Schedules
2) List of "Past Practices"
3) Job Outsourcing
4) Absenteeism
5) Paid Days Off
6) Severance Packages & Contracts
7) Average Age
8) Benefits Compared to Competitors
9) Union History & Influence
10) Vehicle Program
11) Organizational Chart
12) Incentive Plans
13) Employee Handbook/Contract

PROCESS STUDY OBSTACLES

To establish *Best Practices* for every job and process, thorough process study and operator input must be gathered. Below are some potential study pitfalls:

1. The study can pit individuals against each other.
   a) Emphasize it is not about individual performance but about process improvement issues and building better Best Practices (BP's).
   b) Never post the individuals' names when ranking performances.

2. Results commonly reflect only short periods, thus they do not show the full picture.
   a) Make sure to include the full shifts and include spans over numerous situations to assure results are representative.

3. A method of self-evaluation is not provided.
   a) Give feedback to employee privately and share benchmarking goals.

4. Feedback is not immediate.
   a) Do a quick download before auditor leaves section and then make sure results are conveyed back to the operators promptly.

5. Time studies can encourage speed and short cuts over Best Practices.
   a) Make sure study is balanced and all parameters are evaluated.

6. Some processes are not represented well by this technique.
   a) Be sensitive to this and include observer comments to help explain intangible effects, along with measurable performance indicators.

7. All bottlenecks are not identified.
   a) Auditor must review micro and macro effects.

8. Auditors are commonly inexperienced, poor teachers, and/or weak analyzers.
   a) Careful support and training must be offered.

9. The study may seem to be under-cutting first management authority.
   a) Auditors should go out of their way to emphasize the process study is for the purpose of gathering information and will be important in reducing delays and process bottlenecks.

BUILDING INTEGRITY   APPENDIX B.04

MINE ECONOMICS 101

General Case Truths*

1. In Mine Economics, Fixed Cost represents approximately 50% of the total cost. Thus the actual tons produced influence only 50% of the final Total Cost.

2. Downtime cost is estimated at $100/minute. This is assuming extra production is gained through reduced downtime during the normal shift, and can be sold at normal prices. It is not the same as the profit per minute of the budgeted base tons. The referenced downtime is the production time lost.

3. Many variables affect every cost category, thus every decision will have varying trickle effects.

4. Production decisions and schedule changes must be based on incremental costs vs. revenues for that specific operation. Incremental costs are the extra costs associated with the change in production.
    a) Cost breakdown for incremental tons (Fixed vs. Variable)**

	Total Cost	Fixed Cost	Variable Cost
Labor			
Salary/Wage	$14.00	$14.00	-
Benefit Charges	$6.00	$6.00	-
Roof Support	$4.00	$0.40	$3.60
Maintenance	$6.00	$1.00	$5.00
Supplies	$6.60	$1.10	$5.50
Power	$2.50	$2.00	$0.50
Fuel/Oils	$1.50	$1.00	$0.50
Miscellaneous	$3.00	$1.00	$2.00
Transportation	$6.00	-	$6.00
Royalty	$8.40	-	$8.40
Insurance/Taxes	$6.00	$3.00	$3.00
Preparation Plant	$8.00	$5.00	$3.00
Administration	$3.00	$3.00	-
Total Operation Cost	$75.00	50% = $37.50	50% = $37.50

    b) Downtime Cost (sales opportunity lost)
        Assumed: - Base production is set at 400 clean tons/shift.
                          - Shift time of 9.5hrs × 72% production availability
                          = 410 production minutes/shift
                          thus 400 clean tons/shift ÷ 410 production minutes/shift
                          ≈ 1.0 clean tons/minute
        Potential Extra Tonnage Gain   = Production Rate × (Revenue - Variable Cost)
                                          = 1.0 clean tons/minute × ($135/clean ton - $37.50/clean ton)
                                          = $100/minute

    c) Condition Effect***
        If coal thickness varies from 42" to 45" = 0.6% yield, thus cost of savings of $0.73/ton. If extra rock reduced from 6" to 3" = 5.1% yield, thus cost of savings of $5.64/ton.

*Every operation has details that differ from the General Case.
**The example was based on a moderately productive, low seam height, good quality metallurgical coal mine.
***Assumes no effect on productivity.

SUPER UNIT COMPARISONS

Description:
I. Walking Super
1) Manning – 13
2) Ventilation – usually the intake is brought up one side and returned on the other. Alternatively, the air can be coursed up the middle to reduce downwind dust issues.
3) Three cars are used but only one miner can be operated at a time. As one miner is operating, the other is set-up and ready, thus saving the miner place-change-time and some miscellaneous miner delays.

II. Split-Car Super
1) Manning – 15 (add extra face boss and a 4th car driver)
2) Ventilation – the intake is brought up the middle and split to return off each side.
3) Four cars are used but three cars stay together and one car stays with the miner that is cleaning up or moving. Some companies put two cars on each miner all the time, but coal is lost when the miner is moved. The other issue with putting two cars on each miner, as compared to three, is that the loading time per place is lengthened. This usually translates into longer delay times for the roof bolters.
4) There are only four situations in which dual loading should occur (if the roof bolters are considered the bottleneck).
    A. First car of the place.
    B. Last two cars of the place.
    C. If the roof bolter's pace improves and the combined loading rate can be sped up, both miners can operate simultaneously with two cars reporting to each, as long as an operating standard of no more than "x" not bolted anytime during the shift is not exceeded.
    D. Immediately before a *bolter catch-up time* (i.e. third shift, scheduled production delays), as long as an operating standard no more than "y" not bolted will be left at a time.

Split-Car Super Advantages
- Less dust exposure for roof bolters, due to staying on intake air side more consistently.
- Removes the chance of dual loading on one air split.
- Improved cleanup for mined-out place.
- Fourth car driver helps flow, downtime reduction, and speeds up miner move/set-up.
- Second section foreman helps flow and accountability.
- Competition between foremen/crews.
- Better utilization of equipment and manpower.
- The gain is conservatively at least three cars per place.
- Ability to increase the production rate by splitting cars and running both miners, if the roof bolting rate can be increased.

Pushing-out the Bolter Bottleneck

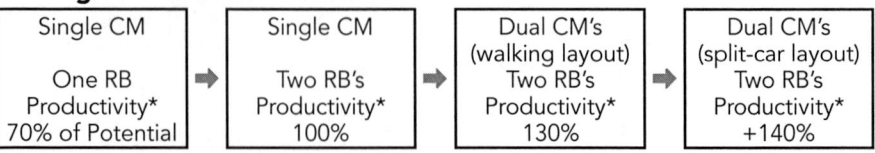

(CR - Continuous Miner)
(RB - Double Boom Roof Bolter)
*Extremely site- and operating-specific

CRITICAL PERFORMANCE EFFICIENCY RATIOS (ER'S)

I. Production Efficiency Ratio (A key if production crew limited)

$$\frac{\text{Total Footage Cut}}{\text{Total Shift Minutes} - \text{Total Production Delay to Load (all codes)}} = \frac{\text{feet}}{\text{up minute}}$$

II. Bolting Efficiency Ratio (A key if bolting crew limited)

$$\frac{\text{Total Footage Bolted}}{\text{Total Shift Minutes} - \text{Total Bolter Delays}} = \frac{\text{feet}}{\text{up minute}}$$

III. Operational Availability Ratio (A key if non-maintenance delay limited)

$$\frac{(\text{Total Shift Minutes} - \text{Non-maint. Delay to Load (100+300+400 series codes)})}{\text{Total Shift Minutes}} = \%$$

IV. Belt Availability Ratio (A key if belt availability limited)

$$\frac{(\text{Total Shift Minutes} - \text{Belt Delay to Load (200 series codes)})}{\text{Total Shift Minutes}} = \%$$

V. Maintenance Availability Ratio (A key if equipment availability limited)

$$\frac{(\text{Total Shift Minutes} - \text{Maint. Delay to Load (500 series codes)})}{\text{Total Shift Minutes}} = \%$$

Note: Delay Code Series
- 100 – Outby
- 200 – Belt
- 300 – Conditions
- 400 – Operations
- 500 - Maintenance

MINE PLANNING 201

Correct Mine Planning facilitates effective operations, support flow, and minimizes variation.

1. Lay out panels perpendicular to questionable geology; mining can be truncated as production economics erode.

2. The number of entries driven should be based on a number of variables: the mining system process bottleneck, long-term ventilation needs, roof and floor sensitivity to advancement rate, unit width with respect to vertical and horizontal pressure, effect of water infusion on the mining process, and the reserve geological dimension restrictions.

3. Pillar dimensions should not only be calculated from roof control needs, but also haulage constraints, cut-depth restrictions, and their effect of various process bottlenecks.

4. Angled cross-cuts should be considered, as they speed-up turning the cross-cut and can enhance haulage rates.

5. Unit lay-outs should favor past practice unless a material improvement can be expected. If a change is warranted, explain it thoroughly, vet all effects, and plan the transition.

6. Partiality should be given to lay-outs with minimal moves and set-ups, unless the productivity of the system is overwhelmingly net-positive. Consistent production usually pays dividends.

7. The best production cut sequence should be carefully laid out to compensate for the haulage, ventilation, dust exposure, bottlenecks, and expected variations.

8. An investment made into a mining hazard map almost always pays dividends.

9. Trends in relationships between surface topography, linears, faulting, roof lithology and coal characteristics can give clues to future expectations (e.g., water infusion, sulfur trends, etc.).

10. Mining direction with respect to the grade and strike should trigger a list of pro-active rules to mitigate effects.

11. Horizontal stresses can commonly be downplayed if entries are aligned with the favored direction.

12. Linears in many cases will forecast potential problem areas, especially where they intersect.

13. Surface topography and stream channels usually map corresponding underground issues (water infusion, roof control, seam thinning, soft bottom). The exact correlated location underground can commonly vary by 200 ft. left or right.

14. Mine lay-outs should minimize outby work where possible (i.e. seal areas vs. ventilating old works).

15. Parallel entries and extra overcasts not only reduce air resistance, but they provide alternative access routes, if isolated roof falls become an issue.

16. Beltlines should be dimensioned so that an inspection/service vehicle can be driven alongside.

17. Air courses should be laid out so inspections can be made with a permissible vehicle.

18. High-grading a reserve maximizes short-term economics, but restricts life.

19. Return-side paneling is the favored general ventilation guideline.

20. Sealing old works keeps the mine focus and resources on current productivity and the future.

21. General rule of thumb is to keep crew-travel times under 45 minutes each way. Longer distances have marked effects on personal and system productivity rates.

22. The water discharge system should be forward-planned. The goal should be a closed water feed system, with pro-active silt retention, water quantity and quality control, and storage flexibility.

23. Most mines only achieve 30% of fan air making it to the working face.

24. Setting ventilation goals at twice the legal minimums is a prudent design criteria.

TYPICAL TIME DISTRIBUTION (SHIFT)
Single Miner Unit-bolting limited, shuttle car haulage

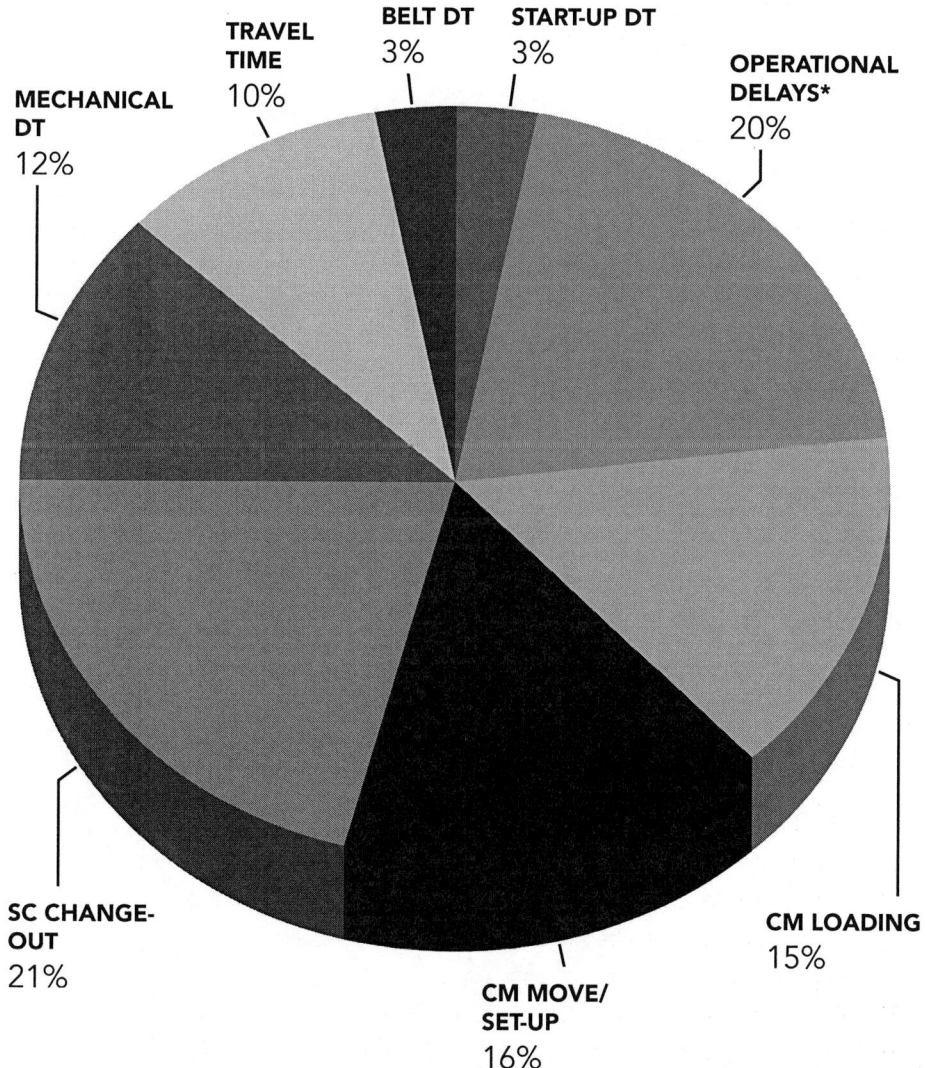

*Operational Delays (20%) = Downwind (5%) + CM Bit Change (4%) + Scoop/Dust (3%) + Misc. (8%)

COST OF LOSS: SAFETY

The largest cost concern of an incident is the actual or potential personal harm to one of our family members. We have a moral responsibility to protect each other. Thus, the actual cost of an injury is unmeasurable.

I. INJURY*

1) Fatality
Direct costs are conservatively estimated over $1 Million. If legal issues are involved, costs will skyrocket further. Many companies originally book estimates at $3 to 5 Million/fatality.

2) Loss Time Injury
Direct cost average is $29,000 (MSHA records) and usually averages over 20 workdays lost/incident.

3) Back Injury
Direct cost average is usually over $75,000/employee claim. Studies have shown over 60% of underground miners will have back issues and most will lose an excess of two months of work-time during their career.

4) Black Lung Claims
Company records studied show average settlements of over $200,000/claim are the norm.

II. VIOLATION

1) Order
-Fines range from $2,000 to +$60,000 – commonly average +$7,000/order

-Lost work time per order often averages $96,000
(2 units × 8 hours/shift × $100/minute)

2) Citation
-Non S&S violation- $100 to $1,000 – average penalty of +$150/violation is normal.

-S&S violation- $1,000 to +$10,000 – commonly average $3,000/violation

---

*OSHA/MSHA studies have reported indirect injury costs average 4.5 times more than the direct costs. Indirect costs include incident related downtime, lower morale, replacement worker training/inefficiencies, insurance costs, corrective action costs, and property damage.

COST OF LOSS: PRODUCTION
A Sample Section*

#	Item	Benefit		Improvement	Realization	Minutes gained per shift	Footage gained per shift	Dollars saved per month ($100/min)
1	Increase morale (attitude)	10	% productivity gain	apply to ft/shift	100%	40.0	20.0	$176,000
2	3rd shift production***	37	ft/day	AFTER maint, bolting, set-up	10% to 80%	100%	26.0	13.0	$114,400
3	Improve utilization of downtime	-20	min/shift	two losses adverted	20% to 100%	40%	12.8	6.4	$56,300
4	Operate 3 SC's instead of 2**	20	% productivity gain	apply to ft/shift	0% to 70%	20%	16.0	8.0	$50,600
5	Increase 3rd shift bolting***	50	bolted ft/day		30% to 80%	60%	14.4	7.2	$43,560
6	Decrease bolt Installation time	-10	% install time	2.5 min/bolt (normal)	0% to 80%	40%	9.6	4.8	$42,240
7	Decrease OSD (roof or floor)	-2	in (+4% yield)	apply to ft/shift	40% to 100%	20%	8.0	4.0	$35,376
8	Reduce absenteeism**	-20	min/shift	efficiency, morale effected	50% to 100%	60%	12.0	6.0	$33,000
9	Eliminate cut sequence delays	-20	min/shift		0% to 80%	40%	6.4	3.2	$28,160
10	Increase SC tram time	-10	sec/trip x 2 trips/car	120 cars/car	0% to 80%	20%	6.4	3.2	$28,160
11	Pre-cut coal for SC during changeout	-30	sec/car	120 cars/shift	50% to 100%	20%	6.0	3.0	$26,400
12	Increase SC payload	20	% of payload	5 to 6 tons/car	40% to 100%	20%	6.0	3.0	$26,400
13	Reduce downwind bolting delays	-30	min/shift		20% to 70%	40%	6.0	3.0	$26,400
14	Decrease mechanical downtime⁵⁵	-20	% of delay	68 min/shift DT	100%	20%	5.4	2.7	$23,936
15	Maximize Hot Seat	-15	min/shift		0% to 80%	40%	4.8	2.4	$21,120
16	Decrease cable "pull-up" delay⁵⁵	-15	min/shift		0% to 80%	40%	4.8	2.4	$21,120
17	Increase CM cut rate	.4	min/place	8 places per shift	0% to 70%	20%	4.4	2.2	$19,712
18	Move SC changeout inby (1 cross-cut)	-10	sec/trip x 2 trips/car	120 cars/shift	20% to 70%	20%	4.0	2.0	$18,024
19	Decrease bolt drilling time	-10	% bolt time	1.5 min/bolt	0% to 80%	40%	3.9	1.9	$16,896
20	Increase cut depth⁵⁵	2	ft/place	8 places per shift	0% to 80%	60%	3.7	1.8	$16,220
21	Reduce SC cable delays	-50	% of delay	30 min/shift	100%	20%	3.0	1.5	$13,200
22	Decrease start-up delays	-30	% of delay	15 min/shift	100%	60%	3.0	1.5	$13,200
23	Decrease travel time	-10	% of trip time	30 trips x 2 trips/shift	0% to 80%	60%	2.9	1.4	$12,672
24	Decrease time for vent/gas check/sights for CM⁵⁵	-50	% of delay	4 min/place	20% to 100%	20%	2.0	1.3	$11,264
25	Decrease CM move time⁵⁵	-20	% of delay	8 min/place	0% to 80%	20%	2.0	1.0	$9,012
26	Decrease belt downtime	-50	% of delay	15 min/shift	100%	20%	1.4	0.7	$6,600
27	Decrease CM clean-up time⁵⁵	-25	% of delay	4 min/place	0% to 80%	20%	1.2	0.6	$5,632
28	Decrease RB loading time	-20	% of loading time	8 min/bolter x 2	0% to 80%	40%	1.0	0.5	$4,506
29	Decrease CM bit changeout time⁵⁵	-25	% of delay	50 bits/shift x .5min/bit	0% to 70%	20%	0.8	0.4	$3,520
30	Decrease SC dump time	-10	% of delay	40 sec/car	100%	10%	0.8	0.4	$3,520
31	Decrease scoop or RB blocking cars	-30	% of delay	15 min/shift	0% to 80%	20%	0.8	0.4	$3,520

*Every operation will change assumptions
**Add a person
***Add two persons
⁵⁵Does not affect super section

Realization if related to: Bolting 40% / Loading 20%

Unit: Single CM, 2 RB

Bottleneck in the cycle: 1st = bolting / 2nd = production / Many items overlap

ASSUMPTIONS

- 42* inches: coal height
- 6* inches of Out-of-Seam Dilution (OSD)
- 68%* plant yield
- 5* tons per car
- 25* ft. cut depth
- 22* days per month
- 9.5* hour shifts
- 1.2* bolts per foot of advance
- 120* ft/shift RB bolting rate
- 5.0* clean tons per minute CM load rate
- $100* lost per minute of downtime
- $300* wages per day of a single employee
- 1.5* x wages = Total Labor Cost
- 120* cars/shift
- 8* places/shift
- 2.00* clean tons per foot of advance
- 400* ctpus clean tons/unit-shift
- 410* available production minute/shift
- 200* feet per shift production Base

HEINRICH TRIANGLE[1]

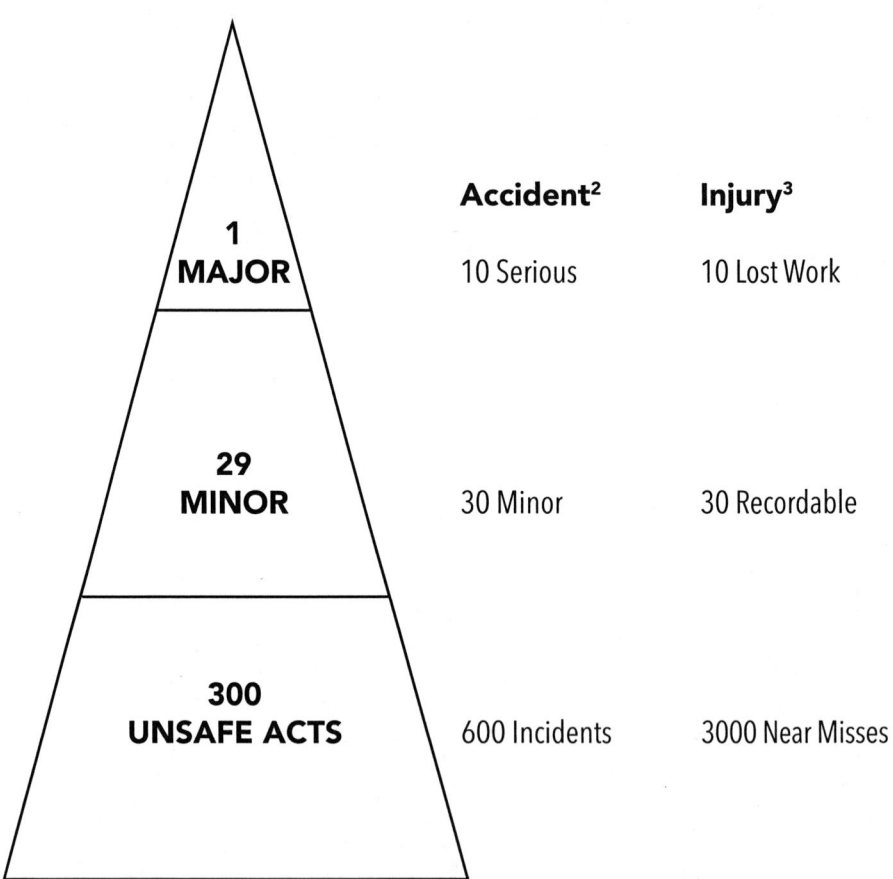

Sources:

1. H. W. Heinrick and E. R. Granniss, *Industrial Accident Prevention: A Scientific Approach* (McGraw-Hill, 1959).

2. F. E. Bird, Jr. and G. L. Germain, *Practical Loss Control Leadership, The Conservation of People, Property, Process, and Profit* (Det Norske Veritas, 1996).

3. Conoco-Philips Study, 2003.

BUILDING INTEGRITY APPENDIX B.12 187

REASONS FOR LOSS

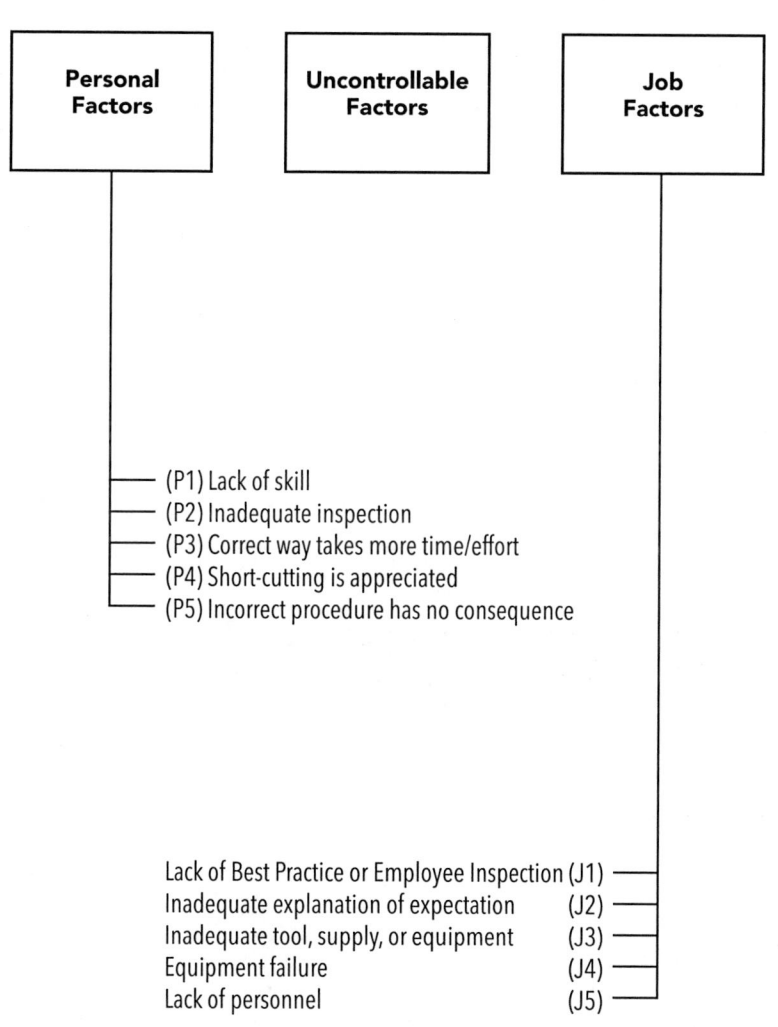

PARALLEL PROCESSES

When a loss does occur:

I. Repair Time for Symptom
(temporary and/or possible permanent solution)

II. Identify the Root Cause

III. Repair Time for Root Cause
(temporary and/or possible permanent solution)

IV. Utilize the Repair Time to Preventively Address:

    1) Other potential loss-resulting events.
(e.g., changing CM bits, pulling up cable, long CM moves, etc.)

    2) A-Level priority work requests that can only be fixed during idle time.

V. Start the Loss Investigation
(find ways to reduce the chance/frequency of the root reoccurrence and to minimize the loss if the loss does repeat)

MAXIMIZED SCHEDULING
Searching for the Win-Win

The true potential of Maximized Scheduling can be realized only if it is built into the corporate business plan. This incorporation of concepts and techniques commonly will exponentially yield gains far beyond current safety, productivity, cost reduction, employee satisfaction, and product quality levels.

The development of the optimum set of work schedules is a dynamic, multi-faceted process. It is a quest and on-going procedure, not a narrow road with a single priority destination. Too often, schedule changes are developed at the last minute without fine tuning the policies, counting the costs, and qualifying the indirect effects. WE are guilty of not taking the time to gather other perspectives and, consequently, shared ownership. A maximized operational plan is where the net savings is optimized against the positive gains minus the resulting losses and costs. We must remember, every change in procedure will result in positive and negative results. Our challenge is to quantify the effects and search for the win-win.

Developing the optimal plan needs to be addressed in a six step manner. The initial stage is to develop a balanced work group. Administration must be represented to provide a broad view and quantify costs. The human resources department (and/or outside consultants) are vital to add the compliance perspective. They will also give insight into litigation potentials and employee preferences. Another important team member will be the operations management group. Their advice on the managerial and application side of scheduling will be invaluable. The final group sector is the workforce. Employee preferences have a heavy influence on the acceptance of new schedules. Their input and suggestions are not only crucial to devising the optimal plan but it is the only way for them to buy into and share ownership.

The second step is to detail a comprehensive list of universal goals to be obtained through the devised operational plan. The goals must be balanced in priorities (safety, productivity, reduced cost, quality, and employee satisfaction) and must be multi-perspective (organization, employees, individual). Trackable yardsticks must also be set up and continually evaluated.

The third critical state is to conduct a comprehensive assessment study. Three general areas can be delineated:

I. Operation specifics	II. Labor	III. Miscellaneous
Safety records & concerns	Openness to change	Communications
Operating conditions	Preferences	Operation goals
Mining system & support functions	Demographics	Priority strengths/weaknesses (safety/efficiency/quality/cost)
Equipment type/design	Skills	Output rates/times
Equipment age/maintenance	Cross-training	
Scheduling history		

The fourth step in the process is to develop the action plan. The action plan will cover work schedules, shift length, supporting rules, and interdepartmental policies. Since all scheduling plans will have many direct and indirect effects, a very analytical approach must be taken to qualify and quantify results-costs. To aid in this review we offer the following considerations:

MAXIMIZED SCHEDULING (CONT.)
Net = Positives - Negatives - Costs

I. SAFETY
1) Accident Rate and History
2) Violation Rate and History
3) Agency and Labor Focus
4) Inspection Schedules

II. PRODUCTIVITY
1) Mining Conditions
2) Mining Type
3) Personnel Support Systems
4) Outby Support Systems
5) Run Scenarios and Production Cycles
6) Operating and Quality Consistency
7) Production Bottleneck Issues
8) Operator Skill on Key Equipment
9) Number of Operators on Each Piece of Equipment
10) Management Style
11) Management Rotation with Respect to Workforce
12) Interdepartmental Cooperation
13) Equipment Type and Condition
14) Preventative/Breakdown Repair Maintenance
15) Rebuild Schedule
16) Shift Length

III. EMPLOYEE SATISFACTION
1) Resistance to Change
2) Operation Continuity
3) Accountability and Responsibility
4) Job Skills
5) Flexibility of Work Schedules
6) Workforce Demographics
7) Morale (Management and Workforce)
8) Undesirable Work Assignments
9) Employee Commuting Time
10) Schedule Compatibility to the Local Area
11) Human Resource Department Functions
12) Frequency of Work Schedule Changes

MAXIMIZED SCHEDULING (CONT.)
Net = Positives - Negatives - Costs

IV. COST REDUCTION (The Net Effect)
1) Total Cost per Saleable Ton
2) Fixed Components
3) Variable Components
4) Maximize Low-Cost Production and Minimize Support
5) Maintenance
6) Absenteeism
7) Premium/Overtime
8) Fringe Benefit
9) Hiring
10) Workforce Staffing
11) Management Staffing

V. BUSINESS PLAN
1) Corporation Direction and Vision
2) Long-Term Gains
3) Short-Term Survival
4) Loss Preventative Attitude
5) Communication System

The fifth stage of Maximized Scheduling is the implementation and communication. This includes presentation timing, how the organizational and employee goals are explained, and the balance of perspectives that were critical to the plan's development. Plan implementation must be shown to be simple/clear, fairly administered, and, at the same time, flexible to employee's needs (within reason).

The final step of the plan development is the follow-up and refining. Even the best plans must change with time, situations, and employee needs. Events will arise and employee input will generate small plan adjustments that are paramount to keeping the operating plan optimized. The painful part of this final stage will be to redirect plan mistakes, correct policy enforcement and mediate one-sided perspectives. A list of *Potential Scheduling Mistakes* and *Techniques to Aid Creative Scheduling* have been included in Lists A and B.

There are many available work schedules and shift length combinations that need to be reviewed. Since there are many excellent papers and books on this subject, we will not reiterate them here. The comment should be added that each schedule has a perfect application and yet no operation can be fitted with the perfect schedule. The moral of the story is that all schedule layouts will need to go through the custom fitting process. For most operations, the ultimate plan will be a number of different schedules and shift lengths under a single roof. This complexity is usually harder to manage, but the rewards of flexibility will generally yield exponential results.

The greatest potential improvement area at most operations is the non-scheduled production hours. If we attack this as a scheduling challenge, and search for ways to balance schedules, employee requests, maintenance needs, staffing, and operating procedures, the quest for survival will be one step closer. We–our industry, corporations, operations, and our employees–can decide to join together or divide. We can decide to dictate or empower. We can decide to adapt to change or resist. But, in the end, some will decide to bend and optimize, and others will break.

MAXIMIZED SCHEDULING (CONT.)

List A Potential Scheduling Mistakes

1. Specific productivity achievements are rewarded by *early outs* for work crews.
2. Extended work shifts are traded for more days off and commonly result in lower efficiency rates.
3. Extra money paid for *special requested* shifts can get out of hand.
4. Favoritism is shown in scheduling certain employees or groups.
5. The majority of the undesirable shifts are being assigned to new employees. This practice has good short-term acceptance from senior employees, but poor long-term effects on new employee quality, absenteeism, and morale.
6. Management and hourly preferences, input, and demographics are not being considered.
7. There is no provision for reduced and/or flexible Saturday and Sunday work scheduling.
8. There is flexibility in allowing different schedules to co-exist (i.e., traditional and weekend crews). This can also get excessive; it is best to find a tolerable balance.
9. The number of schedules and individual request changes can be excessive and distracting (out-of-balance).
10. Negative scheduling rule changes from the original presentation (i.e., fewer days off than originally specified, number of weekends, longer shifts).
11. Frequent changes in shift length and work schedule are disruptive and costly.
12. Excessive work schedule hours tax employee's efficiency and personal lives.
13. Negative safety trends are not addressed that might be affected by schedule changes.
14. Standard inspection checks are not updated when schedules and/or shift lengths change.
15. Long shift lengths on high manual labor positions yield lower efficiency rates.
16. Short-term gains are being emphasized at the cost of long-term losses (e.g., maintenance).
17. The most efficient operators are not maintained on key equipment.
18. Operator-oriented mistakes, which increase with job assignment variations, are not dealt with.
19. Interdepartmental and between-shift communications are not updated as operating and support schedules are changed.
20. Starting time adjustments and escalating transportation delays are not addressed quickly.
21. New decisions may not be correct if old economic rules are used for steering (e.g., overtime cost vs. hiring extra people).
22. Management coverage is not upgraded to handle schedule changes.
23. Poor attitudes of first-line and middle management toward schedule changes are not addressed.
24. Upper management is not present and/or available on off-shifts, in order to maintain operation communication.
25. Neglecting to remember to consider the impact of scheduling changes on supporting functions:
    a) Bathhouse size
    b) Parking lot capacity
    c) Mine transportation system (entrance roads/track, number of vehicles, etc.)
    d) Outby support systems (supply, dusting, etc.)
    e) Safety equipment distribution (SCSR, cap lights, etc.)
26. Employee time keeping, pay check distribution, and human resource information systems are not upgraded to complex scheduling scenarios.
27. Alternative schedules are negotiated by an off-site or non-involved party.

MAXIMIZED SCHEDULING (CONT.)

List B Techniques To Aid Creative Scheduling

1. Cross-training improves staffing flexibility.
2. Personalized absentee follow-up specifically targets solvable problems quickly.
3. Employee attendance responsibility programs reduce absenteeism effects.
4. Absenteeism reduction incentive plans utilizing peer/family pressure can be extremely effective.
5. Overtime after 40 hours yields strong financial returns.
6. Holiday pay earned only if pre-days and post-days are worked fosters employee self-management.
7. A *request-off procedure* that is based on consistent rules is critical to maintain good morale.
8. *Special days* flexibility (e.g., hunting season, voting, employee funerals) commonly has a positive net effect.
9. Vacation scheduling flexibility can have strong positive gains to employee and operational goals.
10. Desirable days or shifts-trading for less desirable ones usually nets more work shifts.
11. Most employees do better with undesirable days and shifts spread out (personal surveys usually show differently).
12. Weekend work handled through an equal sharing or *compensated crews* plan is viewed positively by employees.
13. Employees on undesirable schedules being allowed to return to traditional schedules after a while (i.e., family burn-out) is well received.
14. Over-schedule Mondays, Fridays, and special periods to compensate for high absenteeism and to allow for more requested days off.
15. Support function work reduced on Friday, Saturday, Sunday, and Monday, in order to allow extended weekends and/or to lower weekend labor-needs, pay dividends in morale.
16. More scheduled days off being allowed during the week will reduce Friday, Saturday, Sunday, and Monday requests and thus will net more consistent staffing.
17. Most operations find rotating days and seconds with a fixed midnight is the most productive.
18. *Swarm Maintenance* philosophy can utilize shorter maintenance times and improve production and maintenance departmental barriers.
19. Flexible prep-crews and/or maintenance groups that can be integrated into the system successfully will commonly reduce production delays (e.g., servicing equipment).
20. Some supporting crews being staggered to cover *between shift* loss prevention projects builds production consistencies.
21. Open communication is the key to maximized gains and buy-in to all priorities with consideration for all perspectives.
22. Employee buy-in is improved if their input is sincerely valued and management's credibility is maintained.
23. The importance of developing a win-win relationship in the operation must be taught and encouraged.
24. Sensitized employees, with respect to absenteeism cost and production delay losses, are more open to change. (The *need to change* must be understood first.)
25. Easy-to-read literature and calendars must be distributed first on non-traditional schedules. Keep these simple and clear.
26. Follow-up surveys at predetermined dates from all employees are vital to keeping schedules refined.

Originally presented at the "2000 Las Vegas Coal Show" by Mark A. Bartkoski, P.E.

MINE SUPPORT 301

Proper support planning can minimize cost and maximize *value added* components to the production process.

1. Roadway conditions have a large effect on daily travel times, vehicle maintenance costs, and employee morale. Pro-active road maintenance will pay-off.

2. Main travel-way appearances (cleaning, lights, dusting, cable routing) pay enormous dividends on first impressions and daily morale. It reinforces the *expected standard*.

3. High voltage cable routing should be accessible, yet well protected.

4. Brattice leakage should be reviewed and repairs made regularly.

5. Elaborate real time mine monitoring systems that track potential problem developments can be very beneficial. Alarm ranges should be set as warnings.

6. Continuous monitoring of air quantities will ensure *immediate flags* of changes.

7. Continuous monitoring of air qualities can be correlated to barometric pressures and changes. Effects should be closely analyzed in real time.

8. Back-up equipment should be minimized or rotated regularly into service. Less equipment maintained better, usually is best.

9. Parts stocking should be grouped in a five location plan:

    a) Vendor/OEM Location

    b) Corporate Warehouse (owned and consignment parts)

    c) Operations Office/Site

    d) Outby Location at the Operation

    e) On the Working Section

10. Parts stocking and inventory levels should be checked against their effect on downtime and vendor delivery times. The downtime costs must be the primary driver.

11. Roof control specifics (e.g. How long can a place be left *not bolted* before weakening is realized?) should be incorporated into the cut sequence, shift lengths, equipment choices, and non-production shift work assignments and staffing.

PRO-ACTIVE EMPLOYEE RELATIONS PROGRAMS

1. Action Teams
2. Advanced Training/Education Opportunities
3. Bulletin Board Information posted/monitored
4. Certification Incentive Pay
5. Compensation Review
6. Corporate Communication Plan (Meetings–annual corp., monthly operations, weekly crew)
7. Current Events/Laws posted
8. Cross-Training
9. Employee Appreciation Card (births, birthdays, graduations, anniversaries ...)
10. Employee Development Program
11. Employee Ideas involvement encouraged (Best *Kaizen Idea Award* per month)
12. Family Picnic and Operation Tours
13. First Line/Middle Management Incentives
14. Flexibility and Fairness in Scheduling and Overtime Offerings (no favoritism)
15. Handbook, updated annually
16. Home Informational Letters
17. Increase Number of EMT's
18. Interactive Training Programs
19. Job Placement Book
20. Light Duty Release Program
21. Open Door Policy
22. Performance Incentives
23. Questionnaires on Employee Suggestions/Input
24. Safety Priority Established (Balanced Prevention Business Plan)
25. Senior Employees Respected/Honored
26. Strong Crew Acknowledgement Program
27. Suggestion Box Q&A
28. Union Effects and Motives pros/cons discussion
29. Vacation Pre-Scheduling
30. Weekly Foreman Communication Meeting
31. Work Request Program

DEEP MINE PRODUCTION PERFORMANCE INDICATORS (PI's)

1. Injuries
2. Violations
3. Staffing
4. Feet Mined
5. 2nd Hour Call-Out
6. Distance of Car Change-Out (to the Miner)
7. Cut Time
8. Bolt Time
9. Place Change Delay
10. Cut Depth
11. Production Delay Total
12. Outby Delays
13. Belt Delays
14. Condition Delays
15. Operational Delays
16. Maintenance Delays
17. Feeder Location
18. 3rd Car use percentage
19. 2nd Bolter use percentage
20. Car Counts (per car)
21. Roof Bolts Installed (per bolter)
22. Cavity Heights vs. Goals
23. Cable Splices Reworked
24. Oil Used
25. Install Time/Bolt Row
26. Car Change-Out Time/Car
27. Cutting Time/Car
28. Load Time/Car
29. 1st Car Dumped
30. Last Car Dumped
31. Not Bolted-Start
32. Not Bolted-End
33. Last Open Air
34. Miner Bits Used
35. Roof Bolter Bits Used
36. Rock Dust Used
37. Bolting Efficiency Ratio
38. Production Efficiency Ratio
39. Belt Availability Ratio
40. Maintenance Availability Ratio
41. Operational Availability Ratio
42. Miner Cutting Time/Conveyor Time Ratio

KEY PERFORMANCE INDICATORS (KPI'S)

I. BUSINESS RESULTS
1) LTI Rate (Lost Time Injuries)
2) Violation Density (Violations/Inspector Days)
3) Total Clean Tons
4) Cost/Clean Ton (Mine Cost)
5) Plant Yield

II. PREVENTION
1) RI Rate (Reportable Injuries)
2) Lost Investigation #
3) Risk Assessment #
4) Kaizens Completed
5) Efficiency Audits (# and Score)
6) Work Request Backlog
7) Improvement Projects Savings

III. UNDERGROUND MINES
1) RI Rate
2) Violation #
3) Production Efficiency Ratio
4) Bolting Efficiency Ratio
5) Operational Availability Ratio
6) Maintenance Availability Ratio
7) Belt Availability Ratio
8) Production at *2nd Hour Call-out*
9) Production Rate Per Shift

IV. PREPARATION PLANT
1) RI Rate
2) Violation #
3) Run Time Availability
4) Recovery Efficiency
5) Magnetite Usage
6) Quality
7) Cost/Clean Ton (Departmental)

V. SUPPORT DEPARTMENTS
1) RI Rate
2) Violation #
3) Reserve Addition
4) Drilling Feet/Rig
5) Client Survey Score
6) Support vs Face Employee Ratio
7) Outside Contractor Cost/Month
8) Cost/Month (Departmental)

*KPI's will vary depending on the major driving issues at that time and the audience they are discussed with (e.g. a CFO and a mine foreman would have different KPI's).

TRENDING CATEGORIES

Set Goals & Benchmarks on Specific Performances not General Outcomes
People will accept accountability and be motivated to improve on results they can control.

I. BUSINESS RESULTS (BR's)   -3rd week of the month
   1. Mine to Total Property, Mine's History, and Projections   & month end

II. KEY PERFORMANCE INDICATORS (KPI's)   -3rd week of the month
   1. Mine to Total Property, Mine's History, and Projections   & month end
   2. Crew to Total Property, Mine, Unit, Crew's History, and Projections

III. PERFORMANCE INDICATORS (PI's)   -3rd week of the month
   1. Mine to Total Property, Mine's History, and Projections   & month end
   2. Crew to Total Property, Mine, Unit, Crew's History, and Projections

IV. COST   -3rd week of the month
   1. Mine Categories to Total Property, Mine's History, and Projections   & month end
   2. Mine Items Frequency to Total Property, Mine's History, and Projections

V. GROUPINGS (Top 5 items to be separately reported)   -month end
   1. Cost
      a) Total Mine Cost Category to Total Property, Mine, Equipment Type
      b) Item Mine Frequency to Total Property and Mine

   2. Downtime
      a) Equipment to Total Property, Mine, Crew's History, and Projections
      b) Unit to Total Property, Mines, Crew's History, and Projections
      c) Delay Code to Total Property, Mine's History, and Projections

   3. Maintenance Time
      a) Equipment to Total Property, Mine's History, and Projections

   4. Operating Cost
      a) Equipment to Total Property, Mine's History, and Projections

RESTRUCTURING FORECAST

I. MANPOWER

	Current		Proposed	
	Production: Single CM Section	Employee Count[1]	Production: Super-Section	Employee Count[1]
Deep Hollow Mine	4	205	-	-
Lucky Road Mine	2	110	-	-
Lucky Star Mine	1	60	2	134
Straight Ridge Mine	2	105	3	191
Taurus #1 Mine	3	155	3	191
Shortage due to unfilled positions		-36		
	12	599	8*	516**

$$* \ \frac{8 \text{ (proposed \# of sections)} \times 140\% \text{ (super section rate}^2\text{)}}{12 \text{ (current \# of sections)} \times 100\%} = 7\% \text{ Production Reduction}$$

$$** \ \frac{516 \text{ (proposed count)}}{599 \text{ (current count)}} = 14\% \text{ Labor Reduction}$$

II. PRODUCTION EFFECT OF THE NEW PROPOSAL

1) Economy of scale[3] - better management control, fewer operating mines but manageable size   +2%

2) Improved Personnel Quality (management and hourly) - reducing 14% of the uninspired   +5%

3) Operating with Full Crews - not the normal *one man/crew short*   +10%

4) Reduction of Downtime - estimated 15% more uptime nets 10% increase in production, due to equipment upgrading and purchases, and the super-section layout   +10%

5) Reduction of # of Sections - partially off-set by higher production rate of super section vs. single CM   -7%

                                               Total Prod. Increase =   +20%

Note:
1) A single mine section is budgeted at 11 people/shift and a super-section at 15 people/shift.
2) Super-section production improvement is assumed at 140% of a single miner rate.
3) The optimal operation size is totally site and management specific, but was assumed that 3 super-section (union-free) and 2 super-section (union) was ideal, unless an increased senior management structure was enacted.

PROCESS COORDINATOR RESPONSIBILITIES
Typical Month

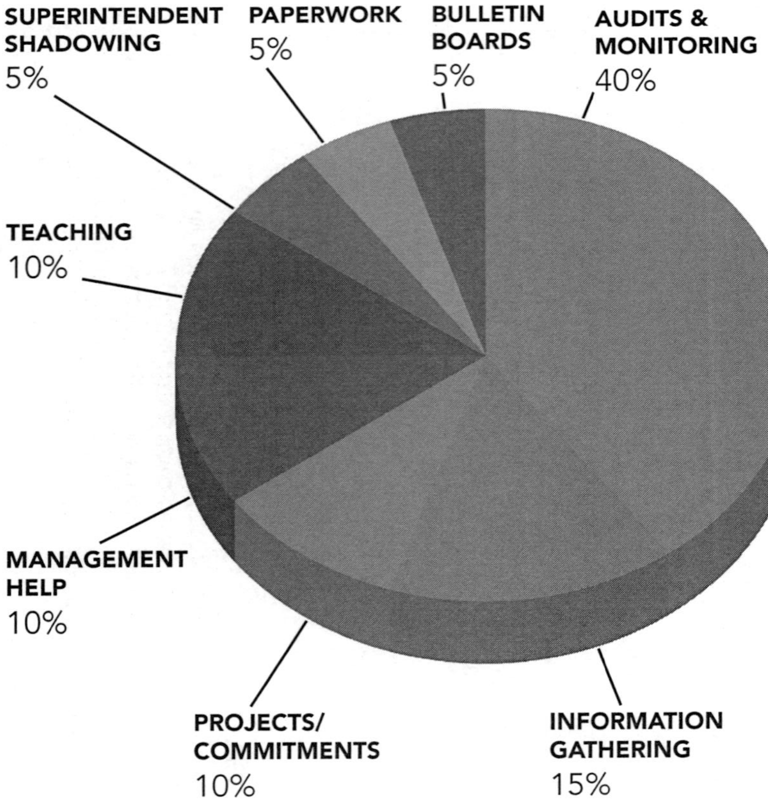

TIME BREAKDOWN EVOLUTION

	1st 6 mo	6-24 mo	+24 mo
	5%	20%	40%
Audits and Monitoring	5%	20%	40%
-Efficiency Audits			
-Process Studies			
-Loss Investigation/Solutions			
-Risk Assessment/Solutions			
-Major Initiatives			
-Trending of Info			
Information Gathering	5%	15%	15%
-Surveys, Studies			
-Reports			
-Suggestions (Action Teams, Suggestion Box)			
-Weekly Communication Meetings			
Projects/Commitments	5%	10%	10%
-Kaizen Ideas			
-Coordinator Intra-departmental Projects			
-Self Assigned Project/Follow Up			
Firstline/Middle Mgt Help	10%	20%	10%
-Communicating Requests			
-Sharing Trend Analysis			
Teaching	60%	20%	10%
-Foundational Values			
-Reporting Systems			
-Best Practices			
Superintendent Shadowing	5%	5%	5%
-Mentoring			
-Fill-In			
Paperwork	5%	5%	5%
-Suggestion Box Answers			
-Backlogs (WR, PM)			
-Return on Investments			
-Cost of Loss			
Bulletin Boards	5%	5%	5%

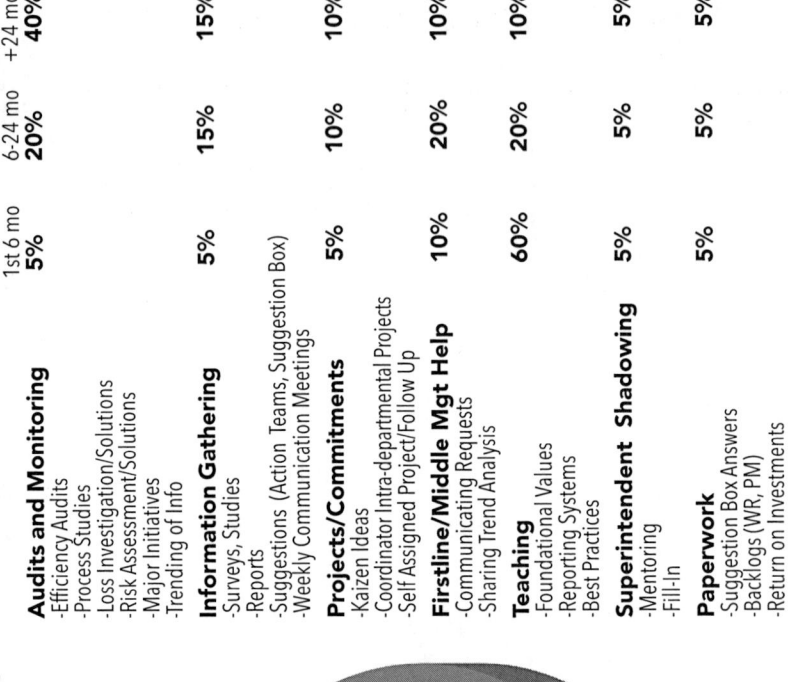

- SUPERINTENDENT SHADOWING 5%
- PAPERWORK 5%
- BULLETIN BOARDS 5%
- AUDITS & MONITORING 40%
- INFORMATION GATHERING 15%
- PROJECTS/COMMITMENTS 10%
- MANAGEMENT HELP 10%
- TEACHING 10%

CORPORATE TRANSFORMATION DOWNFALLS

1. Not establishing a common corporate goal between the owners, management, workforce, and community.

2. Failing to paint a vivid picture of "where are we going?" and "how are we going to get there?"

3. Incompletely uniting behind common principles (i.e., Foundational Values).

4. Working under an imbalanced agenda (i.e., safety is our main goal). Efficiency must be our main goal–with efficiency defined as maximized safety with optimized productivity. Safety is considered to be an uncompromisable core value.

5. Leadership style that is incompatible with the company's values.

6. Failure of senior management to visibly lead and support the change. An outside change agent can only work as a facilitator.

7. A change facilitation does not earn trust, is not viewed as sincere, and not viewed by others as invested in the long term.

8. Not taking steps to ensure that middle- and first-line managers are 100% selling and supporting the change.

9. Not presenting the Plan from the employees' perspective.

10. Failing to develop a two-way Communication Plan.

11. Not developing the Plan in an intentional, coordinated manner (i.e. shotgun start), so the team experiences confusing *inconsistencies in expectation* from the beginning.

12. Operating under a one-size-fits-all, inflexible canned program. Failure to customize *the process* based on the operation's history, growth needs, and management/workforce personality restricts or reduces the company's opportunity of reaching its full potential.

13. Use of a weakly structured and poorly monitored operating plan.

14. Inadequately thinking through the plan, especially the timing.

15. Failing to respectfully follow-up on and address all employee suggestions and corporate promises. *Trust in management* is lost.

16. Not continually refining and updating the change process. Change is not a static event; it must be dynamically orchestrated.

17. Letting uncontrolled management politics undercut the common vision and foundational values.

18. Not sharing accountability at all levels of the operating team.

19. Poorly utilizing assets, equipment, and technology.

20. Incorrectly positioning personnel (management and workforce).

21. Not pro-actively addressing legal/safety changes that can be foreseen.

PREVENTION TENETS

1. Focusing on preventing all losses (injury, violation, downtime, rework, and waste) results in balanced success and earned security.

2. Reducing losses is a win-win for everyone.

3. Prevention must be the attitude and a foundational value, empowerment, and accountability are the fuel.

4. 80% of the losses come from the same repeating issues, processes, and/or people.

5. Eliminating only the symptom results in reoccurrence, and thus, until the root is eradicated, a loss will repeat.

6. Safety, productivity, and quality are the result of prevention; it's doing a job right.

7. The first focus after a loss is to identify the root cause. The second is to at least immobilize the root cause from reoccurrence and any safety repercussion until a full repair can be made. The third priority is to address the symptom, temporarily and eventually, permanently. The fourth parallel focus is to utilize the downtime on other loss prevention projects.

8. Proactively searching for the next bottleneck is the next order of business, when a solution is achieved.

9. The company's total commitment to preventing injuries proves the value they put on their people.

10. *At risk behavior* is the ultimate enemy.

11. A loss is usually the result of an unaddressed or lingering problem.

12. Everyone is responsible to keep trying to expand their own *circle of influence*.

13. "That is not my job," is a quote from an undependable and failing business partner.

14. Prevention protects efficiency, which is defined as maximized safety with optimized productivity at a minimized cost per unit sold.

15. The initial step in a prevention process is always a thorough employee inspection.

16. Looking pro-actively for potential issues is not normally the natural step. Reacting after the loss is usually the norm.

17. Prevention is a state-of-mind, before it's an action.

18. The value of openly monitoring *extra concern areas* far exceeds the negative consequences from compliance agencies.

19. Minor losses eventually lead to major losses.

20. The result of an incident could be a loss in any one or a combination of the loss categories (injury, violation, downtime, rework, or waste).

21. Best practices must be developed and upgraded with a thorough understanding of the *Cost of Loss*.

22. Every employee is a standing member of the Safety Department.

CORPORATE COMMUNICATION PLAN

	FREQUENCY
1. Open Door Policy	On-going
2. Bulletin Board Updates (Appendix B.25)	On-going
3. COO/Supt Communication Meeting	Weekly
4. Supt/Mgr Communication Meeting	Weekly
5. Mgr/Crew Communication Meeting (Appendix B.26)	Weekly
6. Supt/Crew Communication Meeting	Monthly
7. Suggestion Box Q&A	Monthly
8. Kaizen Ideas Input/Response	Monthly
9. Action Teams Notes	Monthly
10. Employee Efficiency Surveys	Monthly
11. Key Performance Indicator Charting	Monthly
12. Loss Grams (posted Incident Reports)	As occurs
13. Business Workshops	Quarterly
14. Company Newsletter	Quarterly
15. Employee Development Programs	Annually
16. Employee Input Surveys (sent to everyone's home)	Annually

BULLETIN BOARD COMPONENTS

1. Key Performance Indicator Charts (Business Results, Department Focus Areas)

2. Clip Boards
    a) Responses to Suggestion Box Questions/Suggestions
    b) Kaizen Ideas Updates
    c) Prevention *Action Team* Meeting Notes
    d) Fatal Grams (Industry Bulletins)
    e) Loss Grams (Company Incident Reports and Near Misses)
    f) Safety Meeting Handouts/Postings
    g) Violations
    h) Loss Investigations
    i) Risk Assessments
    j) Communication Mtg/Workshop Power Points

3. General Information of Corporate Business and Industry News

4. Appreciation Notes (Leaders in Certain Areas/KPI's, special mentions)

5. Major Initiative Results

6. "Why We Work" Section (family/hobby photos)

7. Recognizing Hazard Pictures (staged pictures at the actual operations depicting potentially dangerous situations)

8. Training Schedules

9. Incentive Scorecards

10. Miscellaneous Charts and Postings

BUILDING INTEGRITY   APPENDIX B.26

WEEKLY CREW COMMUNICATION MEETING

Date _____   Foreman _____   No. of Employees _____

I. Safety Results _____
_____

II. Productivity Results _____
_____

III. Operation Plans _____
_____
_____
_____
_____

IV. Crew discussion
    1) Safety-specific areas of concern
_____
_____
_____

    2) Efficiency-specific area our department needs to work on to reduce delay time
_____
_____
_____

    -specific area our crew needs to work on to improve process productivity
_____
_____
_____

    -specific area our crew has done well lately
_____
_____
_____

Ideas of suggestions to help prevent losses (injury, violations, delays, rework, or waste):
-please include employee's names so they can be recognized (if they do not mind)
_____
_____
_____

Questions or Comments for the Superintendent (add to the back of this form)

TRAINING LAY-OUT

Our corporate growth depends on the commitment to first build each individual in:

I. FOCUS AREAS

1. Prevention (Types of Loss, Flow Analysis, Root Cause, Risk Analysis, Prevention Techniques, Accountability)

2. Skills (Mining Principles, Best Practices, Basic Maintenance/Servicing, Technical Areas, Time Management, Communication, Management/Leadership)

3. Business (Mine Economics, Cost of Loss, Market Issues, Absenteeism Effects)

4. Teamwork (Attitude, Intra-departmental Effects, Motivation, Cross Training)

5. Problem Solving (Loss Investigations, Risk Assessment, Brainstorming, Creativity, Kaizen Idea Development, Prioritization, Multi-agendas, Contingency Planning, Action Plans)

II. IMPLEMENTATION

1. General - All communication and training plans will be laced with the five areas listed above

2. Specific - Certain positions will mandate detailed technical training in addition to the normal schedule

3. Developmental - Every employee will have incentives to excel in training and/or certification in their area of expertise and new areas of interest.

III. FOLLOW UP

1. Every employee will have a self-planned and directed Development Program and an annual feedback. They will be offered by their supervisor on the following:

   a. Adherence to plan

   b. Competence in training

   c. Growth skill and certification

IV. A bonus award will be granted to employees based on their progress

DEFINITIONS OF COMPLACENT

Which statement describes you best on a bad day?

1. Content to a fault, unconcerned. Low buy-in. Politically a safer position.

2. Satisfied with deficiencies. Acceptance of second best. Conserves my energy.

3. Not aware of deficiencies or dangers. Mentally soft at pushing myself to find out WHY?

4. A feeling of contentment or self-satisfaction coupled with the sense that things can't get better.

5. Happy or satisfied with myself to a fault. Coasting is an acceptable state.

6. Too many things are out of control, so I just accept the outcome.

7. Accepting status quo is okay, since the conditions are so dynamic.

8. Pleased to the point of doing nothing and allowing circumstances to remain as is. The *do nothing decision* is safest.

9. A feeling of pleasure or security while unaware of potential dangers. *I did not know of the pr* is an acceptable response.

10. Low level involvement protects me from being accountable for the situation.

11. Being patient for the next tide to change, someone will eventually fix it.

12. Accepting the situation; the inconvenience or controversy of change is not worth the pain of action.

13. Acquiesce to current processes, since management may not accept and support potential solutions.

14. Accepting the situation, because no obvious solutions are in sight.

REASONS (EXCUSES) FOR NOT BREAKING A HABIT

I. DID NOT ACCEPT
   1) Not Heard (poor communication)
   2) Not Believed (inadequate presentation)
   3) Not Worth the Effort (pain was not worth the gain)

II. DID NOT DO
   1) Not Remembered (poor follow-up)
   2) Not Made a Habit (repetition not long enough)

INTEGRITY PROCESS BASICS

I. The Transformation Plan:
Mission Statement
Values - Foundation to Build on
Process Pillars

II. Principles of the Process:
Gather Information
Suggestion Box, Foreman Notes, Meeting Input, Employee Surveys, Efficiency Surveys, Process Studies, Action Teams, Loss Investigations, Risk Assessments, Shift Reports, and Employee Inspection.

Refine Process
Kaizen Ideas, Best Practices (Job and Process), Major Initiatives, Failure Maintenance, Preventative Maintenance, and Work Requests.

Monitor Results
Efficiency Audits, Results Tracking/Trending, Operating Cost/Equipment, Backlogs, Return on Investment, and Cost of Loss.

Once the wheel is rolling, the direction is our choice.

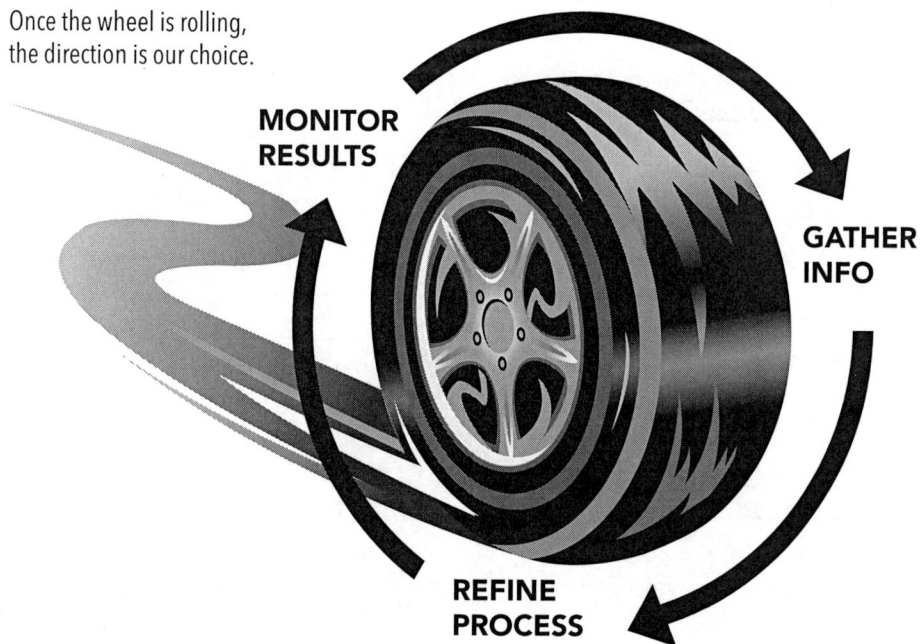

If the wheel slows down, it will fall over or roll in reverse with no method of steering.

210 BUILDING INTEGRITY   APPENDIX B.31

WORK REQUEST FLOW CHART

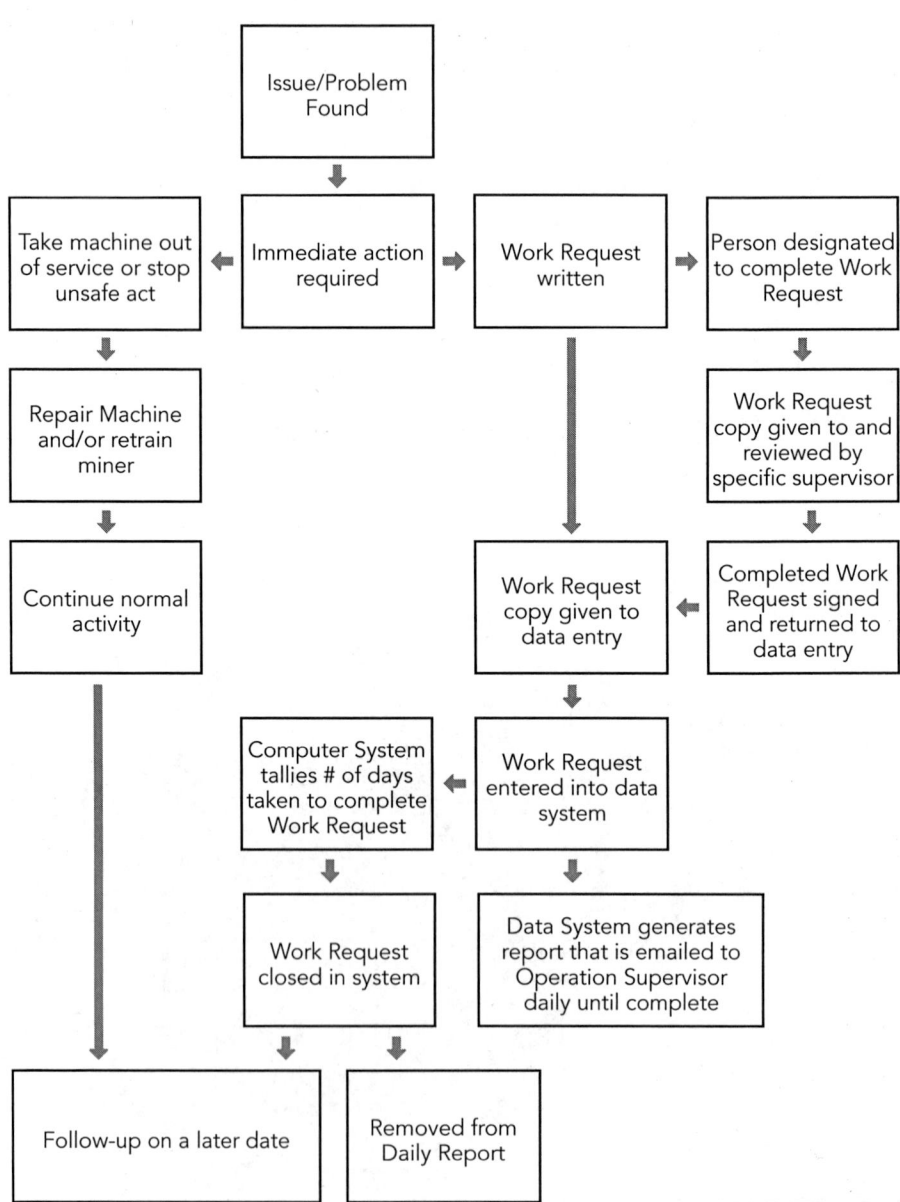

PREVENTION PROJECTS FORM

Department _____   Updated _____

#	Priority	Project/Initiative	Target Date	% Complete

* Projects that have supporting Action Plans.

ACTION PLAN FORM

Action Plan Form

Mine:				Date:
	Major Initiative:			
Action Item	Resources Needed	Responsible Person	Monitor	Completion Date	Percent (%) Complete
Results Expected:				Assumption:
KPI:				

LOSS SYMPTOM VS. ROOT CAUSE

Category – Case	Common Potential Symptoms	Common Potential Root Cause
I. INJURY		
1) Rock fell on roof bolters hand while on drill boom	-Rock fell from roof	-Not wearing correct gloves -Incorrect hand placement -Hydraulic pressure not correct on roof support -Lack of scaling roof rock -Conditions
2) Slipped on slick concrete	-Water on surface	-Water leak -Incorrect drainage -Water pump by-passing
II. VIOLATION		
1) Water pressure too low	-Coupling leaking -Pressure too high caused leak	-Pressure reducer broken -Incorrect setting -Line restriction
2) Dusty beltline	-Poor rock dust plan -Poor inspection or problem communication	-Scraper failure -No v-wiper on bottom belt -Belt alignment -Inadequate water between belts -Poor transfer chute
III. DOWNTIME		
1) Cable splice failure	-Splice failure	-Normal wear -Backlashing cable -Rock cut cable -Ran out of cable
2) Long car change-out distance	-Entry restricted	-Cable length -Cable routing -Haulway conditions
IV. REWORK (Equipment Damage)		
1) Cutter motor down	-Motor failed -Bit block maintenance	-Bit type -Voltage level -Conditions -Product quality
2) Shuttle car spillage	-Tore off sideboards	-Poor design -CM loading technique -Coal height
V. WASTE		
1) Damaged roof bolts	-Bent bolts	-Operator error -Packaging size -Product quality -Bolter machine condition
2) High roof bit usage	-Broken bit	-Hard drilling -Product quality -Drilling pressure -Operation techniques

PREVENTATIVE MAINTENANCE (PM) SYSTEM

I. The information feed is continuously evolving the PM system through:

1. OEM recommended checks/servicing
2. Preventative inspections are based on components rules:
    a. Some items are inspected at 80% of historical life
    b. Some items are evaluated after first failure
    c. Some items are regularly monitored for wear
3. High monthly operating cost per equipment (includes downtime charges, parts cost, and maintenance time charges) will be monitored and addressed. They will have preventative inspections until they come back in line.
4. Oil usage tracking and sampling program may target potential issues.
5. Continuous Output Monitoring will flag eroding indicators. Computer based tracking will highlight certain items as ambient levels are exceeded:
    a. Oil pressure, bearing temperatures, RPM's, vibrations, thermal scans, pump water levels, amp draws, ventilation quantities, air qualities, etc.
6. All equipment downtime, failure analysis, loss investigations, risk assessments, and work request reviews will be made to reveal root causes. If those findings reveal preventative inspections, adjustments, or repairs are needed to prevent repeat losses or failures, the PM system will be refined.

II. The System will require:

1. Work assignments to be:
    a. Prioritized
    b. Responsible party assigned
    c. Maintenance scheduled when necessary
    d. Completions recorded
2. Open backlogs trended and followed-up on
3. Audits for repeating failures conducted regularly:
    a. A department-neutral analysis is critical for this review
    b. Trends should be reviewed by mine, department, crew, shift, equipment/process, loss classification, and root cause
4. Equipment rebuild decisions will be based on:
    a. PM system history
    b. Actual operating cost
    c. Availability
    d. Life of the equipment/component

III. Scope will be expanded from equipment to all processes (e.g., ventilation systems, pumping)

INTEGRITY GROWTH ASSESSMENT
How do we score?

	Good 1	2	3	4	5 Great	
1. Rule Driven	○	○	○	○	○	Principle Guided
2. Address the Person	○	○	○	○	○	Attack Process
3. Emphasis on Standards	○	○	○	○	○	Emphasis on Judgment
4. Conformity to Group	○	○	○	○	○	Diversity of Ideas/Opinions
5. Compliance	○	○	○	○	○	Commitment
6. Micro-management	○	○	○	○	○	Self-Management
7. Individually Rewarded	○	○	○	○	○	Team Celebrated
8. Rigid-Goal Oriented	○	○	○	○	○	Improving Benchmarks
9. Competition Among Crews	○	○	○	○	○	Improvement % Trend
10. Follow Parameters	○	○	○	○	○	Continually Refine Strategy
11. Standardized Procedures	○	○	○	○	○	Improving Best Practices
12. Optimize Employee Skills	○	○	○	○	○	Maximize Cross Training
13. Defined Maintenance Crews	○	○	○	○	○	Expand Maintenance to Everyone
14. Assign Individual Action Plans	○	○	○	○	○	Group Developed Action Plans
15. Reactive Loss Investigations	○	○	○	○	○	Proactive Risk Assessments
16. Symptom Focused	○	○	○	○	○	Root Cause Driven
17. Negative Attitudes Suppressed	○	○	○	○	○	Distractors Rejected
18. Lean Staffing Lowers Cost	○	○	○	○	○	Consistent Staffing Protects Flow
19. Individual Responsibilities	○	○	○	○	○	Team Accountability
20. Profit Centered	○	○	○	○	○	Security Focused
21. Top-Down Management	○	○	○	○	○	Servant Leadership
22. Analog Gauge Checks	○	○	○	○	○	Visual/Automated Alarms
23. Audit Scoring	○	○	○	○	○	Audit Reinforcement
24. Management Inspections	○	○	○	○	○	Employee Checks
25. Clean-Up Projects	○	○	○	○	○	Process Redesigned
26. Employee Evaluations	○	○	○	○	○	Indiv. Development Plans
27. Backlog Rates	○	○	○	○	○	Backlog Trends
28. Complacent with Stress	○	○	○	○	○	Continuous Improv. Challenge
29. Isolated Department Goals	○	○	○	○	○	Complete Process Flow
30. Cost Cutting Focus	○	○	○	○	○	Value Adding Priority

PERSONAL EFFICIENCY CHALLENGE

Monthly grade yourself (Score 1-5; 1=Poor, 5=great) on the below points

MONTH:

1. Pre-plan and balance spiritual, family, career, and personal goal
2. Weekly and monthly planning of your prioritized list
3. Reprioritize items (projects and goals) regularly
4. Pre-plan phone calls, computer follow-up, reviews
5. Develop outside reading schedule
    1) Daily devotional/inspirational reading
    2) Medium term book plan
6. Preschedule TV time
7. Take proactive responsibility for time choices
8. Act on initial readings (e-mails, reports) - avoid double handling
9. Minimize conversation/phone/e-mail time respectfully w/o alienating people
10. Maximize available time
    1) Optimize sleep schedule
    2) Minimize disruptions (e.g. radio)
    3) Reduce distracting projects- evaluate cost/hour vs. return
11. Continue improving report reading/follow-up efficiency
12. Maximize delegation with follow-up
13. Meeting minimization with respect to number and time length
14. Sharpen concurrent multi-tasking skills
15. Make sure back-up plans are in place
16. Visually walk and list follow-up items
    1) Offices
    2) Sites
    3) People
17. Maximize observations
    1) Travel different routes
    2) Disciplined focus
18. Use voice recorders for personal notes during non-writing time (i.e., driving, bedtime)
19. Continue updating organizational technology
    1) Cell phone
    2) Tablet/laptop
    3) Day planner
20. Look for situations to serve others and *your calling*
21. Semi-annual performance review with your supervisor follow-up

Total

EXAMPLES OF CREEP

Creep is defined as the negative erosion on processes, jobs, and/or projects. It normally has detrimental effects in the medium- and long-term, if not held in balance.

Solution: Develop common sense, updated Best Practices for jobs and processes, and follow-up on their compliance. Efficiency Surveys and Audits along with Process Studies will delineate if system or process upgrades are needed. Potential examples of *creep* are as follows:

1. Production of coal on third shift can be good, as long as dayshift is correctly set-up and maintenance projects are completed. Otherwise morale will be damaged badly and repeating problems will worsen.

2. Shift-to-shift competition commonly increases the more aggressive crew's rate, but it can encourage some crews to take process short cuts that have a net negative effect.

3. Manually filling inby beltlines, if the outby belts go down, works as long as the belt drive horsepower and belt strengths can handle the extra start-up loads.

4. Doubling up in the middle entries on the miner cut-sequence produces extra short-term production at the high cost of inefficient cut-sequence issues over the mid-term, if the cut cycle is not brought back in-line.

5. The pressure from a *time study* helps the immediate shift-pace and bottleneck reduction at the potential cost of morale issues if not done in a positive manner.

6. Not regularly changing a miner's bits saves immediate delay-time but causes problems with cutting rates, dust generation, and numerous maintenance issues.

7. Roof bolter operators not bolting tight to the face speeds their exit time for that place, but reduces their over-all efficiency rates which can lead to roof control issues, and will increase miner's total move time.

8. A miner operator not cleaning up after a cut saves a little time, but if the bolter crew is delayed, a more substantial net loss may be incurred.

9. Section roadway and feeder cleaning not done in-cycle may reduce some short-term delays, but we are gambling on larger long-term delays and compliance issues.

10. Running all weekend idle shifts yields a short-term benefit, but can have strong negative effects on morale and maintenance backlogs.

11. Running short-handed saves immediate labor costs but commonly causes MANY other operating problems.

12. Frequent spending restrictions can change operating processes and standards, thus breaking consistency and flow.

13. Cannibalizing unused equipment helps immediate parts costs short-term but eliminates available spare equipment and in the long-term increases maintenance time requirements.

14. Reducing inventory level helps supply cost, but can have potential higher downtime effects.

218 BUILDING INTEGRITY APPENDIX B.39

INTEGRITY PROCESS FLOW CHART

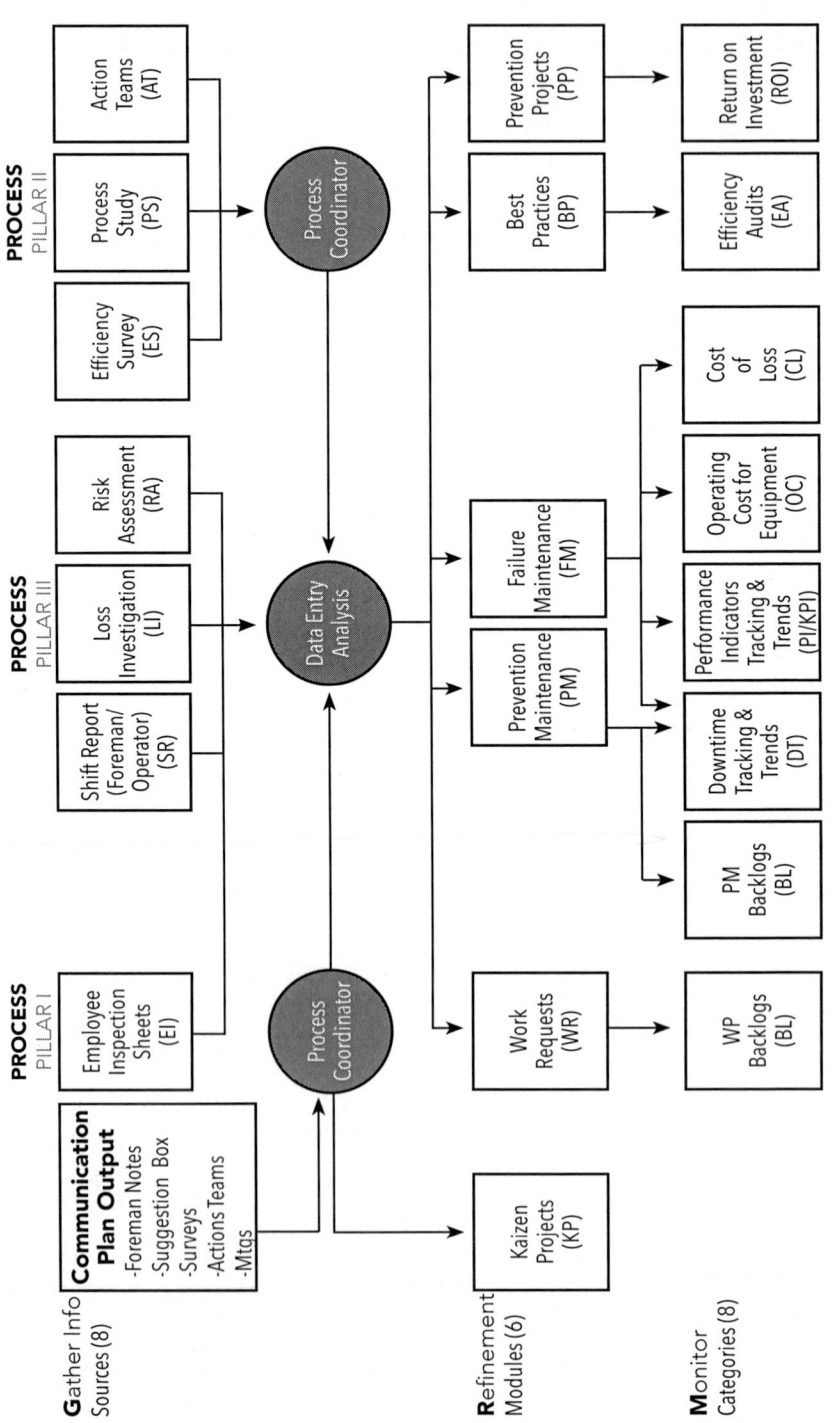

THE **SHARE** PLAN

S **Safety Record**
Goal - Monthly Average below .... Violations/inspection day.
Actual - _____ Violations/inspection day   (0 or $50)   +_____

H **Health Record**
Goal – no Medical Treatment Injuries in the mine for the month.
Actual - _____ Medical Treatment Injuries   (0 or $50)   +_____

A **Ash Record**
Goal - Monthly Average below "x"% ash. (...............)
Actual - _____ % Ash

Calculation: { .... % (goal) - _____% (actual)} x
                 .... % [To be set from Market/Budget]
                 = -/+ _____

R **Revenue**
(assumes market pricing stays at budgeted levels)

E **Efficiency Record**
Goal – Monthly Average above "y" feet/shift (...............)
Actual - _____ feet/shift (actual measure-up)

Calculation: {_____ (actual) – .... "y" feet/shift}
                 x $/ft. [To be set from Market/Budget]
                 = -/+ _____

                                 Total Ash and Efficiency Earnings   +_____

TOTAL "SHARE" PAYMENT =   ═══════════════

Qualifications:
I. To be individually qualified for the monthly payment, each employee must operate within their scheduled days.
II. A loss time injury at the mine disqualifies the entire mine for any SHARE monies for the month.

DIGGING DEEPER...INTO THE SOURCE

Integrity: *a personal choice of uncompromising honesty and sincerity of heart & character.*
Psalm 18:20 The Lord rewarded me according to my righteousness (my conscious integrity and sincerity with Him); according to the cleanness of my hands has He recompensed me. (Amplified)
Proverbs 2:7 He hides away sound and godly Wisdom and stores it for the righteous (those who are upright and in right standing with Him); He is a shield to those who walk uprightly and in integrity (Amplified)
Deuteronomy 16:19-20 | **1Kings** 9:4 | **Job** 2:3, 31:6 | **Psalm** 5:12, 7:8-9, 14:4-6 | **Proverbs** 1:3, 11:3

A divided house: Mark 3:5 And if a house is divided (split into factions and rebelling) against itself, that house will not be able to last. (Amplified)
Matthew 12:25

Accountable: *answerable; responsible; obligated to report, explain, or justify.*
Romans 3:19-20

Anoint: *to authorize or set apart a person for a particular work or service.*
Exodus 29:7, 37:29 | **1Samuel** 26:9 | **John** 6:69, 17:3, 20:31 | **Acts** 26:23 | **Romans** 5:1, 5:8, 6:9 | **2Corinthians** 1:21 | **Ephesians** 4:15

Arrogant: *having/showing insulting attitude of being better/smarter/more important; looking down on others.*
Job 36:9 | **Psalm** 17:10, 75:4, 94:4, 101:5 | **Proverbs** 16:5 | **Malachi** 4:1 | **1Timothy** 6:4, 6:17

Attitudes: *way you think/feel about someone/something; feeling/way of thinking that affects behavior.*
Job 36:5 | **Proverbs** 13:1, 14:6, 15:12, 17:16, 17:24, 21:11, 23:9 | **James** 1:21 | **Revelation** 3:17-19

Balance: *when various parts form a satisfying/harmonious whole; no disproportion.*
Leviticus 19:36 | **Job** 31:6 | **Psalm** 62:9 | **Proverbs** 11:1, 16:11 | **Isaiah** 40:12 | **Romans** 4:25 | **2Timothy** 1:7 | **1Peter** 5:8

Belief: *reliance, support, confidence, trust, conviction, adherence to.*
Proverbs 22:19 | **Luke** 17:5 | **1Corinthians** 13:13 | **2Corinthians** 1:24, 5:7; **2Thessalonians** 2:13 | **Hebrews** 12:2 | **1John** 2:18 | **Jude** 1:3

Biblical Talents Parable: Matthew 25:14-30

Build: *dig a deep, firm foundation upon the rock; lay a cornerstone to accomplish a goal.*
Psalm 102:15-17, 127:1 | **Luke** 6:48, 20:17 | **Acts** 4:11 | **1Corinthians** 3:9-13 | **1Thessalonians** 5:11 | **Hebrews** 11:10

Burning bush: *an experience of direction, attention to divine guidance.*
Exodus Chapter 3 | **Mark** 12:26 | **Luke** 20:37

DIGGING DEEPER...INTO THE SOURCE   (CONT.)

Business: *work that is part of a job; a necessity/need/duty.*
Proverbs 22:29, 26:17 | Ecclesiastes 8:15-17 | Luke 2:49, 18:28, 21:34 | John 5:22, 9:4 | Acts 6:3, 19:24-26 | 1Thessalonians 4:6a | 1Timothy 6:4-6

Calling: *a worthy and particular life destiny/vocation; life of service.*
Isaiah 41:4 | Romans 11:29 | 1Corinthians 1:26 | Ephesians 1:18, 4:1-4 | 2Thessalonians 1:11 | 2Timothy 1:9 | Hebrews 3:1 | 2Peter 1:10

Character: *habit/pattern/way of thinking/speaking/acting; behavior.*
Ecclesiastes 12:13 | Isaiah 26:3 | Jeremiah 9:24 | John 17:26 | Romans 5:4 | 1Corinthians 3:13, 10:23, 15:33 | Hebrews 13:5 | James 3:2

Choice: *permission/liberty to pick out and select and do as you please; an opportunity gift from God.*
Proverbs 1:7, 8:10, 8:19, 9:10, 10:20 | Luke 10:21 | Acts 1:7, 15:7 | 1Corinthians 8:9, 10:23, 12:31

Choose whom you will serve: *a desired selection to whom you will show loyal, favored submission.*
Deuteronomy 30:19 | Joshua 24:15 | Malachi 3:14-16 | Romans 14:22

Commit: *lean/rely on, confidently trust; transmit and entrust [as a deposit]; give over to.*
Psalm 37:5 | Proverbs 16:3 | Isaiah 26:3-4; John 8:34 | Acts 20:32 | 2Timothy 1:12 | 1Peter 4:19 | 1John 5:18

Counsel: *guidance or advice in resolving personal issues and emotional challenges.*
Psalm 1:1, 16:7, 32:8, 73:24 | Proverbs 1:5, 13:13, 16:20, 21:30, 27:9 | Isaiah 9:6 | 1Corinthians 15:52 | Ephesians 6:4

Covenant: *a promise; a solemn pledge; a compact; a treaty or agreement.*
Isaiah 54:10 | Ezekiel 20:37 | Matthew 26:8 | Luke 22:20 | 2Corinthians 3:6 | Galatians 3:14-16 | Hebrews 8:6, 9:15, 10:16, 13:20

Creep: *to slowly, deceitfully corrupt; to stealthily enter in by the side.*
Mark 4:19-20 | Acts 20:30 | 1Corinthians 15:33 | Ephesians 5:4 | 2Timothy 2:21, 3:6 | Titus 1:15 | Jude 1:4, 8, 10 | Revelation 11:18

Discipline: *admonishing/calling to soundness of mind/self-control.*
Psalm 94:10, 94:12 | Proverbs 1:3, 6:23, 15:10 | Acts 24:16 | 1Corinthians 9:27, 11:32 | Ephesians 6:4 | 2Timothy 1:7, 3:16 | Hebrews 12:6

Faith: *a firm conviction based on hearing, assurance, confidence, trust, belief, persuasion.*
Colossians 1:23 | Mark 11:22 | Romans 3:3, 25 | 1Corinthians 2:5 | 2Corinthians 1:24, 5:7 | Galatians 3:23

Foundation: *basis/groundwork/support of anything; the moral underpinning of society/religion.*
Proverbs 24:3 | Luke 6:48 | 1Corinthians 3:9-13 | 2Thessalonians 3:3 | 2Timothy 2:19 | Hebrews 11:10

DIGGING DEEPER...INTO THE SOURCE (CONT.)

Fruit: *off-spring of a living organism; works/deeds; visible expression of an act.*
Psalm 128:2 | Proverbs 11:30, 18:20-21 | John 15:2, 4, 5 | Galatians 5:22-23 | Hebrews 12:11 | James 3:17-18 | Revelations 2:7

Giftings: *a special aptitude/ability/power/talent; something of undeserved favor; endowment.*
Proverbs 18:16, 22:6 | John 3:27 | Romans 11:29, 12:6-7 | 1Corinthians 12:4, 10, 11 | 2Timothy 1:6

Goal: *a directed endeavor toward a purpose or mark; an objective.*
Philippians 2:12-13, 3:4

Hard Worker: *industrious/diligent in carrying out tasks/duties.*
1Corinthians 3:13, 15:58 | Titus 2:14

Illuminate: *brighten with light; light up; dispel darkness; to make understandable; clarify.*
Psalm 19:11, 118:27 | Luke 11:36 | Revelation 18:1, 21:23, 22:5

The Joseph story:
Genesis 30:24-25, 33:2, 7, 35:24, Chapters 37-46 | Acts 7:9-16 | Hebrews 11:22

Leadership: *the ability or capacity to lead, guide, give direction to; a guiding or directing head.*
Genesis 49:10 | Exodus 15:13 | Acts 20:28 | Galatians 3:24, 5:16, 18 | 1Peter 5:2 | 2John 1:6 | Revelation 7:17

Morals: *consistently the right things, founded on fundamental principles of right and truth; virtuous conduct.*
1Corinthians 4:19, 15:33 | Galatians 6:10 | 2Peter 1:4 | Revelation 21:27

Passion: *powerful, compelling emotion/feeling/desire, as love or hate; ambition.*
Proverbs 7:23, 14:17 | Acts 1:24-25 | Galatians 5:24 | Ephesians 4:31 | Colossians 2:11 | 2Peter 3:14 | 1John 2:17

Patience: *forbearance under suffering and endurance in the face of adversity.*
Romans 2:4 | Ephesians 4:2 | Colossians 1:11, 3:12 | 1Timothy 1:16, 6:11 | 2Timothy 4:2 | Titus 2:2 | Hebrews 10:36 | James 1:4

Peaceful: *free of war, strife, commotion, violence, disorder, noise, or excitement; quiet; calm.*
1Chronicles 4:40 | Mark 4:39 | Colossians 3:15 | 1Thessalonians 4:11 | James 3:18 | 1Peter 3:4, 11

Pillar: *steadfast/stationary/firm/steady; foundation/support structure; strong/unbendable/unbreakable/permanent.*
Proverbs 9:1, 24:3 | Jeremiah 1:18 | Daniel 6:26 | Hebrews 6:19 | 1Corinthians 15:58

Possible: *having the ability to act and the power to overcome limits.*
Genesis 30:22 | Deuteronomy 31:6 | Mark 9:23, 14:36 | Luke 4:35 | John 3:8-10 | Acts 2:24 | Romans 12:18

DIGGING DEEPER...INTO THE SOURCE   (CONT.)

Power: *the ability or strength to perform an activity or deed.*
Exodus 9:16,15:6 | 1Chronicles 29:10-12 | Job 36:5; Psalms 59:16 | Proverbs 18:21 | John 1:12 | Acts 1:8 | Romans 1:20, 15:13 | Ephesians 6:10

Promises: *announcements with the special sense of a pledge and offer. God keeps His!*
Genesis 6:18, 17:21 | Exodus 13:5 | Numbers 23:19 | Deuteronomy 1:11, 7:9 | 2Corinthians 1:20 | Hebrews 10:36

Rock: *refuge, stronghold, source of strength.*
Genesis 49:24 | Deuteronomy 32:4 | Psalm 18:2,62:6- 7, 71:3, 73:26, 92:15 | Isaiah 26:4, 30:29; 44:8 | Matthew 7:24-25, 16:18, 27:51 | 1Corinthians 10:4

Security: *safe, well-founded confidence; protection; defense; unexposed to danger or harm; a deposit for a debt owed.*
Isaiah 38:14 | Jeremiah 33:6, 9 | Zechariah 9:11-12 | Matthew 16:25 | 2Corinthians 1:22

Servant Leadership: *leadership with a humble and willing spirit of sacrifice and honor.*
Matthew 20:25-28 | Mark 10:42-45 | Luke 22:24-27 | John 13:3-5, 12-15

Sow: *to scatter/plant seed in order to increase returns; to disseminate.*
Hosea 10:12 | Psalm 126:6 | Ecclesiastes 11:6 | Isaiah 61:11 | Matthew 13:1-43 | Mark 4:3-20 | Luke 8:4-15 | 2Corinthians 9:10 | James 3:18

Training: *skills taught for a job/profession or an art; acquisition of knowledge/skills/competencies.*
1Corinthians 9:25 | Ephesians 6:4 | 1Timothy 1:4, 4:8 | 2Timothy 3:16 | Hebrews 12:9

Transformed: *changed radically in inner character, condition, or nature; metamorphose.*
Acts 20:32 | Romans 12:2 | 1Corinthians 15:51-52 | 2Corinthians 3:18 | Philippians 3:10-11, 21

Vision: *a mental process involved in the conceiving/inventing/planning of an idea-process.*
Exodus 31:3-5 | Proverbs 29:18 | Isaiah 32:8 | Ezekiel 12:27-28 | Habakkuk 2:2-3 | 1Corinthians 2:6-8

Wisdom: *ability to judge correctly and follow the best and timely course of action, based on knowledge and understanding.*
Proverbs 3:13, 16:16, 18:4, 21:11, 24:14 | Ecclesiastes 9:13-18 | Isaiah 11:2, 28:29

Scripture references are from the Amplified Bible (AMPL). Another excellent translation is the New King James Version (NKJV).

On-line source: www.biblegateway.com/. Some definitions were aided in part by *The Hayford Bible Handbook*, Jack W. Hayford, Executive Editor, 1995, and from *Vine's Complete Expository Dictionary of Old and New Testament Words*, W. E. Vine, Merrill F. Unger, William White, Jr., 1996.

Refining Integrity - Table of Contents

I. The Art of Orchestrating Change

II. Values Enrichment (9)
   a) Teaching
   b) Encouragement
   c) Accountability

III. Process Principles
   a) Gathering Information (8)
      - Development
      - Training
      - Format
   b) Refinement Techniques (6)
      - Mechanics
      - Upgrades
      - Follow-up
   c) Monitor Systems (8)
      - Data Collection
      - Measuring Areas
      - Scores/Trending

IV. Pillar Dynamics
   a) Inter- within the Pillar
   b) Intra- among Pillars I, II, and III

V. Benchmarking

VI. Motivation and Celebration

Appendices Topics:
1. Timing Clues for Changing Expectations
2. Potential Regulatory Changes
3. CPM Sensitivity Design
4. Flow Analysis Criteria
5. System Efficiency Review
6. Efficiency Training
7. Foreman Efficiency
8. Production Crew Efficiency
9. Roof Bolter Efficiency
10. Support System Efficiency
11. Efficiency Audit Forms
12. Attendance Reform
13. Client Survey
14. Action Team Topics
15. Shift Report Issues
16. Employee Inspection Report
17. Production Shift Report
18. Continuous Miner Shift Report
19. Roof Bolter Shift Report
20. Efficiency Survey Example
21. 300 Potential Kaizen Ideas
22. Equipment Selection
23. Equipment & Rebuild Parameters
24. Practical Ergonomics
25. Swarm Maintenance
26. Reducing Failure Maintenance
27. Maintenance Repair Variations
28. Unit Lay-out Effects
29. Cut Sequence Design Parameters
30. Cut Sequence Simulations
31. Unit Playbook
32. Sequencing Protection
33. Shift Transition Worksheet
34. Third Shift Design Criteria
35. Third Shift Report
36. Operational Delays
37. Downtime Utilization
38. Contingency Planning on the Unit
39. Momentum Enhancers
40. Process Study Topics
41. Analyzing Performance Indicator Drivers & Variation
42. Cost of Loss - Potential Survey
43. Unit Improvement Plan
44. Major Initiatives
45. Dust Reduction Techniques
46. Rock Dusting System
47. Automated Tracking
48. Potentials of Ash Analyzers & Selective Cutting
49. Supply System Efficiencies
50. Mining Deeper...Into The Source

BIOGRAPHY

Mark A. Bartkoski, P.E. holds a BS and MS in Mining Engineering from Virginia Tech. His +33 year career has been multi-faceted, but the last 25 years have primarily been focused on company rebuilds along with underground and surface mining operation greenfields. He has also participated in over 50 property evaluation studies and completed numerous efficiency and process improvement consulting projects both domestically and abroad.

ACKNOWLEDGMENTS

The author would like to offer his sincere appreciation for the tireless hours, fervent prayer, and awesome talents of which the following invested: Janet Loos, Shirley and Tenney Fuller, Marjorie Alder, Nicole Hocking, Jeff Hayden, and Jeff Bartkoski. He would also like to thank his wife, Margie, for the inspiration, patience, and support during this endeavor and in the life-long ministry they have shared together. And last, but forever first "...our Lord for His guidance, direction, wisdom, salvation..."

To order additional copies of this book
visit our website at:
IntegrityDevelopment.us